▸ Religions A to Z

▸ Religions A to Z

James A. Beverley

THOMAS NELSON PUBLISHERS
Nashville

Religions A to Z

Copyright © 2005 by James A. Beverley

Published in Nashville, Tennessee, by Thomas Nelson, Inc., Publishers.

Book design and composition by Mark McGarry, Texas Type & Book Works, Dallas, Texas

ISBN 1-4185-0573-0

Library of Congress Cataloguing-in-Publication data available on request.

2 3 4 5 6 7 8 9 — 10 09 08 07 06

This book is dedicated to
Andrea Joy Beverley
and
Derek James Beverley,
my wonderful children.
Their love, wisdom, creativity,
and Christian faith mean
everything to me.

Contents

Preface

This work is a spin-off from my much larger work called *Nelson's Illustrated Guide to Religions*. In both books I attempt to analyze a large number of religious traditions in light of the gospel of Jesus Christ. Both books deal with world and new religions, major Protestant denominations, and various movements or trends within larger religious traditions. *Religions A to Z* deals with fewer groups than the other volume and gives less space to many of the groups. Therefore, I urge interested readers to consult my longer book for further study, and also to pay close attention to the recommended reading and Web sites provided in *Religions A to Z*.

My formal study of religion goes back over a quarter of a century. However, specific work for the *Nelson's Illustrated Guide to Religions* and *Religions A to Z* has been ongoing since a sabbatical leave in 1999–2000. I owe a lot to those friends who have encouraged me in my research and writing over the years: John and Trish Wilkinson, Todd Johnson, Kevin and Jill Rische, Annie McKeown, Gary and Peg LeBlanc, John Reddy, Kevin and Sandy Quast, Rodney Howard-Browne, John Axler, Larry and Beverly Matthews, Randy and Susan Campbell, Siddiqi Rae, John Kessler, Ken and Miriam MacLeod, Marta Durski, Dave Collison, Rick and Charis Tobias, Bruxy and Nina Cavey, Pat Minichello, Gladys Chan, Randy and Cindy McCooeye, and Ralston and Cheryl Nickerson.

I also want to acknowledge the influence of several academics in my life. Eileen Barker, Massimo Introvigne, Don Wiebe, and Gordon Melton are valued friends and constant sources of learning about the world of religion, even when we disagree. I am also grateful for continuing encouragement from Hans Küng, my former professor during PhD work at the Toronto School of Theology. His breadth of learning and courage in theological life has been a powerful source of inspiration.

I gladly acknowledge the contribution of Tyndale Seminary administration to my work: Brian Stiller (president), Earl Davey (provost), and Janet Clark (academic dean). Two former deans, Ian Rennie and Brian Cunnington, have also been particularly supportive of my research work. Thanks also to Toby Goodman and Andrew Smith of the IT department at Tyndale. I am very grateful to several friends who have provided academic assistance and help in research: Agnes Choi, Rachel Collins, and Chad Hillier. David Neff and Mark Galli of *Christianity Today* magazine have supported me as a writer and contributing editor.

I also am in debt to key personnel at Thomas Nelson, including Mark Roberts, Michael Stephens, Lee Holloway, and Michael Christopher. Most significantly, Wayne Kinde, Senior Vice-President and Publisher, Nelson Reference and Electronic and Nelson Impact, has been very helpful in his backing of my work.

I am also encouraged by a great circle of relatives, including Bill and Margaret Bulman, Reta Lutes, Norman and Phyllis Gillcash, Mary Beverley, David and Darlene Keirstead, Cindy Beverley, and Lorne and Linda Gillcash. My twin brother, Bob Beverley, is a constant source of love and enthusiasm. As ever, and most important, I am incredibly grateful to my immediate family: my wife, Gloria; our adult children, Derek and Andrea; and Julien, our son-in-law.

James A. Beverley
Toronto, Canada
August 2005
jamesbeverley@sympatico.ca
www.religionwatch.ca

Introduction

It is no small thing to present an analysis of one hundred different religious movements. Readers have a right to know the perspective that I bring to this study. It will be obvious that this work offers more than simply bare facts about the various groups and leaders covered. Rather, *Religions A to Z* provides opinion about many of the controversial issues that arise in the study of the movements covered in this book. While every entry contains basic material that is beyond dispute, I also provide what I believe are necessary criticisms on relevant and important points.

The various traditions in this work are studied from my perspective as an evangelical Christian scholar. I realize that many readers will not share this paradigm or worldview. However, I ask those who follow other philosophies to grant some epistemic patience for the faith tradition that I bring to this study, one that I believe to be the truth. I recognize, of course, that this book would be different if written from a Buddhist, Muslim, esoteric, or other tradition. It would also be a different book if it adopted the standpoint of relativism, postmodernism, or the perspective of the disinterested academic.

Readers should know from the outset that criticisms are offered only when I believe that they are truly necessary. Even then, none of my points are meant to ignore or downplay the ways in which virtually every religion provides love, identity, and meaning to its followers. It will be obvious that this work does not employ the notion of brainwashing to interpret religious life, though I recognize that many leaders and groups are highly manipulative.

I have written this book with a deep recognition of my own fallibility. I am also aware, as I state below, that evangelical Christians have often been careless in response to other religions. Further, even after years of study of particular groups, it is possible to make mistakes of fact and interpretation. Consequently, I welcome input and correction on what I have written, though I also ask for civility in critique.

To be more specific about my perspective, I have presented in various books a list of ten essentials that form a proper Christian response to religions. These ten principles form the framework I have tried to use in responding to the one hundred movements covered in this book. These core points offer a multifaceted and balanced Christian paradigm for assessing religions. They also are built on appreciation for everything true and valid that can be learned from those in other religions, or from non-Christian academics who provide serious research on new and world religions.

1. *All religions and philosophies are to be measured by the final revelation of God in Jesus Christ.* The Christian must show allegiance to Jesus as the only Son of God and as God's final and ultimate Word to humanity. Contrary to relativism, the Bible does not teach that all roads lead to God. The orthodox Christian tradition has always taught the uniqueness and supremacy of Jesus. Karl Barth, the great Protestant theologian, has stated that Jesus is the one distinction between truth and error.

2. *Commitment to Jesus demands that the study of religion be carried out in love.* Bigotry and ignorance are incompatible with Jesus' command to love. Christian response to other religions has often been marked by hatred, and the evangelical study of religions has frequently been superficial and careless. Though this work includes critiques of various groups, my concerns are raised with the aim of providing truthful and important analysis.

3. *Christian response to religions involves a commitment to truth.* By this is meant not only dedication to Christ as the Truth, but also devotion to accuracy in the world of theology and religion. The commandment not to bear false witness against one's neighbor includes avoiding lies, half-truths, and distortions about the religion of the other person.

4. *Christians must recognize the contradictions and ultimate disunity that exists among the religions of the world.* Contrary to popular opin-

ion, the religions of the world often disagree even on basic points. Buddhists do not believe in God. Jews and Muslims do not accept the Trinity. Mormon males believe they will progress to Godhood in eternity. Unificationists believe that Sun Myung Moon is the Messiah. Jehovah's Witnesses trust the Watchtower Society alone for spiritual guidance. Santeria followers kill animals for religious worship.

5. *Disciples of Jesus must recognize every significant point of agreement with people of other religions, and even with those of no faith.* There is no harm in seeing God's common grace at work in the religions and peoples of the world. Thus, atheists can love their children. Wiccans can be upstanding citizens. Hindus can understand the value of love. Muslims can detest the evils of global terrorism. Non-Christians can serve as moral examples to the Christian community.

6. *Those who trust the gospel of Jesus must note the power of the dominant liberal perspective on religion and religious study.* For over a century the West has seen an increasing emphasis on relativism. Since the 1893 World Parliament of Religions, the acceptance of all religions as paths to God has grown. Mainline denominations have downplayed the missionary enterprise, and liberal theologians have argued that Jesus is not the only Savior. Further, postmodernism has eroded confidence in the Christian Gospel.

7. *The Christian church must affirm that the mercy and love of God shown in Jesus are sufficient to answer all concerns about God's fairness.* The Christian must resist attempts to downplay the supremacy of Jesus or to overstate the unity of religions as a means of making Christian faith more acceptable in a climate of relativism. The wideness of God's mercy is shown best by the grace given at Calvary.

Evangelicals need to continue to emphasize the Lordship of Christ in a world of religions. However, this emphasis must be set in the context of the warnings of Jesus against a judgmental attitude (Matthew 7:1–6). The harsh spirit in conservative Christian theology is inconsistent with the meaning of the Cross of Christ.

8. *Those who trust in the Christian gospel must not forget the wrath of God that stands against the wickedness of a fallen world.* The message of God's justice applies to both secular and religious domains, since the

Lord's name is taken in vain in both. People often carry out evil under God's alleged blessing. The Good News in Jesus is a word of judgment about the folly and sin of a lost humanity.

9. *Christians must repent and be in sorrow for the ways in which we have not allowed the gospel to critique the church through the ages.* Karl Barth has pointed prophetically to the ways in which the message of Christ must be heard by all religions, even Christianity. Barth was correct to recognize that religion can be unbelief, even among those who claim to follow Christ. Christians who engage in self-criticism gain the opportunity to help those in other faiths come to Jesus, the healer and light of the world.

10. *Christian response to religion must include respect for human liberty.* Christians must defend the right of all humans to exercise their free choice on religious matters. A decision for the gospel is real only if made in freedom. Likewise, the Christian respects the freedom of humans to reject any religion, including the Christian gospel. Coercion is antithetical to the way in which Jesus treated others.

Building on this, evangelicals must recognize the importance of building peace between religions, especially on common social and ethical issues. This has been argued best by Hans Küng, in his work for a global ethic.

In each entry in this work I attempt to offer basic facts about history and beliefs, though the contents vary depending on the nature of the group or leader under study. Readers will note that I follow the typology outlined by J. Gordon Melton, my friend and colleague at the Institute for the Study of American Religion. His family model of religions provides a way to make sense of the array of religious groups found in our world. I urge readers to consult his massive *Encyclopedia of American Religions* for more detail.

Religions A to Z

▶ Adidam

Adi Da is the charismatic and controversial leader of the Adidam movement. He was born Franklin Albert Jones on November 3, 1939, in Jamaica, New York. He has four daughters, one of whom—Shawnee Free Jones—is an actress in Hollywood. Since his emergence as a guru in 1972, he has taken several names, including Bubba Free John and Da Free John. His original community was known as the Dawn Horse Communion, then the Crazy Wisdom Fellowship, and it has had several other titles as well.

Adi Da claims to be God incarnate and says that he was born in a fully enlightened state. He was raised in Long Island and studied at Columbia and Stanford. He then pursued Eastern religions, studying with the famous Swami Rudrananda (aka Rudi). Adi Da also claimed spiritual lineage with Muktananda, Bhagavan Nityananda, Rang Avadhoot, and the cosmic goddess Ma. Adi Da broke away from Muktananda in 1973. Adi Da teaches his devotees at the group's main centers in California, Hawaii, and the Fiji Islands.

His followers believe that Adi Da dwells in a state known as "Bright." Chris Tong, one scholar in the movement, states that Adi Da is "the only complete Incarnation of the Divine." Adi Da has taught that two female devotees—Ruchira Adidama Sukha Dham Naitauba and Ruchira Adidama Jangama Hriddaya Naitauba—have reached profound levels of spiritual realization.

Ex-members have accused Adi Da of drunkenness, sexually abusing others, and living a life of splendor, especially with his inner circle. Alice, one of his former "wives," states in one Web forum: "Da is a user. He is abusive and manipulative. In summary, he cares for his own pleasure and amusement and is full of humiliation and inconsideration." This criticism was dismissed as "superficial" by one devotee.[1] Followers often claim that Adi Da can operate above traditional values, as in the "crazy wisdom" teachings in Buddhism that allow an enlightened master to rise above the normal rules of karma.

The devotees of Adi Da adore their guru. Funds are often raised through auctioning Adi Da's possessions among his followers. In one auction the starting price for a Q-tip used by Adi Da was $108.00. His disciples express their commitment to him in very emotive language. Members are often in rapture when they are granted the opportunity to be in his presence (darshan) and experience what they regard as his transcendent love.

The Adidam Web site states this of his darshan in the summer of 2005:

> Darshan is Avatar Adi Da's greatest Gift. When receiving His Dar-
> shan, when sitting in His all-Embracing, all-Blessing Divine Com-
> pany, when receiving His Love-Blissful Divine Regard, you are
> magnetized to His Divine Attractiveness. The Way of Adidam is the
> Way of the relationship to Avatar Adi Da Samraj — a relationship of
> attraction to His Divine Human Body and obedience to His Divine
> Heart-Word of Instruction, for the sake of Divine Self-Realization.

When Adi Da was sick in 2000, Carolyn Lee, one of the leaders in the movement, wrote of her anguish and love: "Please let this Leela [account] of Beloved's Anguish break and convert your heart. Our love for our Beloved Guru is beyond any other love, and yet, we tend to abstract Him, even especially in the moments of His most extreme vulnerability and Distress. Beloved is not only seriously ill, He is in danger of not being able to go on in the Body at all, unless He is relieved of the sense that His Work is failing, and that He is truly pro-tected and Set Apart and Given everything He needs in human terms to Bless and transform the world."

Adi Da

TYPOLOGY	Hinduism advaitist sectarian
WEB SITES	www.adidam.org
	www.aboutadidam.org
	www.beezone.com
CRITICAL SITES	http://lightmind.com/daism

▸ Ahmadiyya

The Ahmadiyya movement is rooted in the life and teachings of Mirza Ghulam Ahmad. Ahmad was born in the Punjab in the late 1830s. He claimed to have special status as one chosen to renew Islam. A movement to support him began in March 1889. He died on May 26, 1908, and leadership transferred to Nooruddin, one of his earliest disciples. Nooruddin led the Ahmadi group until his death in 1914.

After Nooruddin's death, Bashir-ud-Din Mahmood Ahmad, Ghulam Ahmad's son, took over leadership. However, the movement soon divided into two factions, with one group based in Qadiani and the other in Lahore. The crisis in unity revolved around differences of opinion about the founder's prophetic status, the relationship to non-Ahmadi Muslims, and the authority of Mahmood Ahmed. The Qadiani branch followed the founder's son and argued that Ghulam Ahmadi is both a prophet and the Mahdi promised in Islamic tradition.

The Lahore group, led by Maulana Muhammad Ali (1874–1951), argued that Ahmad is the Madhi but is not a prophet since Muhammad is the last of the prophets. Maulana Muhammad Ali denounced the Qadiani group as extremist, particularly over the Qadiani teaching that one cannot be a Muslim unless one believes that Mirza Ghulam Ahmad is a prophet. The Lahore leader also tried repeatedly to get the founder's son to debate about the true understanding of Ahmadiyya Islam.

The Qadiani Ahmadi group relocated its headquarters to Rabwa, Pakistan in the late 1940s. The movement has always experienced persecution from the Islamic Sunni majority. In September 1974 the Pakistan Assembly formally stipulated that anyone who claims that Muhammad is not the last prophet or that someone after him is a prophet in any sense cannot be considered a Muslim. In 1984 the government initiated other legal obstacles to Ahmad religious life.

Ghulam Ahmadi taught that Jesus did not die on the cross.

Rather, He only fainted, was later revived, and moved to India. Given this, he argued that it is wrong for Christians to teach that Jesus rose from the dead and that He is coming again to the earth. Ghulam Ahmad claimed that he fulfills predictions about the second coming of a Messiah like Jesus. The Qadiani Ahmadi followers do not believe that Ghulam's prophetic status is equal to Muhammad, but for them he is certainly second to Muhammad in importance as a prophet.

Mirza Ghulam Ahmad claimed that many things pointed to his messianic role. In one document he wrote: "Is it not enough to establish the truth of my claim that the Holy Quran has discussed in graphic detail the signs of and circumstances relating to my coming?" He also added that his name had been foretold as well as the timing of his birth and the name of his village. He said that his facial features had been noted ahead of time and that both lunar and solar eclipses signaled his messianic reign.

The Qadiani Ahmadis believe that they have reconstituted the Islamic caliphate. There have been five caliphs since the death of the founder of the movement: (1) Hazrat Al-Haaj Maulana Hakeem Nooruddin (1841–1914; rule 1908–14), (2) Hazrat Al-Haaj Mirza Bashir-ud-Din Mahmood Ahmad (1889–1965; rule 1914–65), (3) Hazrat Hafiz Mirza Nasir Ahmad (1909–1982; rule 1965–82), (4) Hazrat Mirza Tahir Ahmad (1928–2003; rule 1982–2003), and (5) Mirza Masroor Ahmad. Masroor Ahmad was born in 1950 and became the fifth caliph in 2003.

Ahmadiyya	
FOUNDER	Mirza Ghulam Ahmad
WEB SITES	Qadiani Ahmadi site, www.alislam.org
	Admadi site,www.muslim.org
READING	Yohanan Friedmann, *Prophecy Continuous* (Berkeley: University of California Press, 1989)

▶ Alamo Christian Ministries

Alamo Christian Ministries represents the work of Tony Alamo. His name is often linked with that of his first wife, Susan, who died on April 8, 1982. The Alamos had a significant street ministry in Hollywood during the hippie revolution of the 1960s. Disillusioned hippies were attracted to their message of the gospel and their call to a new type of communal living. The Alamos carried on their ministry under the name Music Square Church and also the Tony and Susan Alamo Christian Foundation.

Tony was born in Joplin, Missouri, on September 20, 1934, as Bernie Lazar Hoffman. Susan was born Edith Opal Horn and, like Tony, was from a Jewish family. Tony and Susan met in California and adopted Alamo as their last name. After they started their church work in California, they branched out to Arkansas and other Southern states in the 1970s. The Alamos' ministry became the target of both anticult groups, particularly the Cult Awareness Network, and law enforcement agencies. In 1976 the U.S. Labor Department charged that church members who work for the church should be subject to the Fair Labor Standards Act and viewed as employees and not volunteers—a position upheld by the U.S. Supreme Court in 1985.

Tony Alamo has had other brushes with the law. After Susan died, she was buried in a mausoleum on church property in Georgia Ridge, Arkansas. In 1991 Alamo removed Susan's body after the government confiscated the property. Christhiaon Coie, Susan's estranged daughter, charged Tony with stealing her body, and her stepfather had the body relocated under court order. In the 1980s and 1990s the IRS targeted Alamo, the church, and its businesses for income tax evasion. Alamo was convicted on four tax-related charges in 1994 and was sentenced to six years in prison. He was released in 1998.

The movement follows a fundamentalist ideology and views the King James Version as the only valid translation. Tony Alamo adopts conspiracy theories about the Roman Catholic Church and taught that the Cult Awareness Network was a branch of the Vatican. He calls the Catholic Church "the Queen of Whores" and cited John Paul II for his criminal past. Alamo claimed that the Gulf War was a Vatican plot to distract attention from U.S. judicial persecution of Alamo. In 1999 he announced that UFOs are real and are a part of God's end-time prophecy.

The extent of Alamo's conspiracy mind-set can be seen in this description of former president Clinton.

> Check it out for yourself. Clinton, as a child, attended Catholic parochial school, graduated from Catholic Georgetown University, and received a Catholic Rhodes scholarship to Catholic Oxford University in Oxford, England. For political reasons, Clinton temporarily became a Baptist; now as President, he is unashamedly and zealously showing his true Catholic colors. By the way Clinton is obediently performing for Rome, he can, with assurance, predict future bloody Christian massacres. If he continues being faithful to the Popes evil leadership, why maybe he could even plan on being the next Fuhrer.

Alamo Christian Ministries

TYPOLOGY	Christian Protestant fundamentalist sectarian
HOME PAGE	www.alamoministries.com

▸ Anabaptists

The term *Anabaptist* refers to radical or free-church Protestants who departed from the Lutheran and Reformed traditions on infant baptism, church-state relations, use of violence, church government, and separation from the world. There has been vigorous debate about the origins of the Anabaptist tradition in the sixteenth century and the extent to which Anabaptist ideas can be traced to reform movements before Luther as well as to violent reactionary elements after Luther's posting of the ninety-five theses in 1517.

Most scholars are content to trace Anabaptism to the community of Christians who were rebaptized in 1525 in Zürich. On January 18 of that year, Conrad Grebel debated his longtime friend Ulrich Zwingli, the famous Swiss Reformer, on the issue of infant baptism. Those who sided with Grebel chose to renounce their baptism as infants. Zwingli won the city council to his defense of the Lutheran-Reformed perspective, and the Anabaptists were declared heretical. Immediately Conrad Grebel and his followers became victims of persecution. On January 5, 1527, Felix Manz was drowned in the lake near Zürich for his profession of believer's baptism.

The earliest opponents of Anabaptism attempted to discredit the movement through associating it with the practices of Thomas Müntzer, a supporter of the German Peasants War, who was executed in 1525. Anabaptists were also criticized by reference to the apocalyptic rebellion in Münster, Germany, in 1534–35. While the leaders in Münster had connections with some Anabaptist thinkers of the day, it is unfair to associate Anabaptism in any simplistic way with this isolated and bizarre revolution. Most Anabaptists of the sixteenth century and since have repudiated violence and have been staunch defenders of pacifism.

As early as 1527 a group of Anabaptists expressed some of their beliefs in what has become known as the Schleitheim Confession.

Seven articles outlined commitment to believer's baptism, church discipline (the ban), pacifism, participation in the Lord's Supper, separation of church and state, denial of oath taking, and the work of the
Christian pastor. One part of the confession reads: "The government
magistracy is according to the flesh, but the Christian's is according
to the Spirit; their houses and dwelling remain in this world, but the
Christian's are in heaven; the weapons of their conflict and war are
carnal and against the flesh only, but the Christian's weapons are
spiritual, against the fortification of the devil."

We now know Anabaptists through the groups that rose from that
tradition: the Mennonites, Hutterites, Amish, and Brethren. (The
Anabaptist Brethren groups are distinct from the Plymouth Brethren,
the dispensational movement started by John Nelson Darby in the
nineteenth century.) The Bruderhof, a communal group now based in
the United States, are a recent addition to the Anabaptist world.

The Mennonites are the largest Anabaptist group in the world,
followed by the Brethren. The Old Order Mennonites shun many
aspects of modern society, as do the Hutterites and Amish. The latter
groups are famous for their old-style communal living. Harrison
Ford's movie *Witness* brought Amish culture to Hollywood. Ford
played a Philadelphia cop forced to hide among the Amish for protection. The film contrasted the darker sides of mainstream society with
the peaceful Amish community.

Anabaptists

TYPOLOGY	Christian Protestant
HOME PAGES	Mennonite World Conference, www.mwc-cmm.org
	Church of the Brethren (Elgin, Illinois), www.brethren.org
	Brethren Church (Ashland, Ohio) www.brethrenchurch.org
	Fellowship of Grace Brethren Churches, www.fgbc.org
	Bruderhof, www.bruderhof.com
READING	Franklin H. Littell, *The Origins of Sectarian Protestantism* (New York: Macmillan, 1964).

▸ Anglicans

The word *Anglican* refers principally to the Church of England and other churches that are part of the worldwide Anglican Communion. This body of churches submits to the leadership of the archbishop of Canterbury, the primate of the Church of England, who is first among equals of the leaders (primates—also termed *archbishops* or *presiding bishops*) of the various Anglican bodies.

The Anglican Communion includes the Episcopal Church, the official name for the Anglican Church in the United States. There are about 80 million Anglicans worldwide and more than 2 million in America. Outside England the largest numbers of Anglicans are located in Nigeria, Uganda, and Australia. Anglicans trace their roots to the work of St. Augustine in Britain in the sixth century. He is viewed as the first archbishop of Canterbury. Anglicans often consider themselves Catholic and Protestant, signifying a desire to be in apostolic succession from Peter and yet separate from Roman Catholicism. The notorious King Henry VIII led the Church of England away from papal allegiance in 1534.

Generally, Anglicans unite in adherence to the historic creeds, *The Book of Common Prayer*, the decisions of the Lambeth Conferences (held every ten years), and the leadership of the archbishop of Canterbury. Anglican tradition has also been deeply impacted by the Thirty-Nine Articles of the Church of England. These articles contain several classic objections to specific Catholic doctrines, such as purgatory. The famous document also states, "For Holy Scripture doth set out unto us only the Name of Jesus Christ, whereby men must be saved."

Rowan Williams became the 104th archbishop of Canterbury on February 27, 2003. The archbishop is appointed by the British Parliament in consultation with Anglican leaders. The British monarch is the official head of the Church of England. The archbishop of Canterbury has no legal authority with Anglican churches outside the Church of England. Williams succeeded George Carey, who was highly regarded for his evangelical Anglican perspective.

Some Anglican churches are not in unity with the See of Canterbury, the Church of England, and the worldwide Anglican Communion. Melton's *Encyclopedia of American Religions* lists sixty-five distinct Anglican churches in the United States alone. The major breakaway churches are the Anglican Catholic Church, the Anglican Province of Christ the King, and the United Episcopal Church of North America. These churches have usually broken away because of disagreements over alterations in the Book of Common Prayer, biblical authority, the ordination of women, and homosexuality.

The appointment of the openly gay Gene Robinson as the bishop of New Hampshire in 2003 has increased the likelihood of further schisms in the Anglican Communion. Peter Jasper Akinola, archbishop of the Church of Nigeria, has stated that the Nigerian churches are in "impaired Communion" with the Episcopal Church USA. In October 2004 the Lambeth Commission on Communion released the Windsor Report, a document that attempts to address how Anglicans should respond to the crisis created by Robinson's election and by a move to bless gay unions by an Anglican diocese in British Columbia.

Anglicans

TYPOLOGY	Christian Protestant
LEADER	Archbishop of Canterbury
HOME PAGES	Anglican Communion
	www.anglicancommunion.org
	Anglicans Online, www.anglicansonline.org
	Episcopal Church (USA)
	www.ecusa.anglican.org
	Anglican Church in Canada, www.anglican.ca
	The United Episcopal Church of North America
	http://united-episcopal.org
READING	John Moorman, *A History of the Church of England*
	(Harrisburg. PA: Morehouse, 1980)

▶ Apostles of Infinite Love

This is one of various groups that claim to be the true version of Roman Catholicism. Michael Collin, a former priest, founded the Apostles of Infinite Love. The movement is based in Saint-Jovite, Quebec, and is currently led by Gregory Tremblay (b. 1928), who is viewed as Pope Jean Gregory XVII. The group also goes by the title The Catholic Church of the Apostles of the Latter Times. Their Quebec site is home to the Order of the Magnificat of the Mother of God.

The movement claims that its origins lie in the La Salette prophecies, or revelations, given by Mary to Mélanie Calvat and Maximin Giraud, two children, on September 19, 1846, in La Salette, France. The Vatican accepts the La Salette apparition but has condemned groups who have used the revelations in ways contrary to Rome. Michael Collin, who died in 1974, was condemned by Rome in 1951, 1956, and 1961 for his disobedience to Vatican policies.

The first verdict against Collin reads: "By a decree dated January 17, 1951, the Supreme Sacred Congregation of the Holy Office has reduced to the status of a layman the priest Michael Collin of the Order of the Sacred Heart, already dismissed from the said Order, traveling through several dioceses, frequently and in various ways violating rules of the Sacred Canon."

The order, founded in 1962, has this to say about its alleged divine roots:

> In Her loving mercy, the Virgin of La Salette has transported Her great light to Quebec soil, where the Order of the Magnificat of the Mother of God, the Order of the Apostles of the Latter Times, has been formed under Her direction and protection. In a turn of events whose initiative the Virgin took upon Herself, the Order has been developing in Quebec and in many countries all over the world for the past thirty-five years.

In April 1999 an arrest warrant was issued in Quebec against Tremblay and three other members of the group, including two nuns. Police raided the group at the time and took children into custody for examination. The charges involved allegations of sexual abuse and assault. Tremblay surrendered to authorities two weeks after charges were laid, but the Quebec courts dropped the case in 2001 because of insufficient evidence to proceed to trial.

The order claims that it has been the constant victim of persecution.

Time has not altered the rage of the enemy of God and his henchmen—quite the contrary. Those who have followed our progress through court trials, newspaper articles, etc., know that our path has been sown with a thousand snares. The Order of the Mother of God is now founded, but it has been established and is holding its own through opposition and persecution.

Apostles of Infinite Love

TYPOLOGY	Christian Roman Catholic sectarian
LEADER	Gregory Tremblay, aka Pope Jean Gregory XVII
HOME PAGE	www.magnificat.ca

▸ Arcane School

The Arcane School is one of many New Age groups that emerged in the twentieth century. It was founded by Alice Bailey (1880–1949) and her husband, Foster, and is one of the most important schools to arise out of the larger Theosophical tradition. (Helena Petrova Blavatsky founded Theosophy in 1875. Within fifty years, Theosophy had become a dominant part of Western esotericism.)

Alice Bailey was born in Manchester, England, on June 16, 1880. In 1899 she moved to India, where she worked at the YWCA. She was married in 1907 to Walter Evans, her first husband. They moved to Cincinnati, where Walter studied for the Episcopal priesthood at Lane Theological Seminary. The couple separated in 1915 after moving to California. Alice first heard about Theosophy from friends in Pacific Grove, California. She became editor of *The Messenger*, the journal of the Theosophy Society, in 1917. Two years later she met Foster Bailey, the society's national secretary.

In November 1919 Alice claimed to receive channeled messages from a spirit being known as Djwhal Khul, or the Tibetan. This created enormous controversy among Theosophists, who believed that Blavatsky was the final channel. Foster sided with Alice and they were forced to leave the movement. They moved to New York and married in 1921. They formed the Lucis Trust to publish Alice's revelations and also started the Arcane School. Alice died in 1949. Foster led the school till his own death in 1977.

In addition to her alleged contacts with Djwhal Khul, Alice Bailey claimed that as a teenager she had a supernatural encounter with another spirit master. She thought it was Jesus Christ but later learned it was Koot Hoomi, one of the members of the Great White Brotherhood who had first appeared to Madame Blavatsky. Bailey's writings were often rooted in her continuing contact with the Tibetan from 1919 until her death.

The Arcane School flourished at a time when Theosophists had been hurt by the failure of the famous mystic Krishnamurti (1895–1986) to accept his role as the Maitreya, or modern Messiah. Alice Bailey spent considerable time on the message that Christ would reappear, not as Jesus Christ or as Krishnamurti, but as a cosmic spirit who has always dwelt with persons in all religions who pursue love. Bailey wrote: "If people look for the Christ Who left His disciples centuries ago, they will fail to recognize the Christ Who is in process of returning. His advance guard is already here and the Plan which they must follow is already made and clear. Let recognition be the aim."

Bailey is most famous for her transmission of "The Great Invocation," probably the most influential prayer in New Age circles. The prayer went through three versions, with the most popular dating from 1945. It reads as follows:

> From the point of Light within the mind of God
> Let light stream forth into the minds of men.
> Let Light descend on Earth.
> From the point of Love within the Heart of God
> Let love stream forth into the hearts of men.
> May Christ return to Earth.
> From the Centre where the Will of God is known
> Let purpose guide the little wills of men—
> The purpose which the Masters know and serve.
> From the Centre which we call the race of men
> Let the Plan of Love and Light work out
> And may it seal the door where evil dwells.
> Let Light and Love and Power restore the Plan on Earth.

Arcane School

TYPOLOGY	Western esoteric
MAJOR FIGURE	Alice Bailey (1880–1949)
WEB PAGE	www.lucistrust.org

▸ Army of Mary

The Army of Mary is a Quebec-based Marian work founded by Marie-Paule Giguere. She was born on September 14, 1921, and married George Cliche on July 1, 1944. The couple had five children, but Marie-Paule left her husband in 1957. She claims that Jesus and the Virgin Mary have appeared to her since she was a teenager.

Marie-Paule states that God told her of her Marian work in 1954. She also claimed that Jesus told her in 1958 that she would be persecuted by the Church. "It will be those of my priesthood who will crucify you. Like me, you are innocent, but on all sides, voices will cry out that you are hateful, that you are the most infamous of creatures. All those of my priesthood who are sinning through pride, egoism, through sensuality in all its forms, will cast stones at you."

The Army of Mary was officially founded on August 28, 1971, and received endorsement as a Pious Association by Cardinal Maurice Roy, the archbishop of Quebec, on March 10, 1975. Marie-Paule's work was also blessed by Ida Peerdeman (1905–96), a Marian mystic based in the Netherlands. The movement came under scrutiny from the Vatican and from the Canadian Catholic authorities in the 1980s. Suspicion was due in part to the fact that Belgian member Marc Bosquart wrote two books contending that Mary was mystically indwelling Marie-Paule. On May 4, 1987, Cardinal Louis-Albert Vachon, then archbishop of Quebec, revoked the status of the Army of Mary as a Pious Association.

On March 31, 2000, the Vatican formally objected to Marie-Paule's *Life of Love*, a fifteen-volume autobiography. In 2001 the Canadian Conference of Catholic Bishops spoke decisively against the movement. Their verdict was ratified by the Vatican. The Canadian Conference stated:

> The Army of Mary's on-going activities and teachings pose dangers for the Catholic Church in Canada and to the faith of its

members. In view of this and the continuing threat to the integrity and unity of the Catholic faith, the Bishops of Canada declare, and hereby inform all the Catholic faithful, that the Army of Mary, regardless of its claims to the contrary, is not a Catholic association. Some of the teaching it propagates about redemption, the Virgin Mary and reincarnation are profoundly at variance with the teaching and profession of the faith of the Catholic Church.

The Canadian bishops were particularly disturbed by the claims of the Army of Mary that Marie-Paule is a reincarnation of the Virgin Mary. They also objected to the insubordination of Army leaders to the direct wishes of Catholic authorities. "The Catholic Bishops of Canada regret the way the leaders of the Army of Mary continue to defy ecclesial authority and refuse to heed the legitimate pastoral admonitions and injunctions of the Archbishop of Quebec."

On April 4, 2005, Marc Cardinal Ouellet, the archbishop of Quebec and primate of Canada, issued a further warning against the army. He cited these words of Marc Bosquart, given in 2001, as an example of the army's faulty understanding of its leader: "So, let's believe it, let's say it, let's proclaim it: in the Kingdom of the Spirit, in that Kingdom which is coming, in that Kingdom which has already begun, everywhere, side by side, there will be Jesus Christ and Marie-Paule, the Redeemer and the Co-Redeemer of all humankind."

The Army of Mary is based in Lac-Etchemin, sixty miles south of Quebec City.

Army of Mary

TYPOLOGY	Christian Roman Catholic sectarian
LEADER	Marie-Paule Giguere (1921–)
HOME PAGE	www.communaute-dame.qc.ca

▸ Aryan Nations

The Aryan Nations is one of the major racist religious groups in America. The movement teaches a version of "Christian identity," that is, the belief that only Anglo-Saxons are children of God, that nonwhites are "mud people," and that the "Canaanite Jew . . . a child of Satan" is "the natural enemy of our Aryan (White) Race." Richard Butler (1918–2004) founded the Aryan Nations in the mid 1970s, with roots in the Church of Jesus Christ Christian, started by Wesley Swift. Butler worked with Swift from 1961 until the latter's death a decade later. He then moved to Hayden, Idaho, and formed the Aryan Nations.

Nations members believe that Adam is the father of the white race only and that whites represent the twelve tribes of Israel. They claim the swastika as their symbol, believing it was used by early Christians to point to Christ as a cornerstone. Butler taught that his ideology is rooted in a love for the white race that leads him to war with "the anti-Christ Jews, mongrel hordes and liberal White race-mixers." Butler was a great admirer of Adolf Hitler.

Butler's group suffered a major financial blow in 2000 when the Southern Poverty Law Center won a $6.3 million civil suit against the group. Membership in the Aryan Nations costs $35, and the member declares: "I am of the White Aryan Race. I concur that Aryan Nations is only Aryans of Anglo-Saxon, Germanic, Nordic, Basque, Lombard, Celtic and Slavic origin. I agree with Aryan Nations' biblical exclusion of Jews, Negroes, Mexicans, Orientals, and Mongrels." After Butler's death in September 2004, Clark "Laslo" Patterson announced that the group's headquarters would move to Alabama.

Charles John Juba claimed leadership of an alternative Aryan Nations for several years. Juba argued that Butler passed the national director's position on to Ray Redfeairn in September 2001 and that the latter resigned that position the next March. Juba then assumed the position and then claimed that Redfeairn was a traitor to the cause. "Redfeairn is riding Pastor Butler's coattails for power, and trying to bully and intimidate anyone in his way for his grasp for power. In doing so, he has those around him do his bidding like the work of Jews, by trying to rule by dividing and conquering."

Juba announced an alternative to WWJD? in his WWHD? (What Would Hitler Do?), calling for an aggressive campaign against the impact of Jews in American society. Juba also states, "We are *not* a non-violent organization, we believe that our Race is on the verge of extinction, and will do anything in our powers to secure a white safe future for our children and our children's children." Juba lost leadership in the group, and Pastor August B. Kreis III is now national director.

Aryan Nations

TYPOLOGY	Christian identity
FOUNDER	Richard Butler
HEADQUARTERS	Lincoln, Alabama
HOME PAGES	www.twelvearyannations.com
	www.aryan-nations.org
CRITIC SITE	Southern Poverty Law Center
	www.splcenter.org
READING	Michael Barkun, *Religion and the Racist Right* (Chapel Hill: University of North Carolina Press, 1997).
	Mattias Gardell, *Gods of the Blood* (Durham, NC: Duke, 2003).
	Jeffrey Kaplan, ed., *Encyclopedia of White Power* (Lanham, MD: AltaMira, 2000).

▸ Aum Shinrikyo

Aum Shinrikyo is one of the most notorious religious groups of modern times. On March 20, 1995, twelve Japanese died as a result of sarin gas poison released during the morning rush hour in Tokyo. The killings turned out to be the work of key leaders of the movement, with involvement by its founder, Asahara Shoko. Shoko's original name was Chizuo Matsumoto. He was born in 1955 in Kyushu, a southern island of Japan. He claimed to have received enlightenment while alone in the Himalayas in 1986.

The violence in the movement can be traced to 1989. The group was targeted in the media, and its political branch suffered total loss in elections. Aum became the object of public ridicule. In November a prominent opponent of the group, lawyer Sakamoto Tsutsumi, disappeared along with his infant son and wife. Their bodies were discovered almost six years later. Tsutsumi had disproved Asahara's claim that his blood contained unique DNA.

Two hundred members of the group were arrested after the 1995 poisoning incident. Asahara was arrested in a hiding place at the group's headquarters in Kamikuishiki. Some of the accused received death sentences, a few others received long jail terms, while most received short sentences. Asahara was sentenced to death in February 2004. The judge's verdict read in part: "This was an evil and serious series of crimes brought about by the extremely malevolent and fantastic lies of Chizuo Matsumoto, who fed the illusion that his existence was absolute and on par with that of a god and who planned to build the group's forces and rule Japan under the guise of being a savior."

Aum Shinrikyo is an eclectic movement. It combines yoga, Tibetan Buddhist practice and ritual, and apocalypticism. Asahara was obsessed with Nostradamus and the book of Revelation. At one time he received the endorsement of His Holiness the Dalai Lama, but this was withdrawn after the group engaged in criminal activity.

Asahara was adored by his followers both before and after the 1995 poisonings. In 2000 one pro-Asahara Web site stated:

> With divine powers developed through the practice of meditation and with enlightened wisdom, Master Asahara shows his genius not only in the spiritual domain, but in various fields such as science, medicine, music, writing, translation, education, etc. In this age of crisis, his unique leadership with altruism and devotion has a great significance to world peace and the survival of human beings.

Since 2000, however, his popularity among members has diminished radically due to increasing evidence of his involvement in the planning of the gas attacks.

In 2000, former members of the Aum group started Aleph, a new movement built on the nonviolent aspects of Asahara's teachings. Aleph has apologized for the criminal actions of Aum and its founder. The new group has also provided financial remuneration for victims. In spite of this attempt at a fresh start, Aleph members are stigmatized because of their connection with Aum. Since the 1995 poisoning, some government leaders, police officials, and newspapers in Japan have called for laws against "cultic" religions.

Aum Shinrikyo

TYPOLOGY	Buddhist Tibetan sectarian
FOUNDER	Asahara Shoko
SPECIAL NOTE	Aum's founder and top leaders were involved in the 1995 gas poisoning in the Tokyo subway system. The group dissolved, and some former members founded Aleph.
READING	Robert Jay Lifton, *Destroying the World to Save It* (New York: Metropolitan, 1999). Ian Reader, *Religious Violence in Contemporary Japan* (Honolulu: University of Hawaii Press, 2000).
ALEPH WEB SITE	http://english.aleph.to

▸ Baha'i

The Baha'i faith, now considered a distinct world religion, cannot be understood apart from its connections to an Iranian sectarian movement of Shia Islam known as the Babi movement. Shia Islam has a core doctrinal position that the world awaits the return of a *mahdi*, or messiah figure, at the end of time. In 1844 a Muslim by the name of Siyyid Ali Muhammad (1819–50), building on this apocalyptic notion, proclaimed that he was the "Bab," or gate to God.

The Bab was executed in 1850, but his followers continued to experience persecution under orthodox Shia leaders. In 1852 many Babis were arrested, including Mirza Husayn 'Ali Nuri. Husayn 'Ali, born in Persia (now Iran) in 1817, became the founder of the Baha'i faith. He is now known to history as Baha'u'lláh (a name meaning "the glory of God"). Baha'u'lláh was exiled to Baghdad in 1853. In 1863 he proclaimed that he was the *mahdi* promised by the Bab and by all religions. In 1868 he was exiled to Acre, on the coast of Syria. He died there in 1892.

After the founder's death, leadership in the movement passed to Abdu-Bahá, the son of Baha'u'lláh. Under Abdu-Bahá (b. 1844), the Baha'i faith became a world movement, and he helped formulate official teaching on many theological and ethical topics. He was also successful at warding off attacks from his stepbrother, though Baha'is experienced a decade of internal conflict over the competing heirs. Abdu-Bahá died in 1921. He was succeeded by his grandson Shoghi Effendi, who led the movement until his death in 1957.

Shoghi Effendi's death created a crisis in the movement since there was no heir to follow as the One Guardian. Leadership was eventually given to those known as the Hands of the Cause of God and then to the members of the Universal House of Justice in Haifa, Israel. In 1960 Charles Remey, who had designed several Baha'i temples, proclaimed that he was the Guardian. Very few chose to follow him. In the early 1960s Remey taught that there would be an impending catastrophe on the planet, leading to the deaths of two-thirds of the world's population. He died in Italy in 1974.

In spite of its complex Islamic past, the central beliefs of the Baha'i religion are straightforward. The most important ones are the following: (1) all religions are one; (2) religion must conform to science and reason; (3) all humans are one; (4) Baha'u'lláh is the manifestation of God for the present age; (5) women and men are equal; and (6) there should be one universal language. Baha'is also believe that there have been previous manifestations of God, including Moses, Zoroaster, Krishna, Buddha, Muhammad, Jesus, and the Bab.

Christian critique of the Baha'i faith involves two major issues. First, no amount of rhetoric or argumentation can rationally support the view that all religions are the same, even though this perspective is advanced by well-informed scholars like Huston Smith. While the world religions do agree on some general moral principles, they emphatically disagree on other core moral issues and on essential doctrinal matters. Baha'i emphasis on the unity of religions is actually used to lead people in other religions to join the Baha'i faith, a rather unnecessary move if all religions are the same.

Second, Baha'is have a faulty assessment of Jesus Christ. Baha'u'lláh did not believe in the historical reality of the miracles of Jesus. While he did teach that Jesus died on the cross (a departure from his Islamic roots), he denied the physical resurrection. He also misunderstood both the divinity of Jesus and the New Testament doctrine of his Second Coming. Jesus will return as Jesus and not as Baha'u'lláh. In fact, Baha'u'lláh fulfills the prediction of Jesus that false teachers will arise who proclaim that they are the return of the Messiah.

Baha'i	
FOUNDER	Baha'u'lláh (1817–92)
HOME PAGE	www.bahai.org
OTHER SITES	www.bahai.com
	http://bahai-library.com

Juan Cole Research
www-personal.umich.edu/~jrcole/bahai.htm
H-Bahai
www.h-net.org/~bahai
Reform Baha'i movement (Frederick Glaysher)
www.reformbahai.org
Reform Blog
http://reformbahaifaith.blogspot.com

READING Francis J. Beckwith, "The Baha'i World Faith," in Ronald
Enroth, ed., *A Guide to New Religious Movements*
    (Downers Grove, IL: InterVarsity Press, 2005)
Peter Smith, *A Concise Encyclopedia of the Baha'i Faith*
    (Oxford: Oneworld, 2000)
William McElwee Miller, *What Is the Baha'i Faith?*
    (Grand Rapids, MI: Eerdmans, 1977)
Margit Warburg, *Baha'i* (Salt Lake City: Signature,
    2001)

▸ Baptists

Most church historians trace Baptist roots back to the work of two Englishmen, John Smyth (1570–1612) and Thomas Helwys (d. 1616). Smyth was an Anglican priest who dissented from his heritage on church-state relations, ecclesiastical hierarchy, and infant baptism. As part of a persecuted Separatist movement in seventeenth-century England, Smyth fled to Holland. He started a church there in 1609, and his associate Thomas Helwys founded a Baptist church in England in 1611.

Both Smyth and Helwys adopted an Arminian theology and believed that Christ died for all human beings. This represents the General Baptist tradition, in contrast to the Particular Baptists, who advance a Calvinist view on predestination, the extent of the atonement, and eternal security. The Particular Baptist movement started in England in the 1630s when a group of Separatists adopted believer's baptism and a Baptist understanding of the church, yet within a dominant Calvinist theology. The Particular Baptists formulated their theology in the London Confession of Faith of 1644.

Some historians have argued that Baptists can be traced back to the Anabaptist tradition of the sixteenth century. However, this view ignores not only early Baptist objections to being identified as Anabaptists but also the significant differences between the two Protestant paradigms, particularly in relation to pacifism and church discipline.

The view that Baptists have survived in an unbroken lineage since Christ has little scholarly support. This position is often called Landmarkism and created a schism in the Southern Baptist Convention in the mid-1800s. The main proponents were James Graves, James Pendleton, and Amos Dayton. The perspective is defended most famously in *The Trail of Blood* by J. M. Carroll (1858–1931).

Melton's *Encyclopedia of Religions in America* identifies sixty-five distinct Baptist bodies. Of these, thirteen have memberships of more than 100,000. The largest Baptist body in the United States is the Southern Baptist Convention, comprising more than 21 million members, making it the largest Protestant grouping in the United States. In 2004 the Southern Baptists, who have generally avoided ecumenical endeavors, voted to leave the Baptist World Alliance (BWA).

Baptist identity centers on the autonomy of the local congregation and the affirmation of believer's baptism. Baptists historically have resisted acceptance of infant baptism as practiced in Catholic and mainline Protestant churches. Baptists are often perceived as fundamentalists, in part because of the conservative trends in the Southern Baptist Convention and the influence of conservative Baptists such as Jerry Falwell.

Baptist leaders have often placed great stress on religious freedom, in part because Baptists were persecuted by state-sponsored churches in Europe in the seventeenth century. Roger Williams, one of the most famous American Baptists, argued for religious freedom in the early republic. This image of Baptists defending religious liberty is something of an antidote to the popular image of Baptists as narrow-minded and judgmental.

Baptists

TYPOLOGY	Christian Protestant
FOUNDERS	John Smyth (1570–1612) and Thomas Helwys (d. 1616)
HOME PAGES	Baptist World Alliance
	www.bwanet.org
	American Baptist Churches
	www.abc-usa.org
	National Baptist Convention of America
	www.nbcamerica.net
	National Baptist Convention, USA
	www.nationalbaptist.com
	Progressive National Baptist Convention
	www.pnbc.org
	Southern Baptist Convention
	www.sbc.net
READING	William H. Brackney, *A Genetic History Of Baptist Thought* (Macon, GA: Mercer, 2004)

▶ The Branch Davidians and David Koresh

The Branch Davidian movement will forever be identified with the leadership of David Koresh and with the fire that consumed him and many of his followers at their Waco compound on April 19, 1993. But the Branch Davidians trace their origin to the work of Victor Houteff, a native of Bulgaria, who joined the Seventh-day Adventists in 1919. He founded the Mount Carmel Center near Waco in 1935 and spread his version of Adventist doctrine around the world.

Houteff's death in 1955 created a crisis in the movement, but his wife, Florence, assumed leadership. The movement was doing well until her prediction of the world's end on April 22, 1959. That false prophecy caused an exodus of members, internal fragmentation, and financial collapse. Ben Roden took over the Mount Carmel property by purchase from other Davidians. Roden died in 1978, and his wife, Lois, assumed leadership, claiming to be the sixth angel of Revelation 9:16.

In 1981 Vernon Howell joined the group. He gathered his own followers but was forced out of Mount Carmel by George Roden, Lois's son, in 1984. Howell took control of Mount Carmel in 1988 when Roden was jailed for contempt of court. Howell changed his name to David Koresh in 1990. He believed himself to be the Lamb of Revelation 5 and claimed that he would open the seven seals of that chapter, thereby ushering in the second coming of Jesus. Koresh began the practice of taking "spiritual wives" in 1984, stating that he was the male figure to create a new line of God's children. He predicted apocalypse in America, and out of this teaching, he adopted a survivalist mentality, stockpiling weapons and food.

Bureau of Alcohol, Tobacco, and Firearms (BATF) agents raided Mt Carmel on February 28, 1993, after acquiring a search warrant. BATF agent Davy Aguilera filed a probable cause affidavit in relation to the cause for the raid. The BATF was influenced by reports of child abuse from ex-members, most notably Marc Breault. Six Davidians and four BATF agents died in the February 28 raid. Afterwards the FBI assumed control of the situation.

The FBI seige lasted fifty-one days. Koresh was allowed to broadcast a sermon on March 2 but went back on his word that he would surrender. In mid-April he negotiated a deal with his lawyer to give up after he finished his commentary on the seven seals. However, the FBI attacked the Branch Davidian facilities on April 19, and the building erupted in flames. Seventy-four members died that day, including twenty-one children. Thirty-five members exited during the siege (fourteen adults and twenty-one children), nine members survived the fire, and another six were away at the time of the raid.

A few of Koresh's followers continue to visit Mount Carmel and worship in the new sanctuary. Clive Doyle supervised the building of the modest church, and he is viewed as the group's spokesperson. He was a follower of Ben and Lois Roden and then accepted Koresh as leader. His youngest daughter died in the compound on April 19, 1993.

Most people forget that there were six hours between the time of the FBI assault on the compound and the start of the fire or fires that engulfed the compound. This gave Koresh and his followers plenty of time to surrender. They chose not to do so. It is possible that they were scared of being killed by the FBI if they walked out. Further, some members were physically trapped in debris. However, it is probable that many chose to remain inside simply because that is what Koresh, their leader, wanted them to do.

The Branch Davidians and David Koresh

TYPOLOGY	Christian Protestant Adventist sectarian
FOUNDER	David Koresh (d. 1993)
HEADQUARTERS	Waco, Texas
WEB SITES	Davidian Massacre Homepage, http://carolmoore.net/waco/
	Mount Carmel Survivors Site, www.anycities.com/mtcarmel
	PBS *Front Line* "Waco: The Inside Story" www.pbs.org/wgbh/pages/frontline/waco
READING	James Tabor and Eugene V. Gallagher, *Why Waco?* (Berkeley: University of California Press, 1997).

▶ British-Israelism

The term *British-Israelism* refers to the idea that the ten lost tribes of Israel settled in Great Britain and that there is a direct link between the ancient Israelites and the Anglo-Saxon people. British-Israelites even claim that the Stone of Scone used in British royalty ceremonies is the same one that was used in the coronation of King David in Israel.

Theories about a connection between Britain and ancient Jews circulated in some form among Puritans and a few writers of the eighteenth century. Richard Brothers was one of these early British-Israelites. Brothers was born in Canada in 1757 and by the turn of the century was claiming that he was descended from King David and was the proper heir to the British throne. He was committed to an asylum and died in 1824.

Most scholars trace British-Israelism to John Wilson, a native of Ireland who authored *Lectures on Our Israelitish Origin* in 1840. After Wilson's death in 1871, Edward Hine spread his ideas throughout England and the United States. British-Israelism also had some impact on the theories of William Miller and early Adventists. A conscious anti-Semitic element emerged in British-Israelism through the views of Howard Rand of the Anglo-Saxon Federation of America in 1928.

The most popular exponent of British-Israelism in the twentieth century was Herbert W. Armstrong, founder of the Worldwide Church of God. In 1967 Armstrong authored *The United States and British Commonwealth in Prophecy*, a work that owed much to the views expressed by J. H. Allen's *Judah's Sceptre and Joseph's Birthright*, first published in 1902. After Armstrong's death, the Worldwide Church of God abandoned British-Israelism, though many splinter groups retain the ideology.

British-Israelism is advanced today through several organizations, most notably the British-Israel World Federation, organized in 1919. The BIWF has branches in Australia, New Zealand, and Canada. The federation contends that "the Royal House of Britain is descended from King David" and that "the British Monarchs are anointed in the same way as Zadok the Priest anointed the Kings of Israel." The organization also maintains that God's promise that Israel will not be defeated is proved by British victories in World Wars I and II and "in many other great battles such as the Spanish Armada, Trafalgar and Waterloo." The federation argues in its booklet "As Birds Flying over Jerusalem" that the Royal Flying Corps fulfilled a 2,600-year-old Bible prophecy.

British-Israelism is based on superficial Bible study and careless historical judgments. Its claims are refuted in detail in Joseph Hopkins's *The Armstrong Empire* and in Walter Martin's classic work, *The Kingdom of the Cults*. The subtle racism in British-Israelism turns far more sinister in the radical white supremacist movements that have embraced its emphasis on Anglo-Saxons as the people of God.

British-Israelism

TYPOLOGY	Christian Protestant sectarian
HOME PAGE	British-Israel World Federation
	http://www.britishisrael.co.uk
CRITICAL SITES	Worldwide Church of God critique
	www.wcg.org/lit/prophecy/anglo/usbrit1.htm
	British-Israelism and the WCG
	www.wcg.org/lit/prophecy/anglo/howanglo.htm
	Robert Roberts's 1879 reply to Edward Hine
	http://mm91007.tripod.com/book/anglo.htm

▸ Bruderhof

The Bruderhof is a Christian Anabaptist communal group founded in 1920 in Germany by Eberhard Arnold. He died in 1935. Before and during the Second World War, Bruderhof communities were victims of Nazi persecution. Many Bruderhof members relocated to Britain in 1939 to 1941, but they were forced to leave, and so most then settled in Paraguay. Heinrich (Heini) Arnold led the movement from 1935 until his death in 1982.

The Bruderhof started a new community called the Woodcrest Hof in Rifton, New York, in 1954. In 1959 the membership experienced a crisis when Arnold shut down the European community and the one in Paraguay. Many followers were expelled from the group at the time. Details of this trauma in the group's history became public when Ramon Sender, one ex-member, began a network for Bruderhof apostates in 1989 using the *Keep in Touch* (KIT) newsletter. Sender started the Peregrine Foundation to expand the reach of Bruderhof critics. The foundation's press has published Elizabeth Bohlken-Tumpe's *Torches Extinguished*. She is the granddaughter of the Bruderhof founder. Her book is an alternative to the group's work *Torches Rekindled* (Plough Publishing).

The Bruderhof were connected for several decades with two major Hutterite groups, but this tie was severed in 1990. The Hutterite elders were upset that the Bruderhof had an open policy about public education of their children. They also objected to Bruderhof participation in a public rally against the death penalty. "Have we ever heard of Hutterites marching with other denominations, or taking part in such activities? No! Never in Hutterite history or in biblical history."[2] They concluded that the use of candles in Bruderhof worship could lead to idolatry, and the use of courts to settle disputes between Christians was against Hutterite tradition.

The Bruderhof group is now led by Johann Christoph Arnold.

Under his leadership, the spiritual community has taken aggressive steps, including litigation, against KIT members, media groups critical of the movement, and several scholars. The community protested a documentary aired on March 27, 1997, by the CBS newsmagazine *48 Hours*.

Bruderhof leaders also tried to pressure Oxford University Press to stop publication of Julius Rubin's work *The Other Side of Joy*, a study of tensions in the Bruderhof community. Rubin's work was released by Oxford in 2000 after considerable delay. The SPCK publishing house in Britain sold the entire first run of their book *Harmful Religion* to the English Bruderhof community. The first edition of the book had a chapter on the group by Rubin. The legal and media controversies have subsided since 2000.[3]

Typical of other Anabaptists, the Bruderhof are opposed to military service. The group campaigns actively for peace initiatives. Johann Christoph Arnold maintains a presence outside Bruderhof circles. He has met several times with Cardinal Ratzinger, now Pope Benedict XVI, and also had an audience with John Paul II in 2004. In these settings Arnold has worked on Vatican recognition of its persecution of Anabaptists in the sixteenth century. Arnold also speaks publicly with former NYPD officer Steven McDonald for the Bruderhof antiviolence program called Breaking the Cycle. McDonald was shot in 1986 in the line of duty and left paralyzed from the neck down.

Bruderhof

TYPOLOGY	Christian Protestant Anabaptist
HOME PAGES	Bruderhof home page, www.bruderhof.com
	Johann Christoph Arnold, www.christopharnold.com
	Breaking the Cycle, www.breakingthecycle.us
CRITIC SITE	The Peregrine Foundation, www.perefound.org
READING	Elizabeth Bohlken-Tumpe, *Torches Extinguished* (San Francisco: Carrier Pigeon Press, 1993)
	Julius H. Rubin, *The Other Side of Joy: Religious Melancholy among the Bruderhof* (New York: Oxford University Press, 2000)
	Merrill Mow, *Torches Rekindled: The Bruderhof's Struggle for Renewal* (Rifton, NY: Plough, 1990)

▸ Buddhism

Buddhism has probably the best image of any world religion. This arises in general because of Buddhist emphasis on peace, serenity, and compassion. More specifically, Buddhism has great appeal because of the singular impact of His Holiness the Dalai Lama, renowned for his great character, humility, and humor. Buddhism goes back to an Indian reformer named Gautama, who is now known to us as the Buddha.

The different traditions in Buddhism do not agree on the details about his life and teachings. In fact, there is no uniformity among Buddhists or among scholars of Buddhism even about when he lived. However, his life is often captured in twelve crucial acts, the first having to do with his preincarnate state.

1. Waits in Tushita (the eternal realm)
2. Grows in the womb of Queen Mayadevi, his mother
3. Is born out of her side
4. Attains intellectual and physical skills
5. Marries Yashodhara and birth of son (Rahula)
6. Renounces royal life and departure from palace
7. Chooses ascetic path of extreme denial
8. Seeks enlightenment at the bodhi tree
9. Defeats Mara (the lord of Samsara)
10. Attains enlightenment
11. Teaches Buddhist dharma
12. Enters Nirvana

Buddha's life story includes alleged supernatural elements. When he was in his mother's womb, his father could see him sitting in a meditation posture inside a wonderful box. After Gautama was born, he took seven steps and proclaimed, "I alone in the world am the

Honored One." When Gautama's mother died, she became a goddess and her womb is preserved in the heavens. Gautama escaped from the royal palace on his horse Kanthaka. The horse died of a broken heart when Gautama had to leave him, but Kanthaka became a god. When Gautama defeated Mara, he did so, in part, by turning demons into flowers.

Christian critique of Buddhism begins with questions about the historical reliability of Buddha and with contradictions among various forms of Buddhism. For example, the Dalai Lama states in his book *The Opening of the Wisdom-Eye* that Tibetan Buddhist teachings and rituals "were taught by Lord Buddha in person." This claim has two serious weaknesses.

First, there are crucial differences in belief and ritual between the late Buddhism of Tibet and the earlier Buddhisms of India and Sri Lanka. There are similar differences between Tibetan Buddhism and the forms of Buddhism practiced in China and Japan. Some critics, indeed, argue that Zen is so different from any other type of Buddhism that it deserves to be treated as a separate religion.

Second, there is the more serious issue of the historical integrity of the earliest documents about Buddha. These texts, in Pali and Sanskrit, were written between four and five centuries after the death of Gautama. In *A Short History of Buddhism*, Edward Conze, a devout Buddhist scholar, dismisses any "confident assertions" about what the Buddha really said as "mere guesswork." Conze wrote in the introduction to *Buddhist Scriptures*: "Buddhists possess nothing that corresponds to the New Testament."

Christians have always objected to notions of karma and reincarnation in Buddhism. The Dalai Lama writes in one of his books that a person killed by a lightning bolt has earned that fate by some misdeed in a previous life. That example, though grim, does not address the deeper implications of the Buddhist view. What of the many Buddhist nuns raped by Communist soldiers during the purge of Tibet? Was this their karmic debt? Some Buddhist teachers have even contended that those who died in the 2004 tsunami disaster were victims of their misdeeds in previous reincarnations.

Stephen Batchelor, a famous Western Buddhist, has argued that it is not necessary to believe in karma and reincarnation in order to be faithful to Buddhism. He expressed this in his 1998 work *Buddhism Without Beliefs*. He says there is symmetry between humanistic, agnostic Western culture and Buddhism. While Christians share his moral and intellectual objections, it is hard to imagine that a faithful reading of virtually every Buddhist tradition can allow disbelief in karma and reincarnation.

Buddhist teachers in Southeast Asia, Japan, Tibet, and other areas of the world where Buddhism is dominant often have little interest in Jesus Christ. Buddhist teachers who have come to the West, however, have frequently incorporated an appreciation of Jesus into their own teachings about Buddhism. This is particularly true of the Dalai Lama and Thich Nhat Hahn. Thich Nhat Hahn was born in Vietnam in 1926 but was forced to leave in 1966. He now lives in exile in France. He contends that Jesus and Buddha are spiritual brothers. "In fact, they could have taken each other's hands and practiced walking meditation, so why not the two of you, one as a Buddhist and one as a Christian? You are the continuation of the Buddha, and you are the continuation of Jesus Christ."

While every agreement between Jesus and Buddha should be recognized, the gaps between Buddhism and Christianity remain enormous. Buddhism is about salvation through self-instruction. It is largely a works-based system, contrary to the Christian emphasis on salvation through grace alone through Christ alone. Buddhists do not believe that Jesus is the only Son of God, since they either deny or are indifferent to affirmation of God. The Buddhist teaching that the self is not ultimately real is distinct from the Jewish and Christian teaching that the human self, created by God and made in His image, is very real.

Claims that Buddhism is a rational or scientific religion can be sustained only by offering a Westernized version of Buddhism that pays far more attention to science than do more traditional versions of Buddhism. In the forms of Buddhism dominant in Tibet, Japan, Thailand, Korea, China, and Vietnam, for example, the oral traditions and scriptural material contain miracle stories that defy rationality. Likewise, paths to liberation from karma often involve rituals that seem to make no common sense. The elaborate cosmologies in Mahayana and Vajrayana Buddhism are distinct from the discourse of modern science.

Buddhism 101

- The current universe has evolved through natural law.
- Truth has been given through countless ages by various Buddhas, or enlightened beings.
- Gautama Buddha, who lived twenty-five hundred years ago, is the teacher for our time period.
- While salvation depends on individual effort, the Buddhist is to take refuge in the Buddha, his teaching (dharma), and the Buddhist community (sangha).
- The Buddha taught Four Noble Truths: (1) suffering is real; (2) suffering is caused by selfish desire; (3) suffering will cease when selfish desire is eliminated; and (4) selfish desire will cease through following the Noble Eightfold Path.
- The Noble Eightfold Path that leads to nirvana involves having the (1) right view, (2) right resolve, (3) right speech, (4) right action, (5) right livelihood, (6) right effort, (7) right mindfulness, and (8) right concentration.
- All living things are subject to the law of karma, the principle of cause and effect, which controls the cycle of reincarnation.
- The Buddhist is to abstain from killing, stealing, forbidden sex, lying, and the use of illicit drugs and liquor.
- There is no God or Supreme Creator.
- According to Buddhists, their religion is neither irrational, pessimistic, nor nihilistic.

Time Line of Buddhism

566–486/490–410 BC	Siddhartha Guatama, the historical Buddha
486 BC	First Buddhist Council at Rajagrha
386 BC	Second Council at Vaisali
367 BC	Noncanonical Council at Pataliputra
272–231 BC	King Asoka converts to Buddhism
c. 250 BC	Asoka's son Mahinda goes as missionary to Sri Lanka
250 BC	Third Council at Pataliputra
250 BC	Pali Canon finished
247 BC	Mahinda takes Buddhism to Sri Lanka
200 BC	Beginnings of Mahayana Buddhism
Second century BC	Nagasena's famous dialogue with King Milinda

25 BC	Pali Canon written in Sri Lanka
First century AD	Fourth Buddhist Council at Kagmir
First century	Lotus Sutra composed
First century	Buddhism spreads to Central Asia
Second century?	Asvaghosa composes *Buddha-Carita*
Second century	Nargarjuna forms Madhyamika school
Third century	Buddhism spreads to Southeast Asia
310–90	Life of Asanga, founder of Yogacara school
Fourth century	Vajrayana Buddhism starts in India
372	Buddhism spreads to Korea
334–416	Life of Hui-yuan (translator of Chinese texts)
344–413	Life of Kumarajiva, founder of Madhyamika in China
405	Fa-hsien, Chinese monk, arrives in India
420–500	Life of Vasubandhu, author of *Vijnaptiimatra Sutra*
Fifth century	Nalanda monastery founded in India
Fifth century	Buddhaghosa composes *Visuddhimagga* (Path of Purity)
Fifth century	Amitabha (Amida) Pure Land school starts in China
520	Bodhidharma goes to China
538	Buddhism reaches Japan
602–64	Life of Hsan-tsang (Chinese translator and pilgrim)
638–713	Life of Hui-Neng, sixth patriarch of Ch'an Buddhism
Eighth century	Hosso, Jojitsu, Kegon, Kusha, Ritsu, and Sanron schools
Eighth century	Padmasambhava travels to Tibet to help spread Buddhism
Eighth century	Nyingma-pa sect in Tibet begins
767–822	Life of Saicho (founder of Tendai school)
774–835	Life of Kukai (founder of Shingon school)
845	Buddhism under attack in China
Ninth century	Diamond Sutra written in China
983	Szechuan Canon printed
1008–64	Life of Bu-ston, Tibetan textual scholar
1012–96?	Life of Marpa, founder of Kargyupa sect
1040–1103	Life of Milarepa, disciple of Marpa
c. 1040	Atisha (982–1054) starts Kahdam-pa school in Tibet
c. 1050	Sakyapa Tibetan school begins
1123	Death of Milarepa (b. 1040), Tibetan saint
1133–1212	Life of Honen, founder of Jodo, focus on Amitabha
1141–1215	Life of Eisai, founder of Rinzai Zen Japanese sect
1173–1263	Life of Shinran, founder of True Pure Land Japanese sect
1200	Nalanda University destroyed
1200–1253	Life of Dogen, founder of Soto Zen Japanese sect
1222–82	Life of Nichiren
Thirteenth century	Vajrayana spreads to Mongols
Fourteenth century	Bu-ston edits Tibetan Buddhist canon

1360	Theravada becomes state religion in Thailand
1355–1417	Life of Tsongkhapa, founder of Gelugpa Tibetan sect
Fifteenth century	Dalai Lama lineage in Tibet begins
1587	Altan Khan gives Gelugpa leader title of Dalai Lama
1686–1769	Life of Hakuin, famous Rinzai teacher of koans
1862	Sri Lankan monks get reordained in Burma
1862	Western translation of Dhammapada
1870	Birth of D. T. Suzuki, Japanese Zen teacher
1871	Fifth Buddhist Council in Mandalay, Myanmar
1891	Anagarika Dharmapala (1865–1933) starts Maha Bodhi
1893	Buddhist monks at Parliament of Religions in Chicago
1904	Birth of Ven. U. Sobhana (Vispassana reformer)
1907	Birth of Ven. Walpola Rahula, Sri Lankan reformer
1926	Founding of Buddhist Society by Christmas Humphreys
1926	Birth of Thich Nhat Hanh, famous Vietnamese Buddhist
1928–29	T'ai-Hsu (b. 1889), Chinese monk, travels in Europe
1932	Buddhadasa establishes Suan Mokkhabalarama in Chaiya
1935	Birth of Dalai Lama
1950	Communist persecution of Tibet
1954–56	Sixth Buddhist Council at Rangoon, Myanmar
1956	Ambedkar (1891–1956) espouses Buddhism
1959	Dalai Lama flees Tibet
1966	D. T. Suzuki dies
1989	Dalai Lama receives Nobel Peace Prize
1997	Hollywood focus on Buddhism
2004	World Buddhist summit held in Myanmar

Buddhism

FOUNDER	Gautama (566–486/490–410 B.C)
WEB SITES	BuddhaNet, www.buddhanet.net
	DharmaNet, www.dharmanet.org
	Buddhist Studies Virtual Library
	www.ciolek.com/WWWVL-Buddhism.html
	Government of Tibet in Exile (Dalai Lama)
	www.tibet.com
READING	Rick Fields, *How the Swans Came to the Lake* (Boston: Shambhala, 1992).
	Donald S. Lopez Jr., *The Story of Buddhism* (San Francisco: HarperSanFrancisco, 2001).
	J. Isamu Yamamoto, *Beyond Buddhism* (Downers Grove, IL: InterVarsity, 1982).

Charismatic Christianity is a stream of the church that puts emphasis on the "sign-gifts" of the Holy Spirit: prophecy, healings, and speaking in tongues, as mentioned in 1 Corinthians 12. Historians often date the origin of the modern charismatic movement to April 3, 1960. On that day Dennis Bennett announced to his congregation at St. Mark's Episcopal Church in Van Nuys, California, that he had spoken in tongues. Reports in *Newsweek* and *Time* about the ensuing controversy led to national awareness of charismatic gifts in mainline Protestantism. In 1967 charismatic gifts became a significant reality in Roman Catholic worship. One manner in which many Charismatics differ from Pentecostals is that the latter usually believe speaking in tongues is the exclusive sign of the baptism of the Holy Spirit.

Both Pentecostal and charismatic Christianity have been impacted significantly by John Wimber (1934–97), leader of the Vineyard movement. Wimber's music ministry, views on healing and prophecy, and style of leadership influenced Christian pastors and congregations worldwide. Wimber had a significant impact on both the Kansas City Prophets (a movement connected with Mike Bickle) and the Toronto Blessing (a revival movement started in 1994 and led by John Arnott).

Mike Bickle's Kansas City Fellowship (KCF) became a major charismatic center in the late 1980s, following Wimber's embrace of Bickle and the prophets (John Paul Jackson, Bob Jones, and Paul Cain) connected with KCF. Paul Cain was a healing revivalist in the 1950s and began a second ministry with Bickle and Wimber. In the fall of 2004 Cain was disciplined over allegations of sexual sin and alcoholism. Jones is now connected with Rick Joyner, who leads MorningStar Ministries in North Carolina. John Paul Jackson heads Streams Ministries International, based in New Hampshire.

The Toronto Blessing is one of the most famous and controversial renewal movements in the charismatic world. The revival's start is dated to January 20, 1994, when Randy Clark, a visiting pastor, spoke about his spiritual renewal under the ministry of Rodney Howard-Browne, a South African evangelist based in Florida. His preaching led to strange manifestations—people falling over, laughing, screaming, shaking violently, and even behaving like animals.

Aspects of the Toronto Blessing were duplicated in Pensacola, Florida, in the ongoing revival that began on Father's Day 1995 at the Brownsville Assembly of God congregation. Steve Hill, a visiting evangelist, was reporting at the time on his personal spiritual renewal at Holy Trinity Church, Brompton, England. The Brownsville congregation was led by John Kilpatrick from 1981 to 2003.

Hank Hanegraaff critiqued the wilder components in the Vineyard, the Kansas City Prophets saga, the Toronto Blessing, and the Brownsville renewal in his best-selling book *Counterfeit Revival*. On the other hand, Jack Deere, a former Old Testament professor at Dallas Theological Seminary, defended these renewals in his work *Surprised by the Power of the Holy Spirit*. Mainstream charismatic life is chronicled in the monthly issues of *Charisma* magazine, published by Stephen Strang.

A charismatic Christian style is still dominant in parts of the Roman Catholic and mainline Protestant world. More important, much of the incredible growth of Christian faith in the Third World involves a charismatic dimension. Many missiologists argue that the charismatic or Pentecostal worldview ties in with the supernatural worldviews of South American and African cultures.

Charismatics

TYPOLOGY	Christian Protestant
WEB SITES	Toronto Airport Christian Fellowship, www.tacf.org
	Brownsville Revival, www.brownsville-revival.org
READING	Stanley M. Burgess, ed., *The New International Dictionary of Pentecostal and Charismatic Movements* (Grand Rapids, MI: Zondervan, 2002).
	Harvey Cox, *Fire from Heaven* (Reading, MA: Addison-Wesley, 1994).
	Vinson Synan, *The Century of the Holy Spirit* (Nashville: Thomas Nelson, 2001).

▸ Ching Hai

Ching Hai is the leader of the Supreme Master Ching Hai Association. She was born in 1950 in Vietnam with the birth name Hue Dang Trinh. She practices a form of Quan Yin Buddhism.

Before she began her religious teaching, Ching Hai worked in Germany and was married to a German scientist. Ching Hai's followers claim that she left him (with his approval) in order to pursue enlightenment, a path that allegedly took her to thirty countries over seven years. She is said to have reached enlightenment in the Himalayas when she met Master Khuda Ji, who was supposedly 450 years old at the time. She also claims to be his only disciple.

Ching Hai describes her Himalayan trek in austere terms.

> I couldn't afford to hire a horse or a coolie. I had nothing, so I could only walk. Perhaps my continuous walking kept me warm. Otherwise, I would have frozen, as I was wearing wet clothes and shoes amid the rain and snow in the mountains. Some peaks were high and lofty, and looked awesome. I must have been as crazy then as couples who are madly in love, and oblivious to everything else. However, God blesses idiots like me.

Critics of Ching Hai argue that her teaching is rooted in more mundane realities, including study with Thakar Singh (a controversial Sant Mat teacher) in India and with Xing-jing (a Buddhist nun in Taiwan). Her emphasis on light and sound matches the Sant Mat tradition.

Ching Hai gained considerable attention in 1996 when she donated $600,000 to President Clinton for his legal defense. The money was returned to the group. Yet Ching Hai continues to maintain a high profile. She was a featured speaker at the 1999 Parliament of the World's Religions in Cape Town, South Africa. Her mission is supported by sales of her designs in jewelry and fashion clothing.

Ching Hai has an interesting perspective on miracles.

You see, the miracles don't secure a holy personality. Many people have miracle power without being holy. This you know: the black magician, the white magician, they all have miracles, but that doesn't mean they are holy. Jesus had to use these miracles because it was in different circumstances. Nowadays we are more intelligent, we are not as barbaric, we are more technological, more advanced, more civilized, and more scientifically minded. I do not want to use miracles to bait you because I respect your wisdom, I respect your intelligence. Miracles don't make a person holy, that is for sure. You will know my miracles in time if you are sincere, if you have a higher ideal. You will know everything about your Master in time. I'm not selling cheap in the supermarket.

Ching Hai teaches that all humans are divine and that this realization will lead to world peace.

Through enlightenment we come to realize that the God Nature is within us, being an innate quality that we possess from birth. Only through rediscovering it can we realize that we all have the same God Nature and that we are originally one, without any discrimination between friend and foe, or me and you. Then we truly become peaceful and harmonious, and can bring real peace into the world.

Ching Hai

TYPOLOGY	Sant Mat and Buddhist
HOME PAGES	www.godsimmediatecontact.com
	www.godsdirectcontact.org

▶ Christadelphians

Christadelphians trace their modern roots to the work of John Thomas, a native of England. Thomas was born in 1805 and immigrated to the United States in 1832. He was associated for some time with restorationist movements (the Campbellites and the Millerites) but kept refining his own theological positions. He gained a following both in England and the United States and in 1864 adopted the name "Christadelphian" (meaning "brothers in Christ") for his group. Though some of his date-setting and apocalyptic warnings about England created unrest, his followers remained united until his death in 1871. Robert Roberts led the English branch of the movement after the founder's death, while Thomas Williams led the American group.

Christadelphians affirm the inerrancy of Scripture but hold some views distinct from classical Christian orthodoxy. They deny the Trinity and the personal nature of the Holy Spirit. They believe Jesus to be the Son of God but do not believe that He is one in essence with the Father and Spirit. Christadelphians state: "Jesus is a Man, not God!" They also deny that Jesus had a sinless nature. They do believe in the virgin birth of Jesus, accept the Gospel accounts of his miracles, and believe that Jesus will come again to earth.

Christadelphians deny the immortality of the soul, eternal punishment, and the existence of Satan. They affirm the notion of soul sleep and believer's baptism, even contending that baptism is necessary for salvation. They reject the typical Protestant understanding of "grace alone" for salvation, arguing "we reject the doctrine that the Gospel alone will save, without obedience to Christ's commandments." The group also condemns Christian involvement in the military and politics.

The Christadelphians have experienced major internal tensions throughout their history over what constitutes true doctrine. There have been divisions over the understanding of Christ's nature, the issue of biblical inerrancy, and the proper place of leadership within the body. The most significant division occurred in the 1890s over whether the dead who once followed Christ would be raised to judgment. The bitter controversy over a rather arcane point led to an amendment of the Statement of Faith. Some Christadelphians follow the Birmingham Unamended Statement of Faith (or BUSF). The majority follow the Birmingham Amended Statement of Faith (or BASF). Frequent attempts to bridge the schism have failed, though there has been less tension on the issue in recent decades.

Christadelphians have no central ecclesiastical authority, though they are bound by their common heritage from Thomas and by the many doctrines common to both Statements of Faith. There are more than three hundred local congregations in Britain and more than four hundred in the United States. *The Christadelphian* serves as the main magazine for Amended fellowships, while *The Christadelphian Advocate* reaches those who follow the Unamended Statement of Faith.

Christadelphians

TYPOLOGY	Christian Protestant
FOUNDER	John Thomas (1805–71)
HOME PAGES	www.christadelphia.org
	www.thechristadelphians.org
READING	Charles H. Lippy, *The Christadelphians in North America* (Lewiston, New York: Edwin Mellen, 1989)

▸ Christian Science

Christian Science is the popular designation for the Church of Christ, Scientist, the controversial movement founded by Mary Baker Eddy in Lynn, Massachusetts, in 1879. Eddy published *Science and Health with Key to the Scriptures* in 1875. She revised the work several times before her death. *Science and Health* is the defining text of the religion.

Eddy was born in Bow, New Hampshire, on July 16, 1821. She claimed that the turning point of her spiritual life came in February 1866 after life-threatening injuries from a fall on the sidewalk were reversed when she discovered the healing methods of Jesus. Critics dispute not only her account of the healing but also her underlying ideology of sickness and health.

Eddy started public teaching of her method of healing in 1870, founded her church in 1879, and established the Massachusetts Metaphysical College in 1881. The movement grew rapidly in the final two decades of the century in spite of widespread criticism in the media and from religious leaders such as fellow Bostonian A. J. Gordon. The mother church in Boston was dedicated in January of 1895 and the movement published the first issue of *The Christian Science Monitor* in 1908. Mrs. Eddy died on December 3, 1910, at age eighty-nine, in her home in Chestnut Hill.

Christian Science represents Mrs. Eddy's metaphysical understanding of Christian faith. Though the movement uses the standard terms of Christian orthodoxy, it invests them with the ideology of the mind science tradition that was popular in America in the 1800s, most notably through the work of Phineas Parkhurt Quimby (1802–66), a pioneer in the field of mesmerism in the United States. Eddy turned to Quimby in 1862 for medical assistance but later abandoned his approach for her own theories of divine healing.

The movement has faced crisis in the last few decades. Several ex-members have launched massive campaigns against Christian Science for its neglect of the health needs of children. Doug and Rita Swan blamed Christian Science ideology and practice for the death of their son Matthew from spinal meningitis. They formed an organization named C.H.I.L.D. (Children's Healthcare Is a Legal Duty) that monitors Christian Science and other groups accused of putting children at risk.

Caroline Fraser, a prominent ex-member, created controversy when she chronicled the death of Christian Science children in *The Atlantic Monthly* in 1995. Fraser's later work, *God's Perfect Child*, published in 1999, created further turmoil for Christian Science. For example, her work highlighted the case of Robyn Twitchell, a two-year-old who died in 1986 of a bowel obstruction that was treatable. Robyn's parents, David and Ginger Twitchell, claimed that their reliance on prayer alone was allowed under a religious exemption clause that was added to the Massachusetts law on child neglect in 1971. They were convicted in 1990 of involuntary manslaughter.

In recent years Christian Science has tried to appeal to those attracted to the New Age movement and to modern notions of spirituality. Virginia Harris, the current head of the mother church, has campaigned aggressively for a fresh image of the movement. She has appeared on *Larry King Live* and on PBS and has been interviewed by *The New York Times*, *Forbes Magazine*, and *The Los Angeles Times*. Mrs. Harris is also on the board of the Mary Baker Eddy Library for the Betterment of Humanity, opened in September 2002.

Christian Science is one of the few religions in the world that contains in its core a teaching that is often deadly when put into practice. Mrs. Eddy repeatedly taught that matter is not real and that sin, disease, and death are illusions. These denials lead Christian Scientists to avoid doctors and hospitals as they pray for healing from false belief in the reality of sickness. Thus, Christian Science claims of healing are not about reversal of real physical disease but about faith-based denial that disease has any actuality other than in the mind.

Christian Science

TYPOLOGY	Christian esoteric sectarian
FOUNDER	Mary Baker Eddy
SCRIPTURE	*Science and Health*
HOME PAGES	Church of Christ, Scientist, Web site
	www.tfccs.com
	The Mary Baker Eddy Library
	www.marybakereddylibrary.org
CRITIC SITES	Children's Health Care Is a Legal Duty (CHILD, Inc.)
	www.childrenshealthcare.org
	Christian Way
	www.christianway.org
	Ex-Christian Scientists
	www.ex-christian-science.8m.com
	Quackwatch (Stephen Barrett, M.D.)
	www.quackwatch.org
READING	Gillian Gill, *Mary Baker Eddy* (Cambridge, MA: Da Capo Press, 1998)
	Robert Davis Thomas, *With Bleeding Footsteps* (New York: Knopf, 1994)
	Caroline Fraser, *God's Perfect Child* (New York: Henry Holt, 1999)

▸ Christianity

Christianity is the largest of the world religions. David Barrett and Todd Johnson at the Center for the Study of Global Christianity report that in 2005 there are over 2.13 billion Christians in the world. This is almost 1 billion more than the number of Muslims. Nearly one in three people on the planet professes allegiance to the Christian faith.

The story of Christianity, like that of every other world religion, is a complex one. This complexity is illustrated by the various groups that claim to be Christian, with their competing views of truth and different understandings about Christian belief and living. The difference of opinion among the three major divisions in Christendom (Roman Catholic, Orthodox, and Protestant) is merely one signal of the difficult issues raised in the study of Christianity.

In spite of such complexities, some major beliefs are common to the vast majority of Christians and church bodies that have made up Christianity since the time of Jesus of Nazareth. For instance, Christians inherit from the Jewish tradition the belief that there is only one God, the omnipotent Creator. Christians affirm that God is an eternal Spirit being who is perfect and all loving.

Christianity has always taught that God has revealed himself in the person of Jesus of Nazareth. The New Testament confesses that Jesus is the Christ, or Messiah, and that he is the Son of God. He is greater than angels and is the final and ultimate revelation.

Based on the New Testament data about Jesus, Christians came to believe that God exists eternally in three Persons: Father, Son, and Holy Spirit. This doctrine of the Trinity was developed over the first four centuries of church history.

According to Christian tradition, Jesus was born to the Virgin Mary, and his ministry was announced by John the Baptist, his cousin. Jesus was a worker of miracles. The New Testament reports that he had power over nature, the demonic, disease, and death. Even his enemies were amazed by his mighty deeds, according to the Gospel accounts. The earliest traditions about Jesus give significant attention to his miracles—a fact that speaks against Enlightenment skepticism about their value.

Jesus often taught in parables. His preaching and teaching focused on several major items, including his own mission, the nature of God's kingdom, and what it means to follow God. Jesus taught that the most important moral principles involve loving God and loving other humans. Jesus was critical of legalism and religious hypocrisy. He challenged his disciples to a deep understanding of, and obedience to, the moral principles of the Old Testament.

Jesus died as a result of conflict with both Jewish and Roman leaders. His death is viewed in Christian tradition as a sacrifice for human sin. Christians remember the death of Jesus in the sacraments of baptism and the Lord's Supper (or Eucharist). Salvation is a gift of God, not caused by human works, but based on the grace of God, and is to be accepted by faith. Those who follow Christ are to obey God's will, which is made known in the Bible, through prayer, and in duplication of the life of Christ in daily living.

Early Christians believed that Jesus was raised bodily from the dead. His resurrection formed the basis for the rise of the Christian church, for the reception of the Holy Spirit at Pentecost, and for proclamation of his Second Coming at the end of time. Christians believe that God will one day judge all humanity. Christianity affirms both the gift of eternal life through Christ and the peril of eternal death to those outside Christ.

Christians affirm belief in one holy, catholic, and apostolic church. Most Christians have chosen to identify the church with one distinct human organization, whether it is Roman Catholic, Orthodox, Protestant, or some other body of believers. Tragically, strict identification of the church with one body often blinds that group to self-criticism. The true church of Jesus, shown in holiness and union with the apostolic faith, is often at odds with this or that group that claims to be Christ's only bride.

Time Line of Christianity

70	Jerusalem destroyed by Roman army
150	Justin Martyr defends Christianity
155	Church father Polycarp endures persecution
177	Irenaeus writes against emerging heresies
196	Tertullian defends a vigorous Christian lifestyle
205	Origen combines theology with philosophical learning
251	Cyprian argues for the primacy of Rome
257	Sixtus II becomes pope
270	Antony chooses the path of a hermit
311	Donatist schism in North Africa
312	Constantine is converted
313	Edict of Toleration agreed upon by Constantine and Licinius
325	Council of Nicea defines orthodoxy
365	Athanasius defends the doctrine of the Trinity
382	Pope Damascus lists Old and New Testament canon
385	In Milan, Bishop Ambrose defies Roman authorities
387	Conversion of Augustine of Hippo
398	John Chrysostom becomes bishop of Constantinople.
405	Latin Vulgate completed by Jerome
410	Goths sack Rome
416	Council of Carthage condemns Pelagianism
431	Council of Ephesus approves *theotokos* as a title for Mary
432	Patrick returns to Ireland as a missionary
440	Leo the Great becomes pope
451	Council of Chalcedon affirms the Nicene view of Jesus
525	Boethius is executed
529	Benedict of Nursia establishes monasticism
553	Second Council of Constantinople
563	Columba works as a missionary in Iona
590	Gregory I begins papal rule
600	Isidore, bishop of Seville, works as a scholar
619	Boniface V becomes pope
632	Death of Muhammad
664	Synod of Whitby accepts the authority of Rome for the English church
681	Third Council of Constantinople
716	Boniface brings the gospel to Germany
726	Controversy over icons
731	The Venerable Bede writes *Ecclesiastical History*
732	Charles Martel defeats Muslims at Tours

754   Boniface is martyred in Frisia
787   Icons are approved at the Second Council of Nicea
800   Charlemagne crowned emperor
851   Martyrdom of Christians at Cordova by Muslims
863   Serbs evangelized by Cyril and Methodius
877   Death of philosopher Scotus Erigena in Ireland
909   Monastery founded at Cluny
988   Vladimir chooses Orthodoxy for the Russian people
1054   Great Schism between East and West
1093   Anselm becomes archbishop of Canterbury
1095   Start of First Crusade by Pope Urban II
1115   Bernard of Clairvaux starts a monastery
1116   Peter Abelard teaches in Paris
1170   Archbishop Thomas Becket murdered
1173   Peter Waldo initiates reform
1187   Saladin captures Jerusalem
1204   Western Crusaders sack Constantinople
1209   Francis of Assisi chooses the monastic life
1215   The Fourth Lateran Council affirms papal supremacy
1273   Thomas Aquinas completes his *Summa theologia*
1295   Mongol dynasty converts to Islam
1302   Boniface VIII proclaims universal papal supremacy
1321   Dante writes *The Divine Comedy*
1378   Great Schism in papacy
1380   Wycliffe works on Bible translation into English
1415   John Hus burned at the stake by the Council of Con
       stance
1418   *Imitatio Christi* surfaces, attributed to Thomas à Kem
       pis
1447   Nicholas V becomes pope
1453   Ottoman Turks take control of Constantinople
1456   Johann Gutenberg prints the first Bible
1478   Start of Spanish Inquisition
1492   Muslims expelled from Spain
1498   Savonarola, leading Dominican preacher, burned at
       the stake
1509   Erasmus protests abuses in Rome
1512   Michelangelo finishes the Sistine Chapel
1517   Martin Luther posts his ninety-five theses
1521   Luther is excommunicated
1523   Zwingli leads the Reformation in Zurich
1525   Start of Anabaptist movement
1530   Lutherans adopt the Augsburg Confession
1534   Henry VIII becomes head of the Church of England

1536	John Calvin publishes *Institutes of the Christian Religion*
1540	Jesuit movement started by Ignatius
1545	Start of the Council of Trent
1549	*Book of Common Prayer* produced by Cranmer
1553	Servetus burned to death for heresy at Geneva
1555	Latimer and Ridley burned at the stake in Oxford
1560	Reformed Church started in Scotland by John Knox
1562	Socinus teaches Unitarian views
1572	Huguenots killed on Saint Bartholomew's Day in France
1577	Formula of Concord affirmed by Lutherans
1594	Richard Hooker writes *Ecclesiastical Polity*
1601	Matteo Ricci travels to China as Catholic missionary
1609	Start of Baptist movement by Anglican preacher John Smyth
1611	King James Version published
1618	Synod of Dordt condemns Arminianism
1620	Pilgrims arrive in America
1622	Pope Gregory XV creates the Holy Office
1646	Westminster Confession adopted
1648	George Fox establishes the Society of Friends (Quakers)
1648	Peace of Westphalia ends the Thirty Years' War
1654	Conversion of Pascal
1675	Philip Jacob Spener publishes *Pia Desideria*
1676	Innocent XI becomes pope
1678	Publication of John Bunyan's *The Pilgrim's Progress*
1678	Richard Simon engages in Old Testament criticism
1691	Innocent XII becomes pope
1701	Society for the Propagation of the Gospel started in London
1727	Moravian Brethren experience revival
1728	William Law, *A Serious Call to a Devout and Holy Life*
1735	Jonathan Edwards leads the Great Awakening in America
1736	Joseph Butler, *The Analogy of Religion*
1738	Conversion of John Wesley
1740	Benedict XIV becomes pope
1748	David Hume publishes critique of miracles
1778	Death of Voltaire
1780	Robert Raikes starts the Sunday school movement
1799	Friedrich Schleiermacher, *On Religion: Speeches to Its Cultured Despisers*
1800	Pius VII becomes pope
1804	British and Foreign Bible Society started
1807	Slave trade abolished by British Parliament

1966	Archbishop Ramsey meets Paul VI in Rome
1968	Martin Luther King shot to death
1968	Pope Paul VI condemns birth control pill
1970	Hans Küng writes critique of papal infallibility
1976	Election of Jimmy Carter as American president
1978	John Paul II becomes pope
1979	Hans Küng removed as Catholic theologian
1980	Oscar Romero assassinated in El Salvador
1986	Desmond Tutu becomes Cape Town Archbishop
1987	Scandals in Jim Bakker and Jimmy Swaggart ministries
1999	Agreement on justification between Lutherans and Catholics
2000	Vatican issues Lenten apology
2005	Death of John Paul II; Benedict XVI is the new popes

Christianity

WEB SITES

Christianity Today
www.christianitytoday.com
World Evangelical Alliance
www.worldevangelicalalliance.com
World Council of Churches
www.wcc-coe.org

READING

Francis Beckwith, William Lane Craig, J. P. Moreland, eds. *To Everyone An Answer* (Downers Grove, IL: InterVarsity, 2004)

Norman Geisler, *Encyclopedia of Christian Apologetics* (Grand Rapids: Baker, 1999.

Gary Habermas and Michael Licona, *The Case for the Resurrection of Jesus* (Grand Rapids: Kregel, 2004)

C. S. Lewis, *Mere Christianity* (Grand Rapids: Zondervan, 2001)

J. I. Packer, *Knowing God* (Downers Grove IL: InterVarsity, 1993)

Jaroslav Pelikan, *Jesus Through the Centuries* (New Haven: Yale, 1999)

Lee Strobel, *The Case for Christ* (Grand Rapids: Zondervan, 1998)

▶ Church of Christ (Stone-Campbell Restoration Movement)

In the early nineteenth century, in the midst of a proliferation of Protestant denominations, several Christian leaders in the southern United States campaigned for the restoration of a single Church of Christ. The best-known advocates of this return to "primitive" Christianity were Barton Stone (1772–1844), Thomas Campbell (1763–1854), and his son Alexander (1788–1866).

The Campbells were Presbyterian in their roots, as was Stone. Other Restorationists came from Methodist backgrounds (James O'Kelly, 1757–1826) and from the Baptist church (Abner Jones, 1772–1841, and Elias Smith, 1769–1846). Stone and other Presbyterians advanced their new Restorationist outlook in the famous document known as "The Last Will and Testament of the Springfield Presbytery." This was issued in 1804 in Kentucky.

The focus on one Church of Christ rooted in the Bible alone was an ideal never to be realized. Melton's *Encyclopedia of Religions in America* lists sixteen distinct bodies that have emerged from the original movement. Divisions occurred over different understandings of baptism, women in leadership, use of instrumental music in worship, whether to have one cup during Communion, and whether Sunday school is biblical. The movement also experienced schism over charismatic gifts. Pat Boone was excommunicated by the Church of Christ in Inglewood, California, in 1971. As is often the case, a movement designed to restore unity in the church led to greater splintering.

The major restoration groups today are (1) the Christian Church (Disciples of Christ), (2) Christian Churches and Churches of Christ, and (3) Churches of Christ (Non-instrumental). Since the Stone-Campbell movement emphasizes local church autonomy, the various streams in the movement are identified through common doctrine and practice. Likewise, the different groups find unity in their various educational institutions, publications, and conferences.

The controversial International Churches of Christ (ICOC), founded by Kip McKean, are also rooted in the Church of Christ tradition from Stone-Campbell. The ICOC is also referred to as the Boston Church of Christ, the Boston Movement, and the Crossroads Movement. In the 1990s, the ICOC and the mainstream of the Church of Christ movement distanced themselves from each other over a growing list of issues. McKean's resignation from the top leaderhip position in 2002 has created an enormous crisis in the ICOC.

Ultraconservative Church of Christ members deny salvation to those outside their "one church." This verdict is based either on arguments against the validity of baptism in mainline churches or about practices (such as instrumental music in worship) that allegedly illustrate the spiritual death in non–Church of Christ circles. Strict members believe that it is necessary to be baptized as a believer in order to be saved. Moderates in the Church of Christ tradition do not deny salvation to those outside their religious group or have a legalistic view on the necessity of baptism.

Church of Christ (Stone-Campbell Restoration Movement)

FOUNDERS	Barton Stone, Thomas Campbell, Alexander Campbell
WEB SITES	Christian Church (Disciples of Christ)
	www.disciples.org
	Churches of Christ
	http://church-of-christ.org
OTHER SITES	Restoration Movement (Hans Rollmann)
	www.mun.ca/rels/restmov
	The Stone Campbell Journal
	www.stone-campbelljournal.com
	Stone-Campbell Resources (Jim McMillan)
	www.bible.acu.edu/stone-campbell
READING	William Baker, ed., *Evangelicalism and the Stone-Campbell Movement* (Downers Grove, IL: InterVarsity, 2002)
	Douglas A. Foster, Paul M. Blowers, Anthony L. Dunnavant, and D. Newell Williams, eds., *The Encyclopedia of the Stone-Campbell Movement* (Grand Rapids: Eerdmans, 2004)

▶ Church Universal and Triumphant

The Church Universal and Triumphant, or CUT, is one of the best-known New Age groups. Originally named Summit Lighthouse, it was founded by Mark Prophet in 1958. The church has its roots in the Theosophical tradition (Madame Blavatsky) and its offshoot I AM, founded by Guy and Edna Ballard. Prophet was born in 1918 in Wisconsin and claimed to have been contacted by the ascended master El Morya in his teens. He stated that he rejected the supernatural visitor's message until the early 1950s.

In 1961 Mark met Elizabeth Clare Wulf, a former Christian Scientist, and they were married in 1963, after Mark's divorce from his first wife. The new couple moved their headquarters to Colorado. Mark died in 1973. Elizabeth, a native of New Jersey, took over leadership of Summit Lighthouse.

Both Mark and Elizabeth Prophet taught that they were restoring the lost teachings of Jesus, and they argued that Jesus traveled in India and Tibet before beginning His public ministry. Elizabeth taught that she was Catherine of Siena in a previous life, while her husband taught that he had previously existed as the third-century Christian theologian Origen and as Mark the Evangelist, companion to the apostle Peter.

Summit Lighthouse was renamed the Church Universal and Triumphant in 1974 on the basis of an alleged revelation from Pope John XXIII through Mrs. Prophet. At the time, headquarters was near Santa Barbara, though later the church moved to Malibu (at a site known as Camelot) and then to Montana in 1986. The church had previously purchased the former ranch of Malcolm Forbes near Yellowstone Park.

After the move to Montana, Mrs. Prophet's messages became increasingly apocalyptic and stressed a survivalist mentality. The church was mocked for its building of bomb shelters, and critics complained that the movement was stockpiling weapons. Members were encouraged to have supplies that could last for seven years and were given the opportunity to purchase in bulk from the church.

Through the 1980s, Mrs. Prophet taught members that a major catastrophe could possibly hit at some point prior to March 15, 1990. She even observed that the national March obsession with college basketball finals gave America's enemies an opportunity to strike. Cheri Walsh, a former member, writes: "I was on the night shift in the bomb shelter. I was glad because if anything happened it would probably be in the middle of the night and I would already be there." Church membership declined through the 1990s following several major organizational changes and the decline of Mrs. Prophet's health.

In 1999 Mrs. Prophet stepped down from church leadership after being diagnosed with Alzheimer's disease. After her first husband's death, she remarried three times. She has five children—Sean, Erin, Moira, Tatiana (all adults), and Seth, who was born in 1994. All of the adult children left the movement during their teen years, experienced periods of hostility to the church and their mother, and later achieved some reconciliation with her.

Church Universal and Triumphant

TYPOLOGY	Western esoteric
FOUNDERS	Mark and Elizabeth Prophet
HOME PAGE	www.tsl.org
CRITIC SITES	www.lifeincut.com
READING	Bradley C. Whitsel, *The Church Universal and Triumphant* (Syracuse, NY: Syracuse University Press, 2003).

▸ Concerned Christians

Monte Kim Miller, the leader of Concerned Christians, was born April 20, 1954. A native of Colorado, he was converted under the ministry of Bill Bright. Miller was originally connected with the evangelical countercult movement, but in the late 1980s he adopted an isolationist ideology that made him the target of cult watchers.

Miller uses files from his former radio program, *Our Foundation*, to spread his views. In 1996 he claimed to have a message from God for the radio stations that used to run his program: "You are to begin airing the program for free on the air. Do not laugh. He is serious. We will not be sending you any more funds. It is time for you to serve the Lord with all your heart, soul, and mind." He filed for bankruptcy the next year.

Miller denies the common allegation that he predicted that Denver would be destroyed on October 10, 1998. Miller left the Denver area in September of that year. He is also said to have prophesied that he would be gunned down in Israel in 1999 and rise again. Some of Miller's followers were arrested in Israel in late 1998. They were sent back to the United States out of fear they would commit violence in order to bring about their vision of Armageddon, as the end of the millennium approached.

Miller claims that he is "the Prophet" of God speaking God's message to the last days. The tone of his message is expressed in this announcement to the world:

> Fear God, for it is he who gathered athletes from precisely 77 nations on the 770th day of the millennium, February 8, 2002, the Opening of the Winter Olympic Games. It is he who ordained, on the very same day, the completion of his 777th tape and CD of detailed explanations of his coordination of world history, this all

being 7 days before the 777th day of the millennium, February 15, 2002, his day that The Seventh Angel Sounds.

The United States is the target of much of Miller's prophetic wrath.

It is God *or* country, not God *and* country. If a Christian does not denounce in his heart the *Declaration of Independence* principles that America was founded upon, that is, "life, liberty, and the pursuit of happiness," that Christian will be considered by God to have a heart of treason against the Kingdom of Heaven. A man who is willing to die for America is a man who will not enter the kingdom of God.

Miller claims to offer precise details of biblical prophecy. He states that the space shuttle *Challenger*'s destruction was foretold in Scripture. Also, the Manhattan Project was directed out of rooms 5120 and 5121 in the War Department Building in Washington in order to fulfill Jeremiah 51:20–21. Furthermore, God ordained that a recent bomb in the American arsenal be named MOAB (Massive Ordnance Air Burst) since Moab was the son of Lot's daughter. This connection with Sodom proves, according to Miller, that America is the modern kingdom of Babylon.

Early in the new millennium Miller dropped out of sight and his current whereabouts are unknown.

Concerned Christians

TYPOLOGY	Christian Protestant sectarian
FOUNDER	Monte Kim Miller (1954–)
HOME PAGE	www.kimmillerconcernedchristians.com
	(Go to this site via www.waybackmachine.org to consult archives)

▸ A Course in Miracles

A Course in Miracles (ACIM), one of the most popular texts in the New Age movement, has also found its way into a few mainline Christian denominations. The story of its origin has been complicated by stormy litigation surrounding copyright battles over the three-volume work. The standard story is that ACIM is a product of channeling from Jesus to a woman named Helen Schucman. The Jesus of ACIM conforms to standard New Thought teaching, with no emphasis upon Jesus as the unique Son of God.

Schucman, a secular atheist, became associate professor of medical psychology at the Columbia-Presbyterian Medical Center in New York City in 1958. In the summer of 1965, she claimed to experience dramatic dreams in which she heard from a Voice. In October of that year the Voice told her: "This is a course in miracles; please take notes." With the help of William Thetford, her boss, she began channeling almost fifteen hundred pages of material. The process lasted until September 1972 and resulted in *A Course in Miracles*. Schucman died in 1981, followed by Thetford seven years later.

In 1973 the ACIM was edited by Ken Wapnick, who had become friends with Helen and Bill. In 1975 the text was shown to Judy Skutch, president of the Foundation for Parasensory Investigation. Skutch changed her organization to the Foundation for Inner Peace (FIP) that same year and registered the copyright of ACIM under "Anonymous (Helen Schucman)." In these formative years it was regularly claimed that Jesus was the ultimate source of ACIM. In fact, Wapnick stated at one point, "It was very clear to me that Helen could not have written it and I just could not imagine it having any other source than Jesus himself."

In 1995 the Foundation for Inner Peace reached an agreement with Penguin Books to allow the publisher to hold copyright for

ACIM. The next year the New Christian Church of Full Endeavor was sued for distributing ACIM on its own. That began a lengthy legal battle and period of turmoil among the groups (including Robert Perry's Circle of Atonement) that use the text as a source of truth. Litigation continued until April 2004, when the court ruled that *A Course in Miracles* could not be copyrighted. That decision rose largely because the earliest versions of ACIM were not distributed with copyright notice.

The fame of *A Course in Miracles* has been extended through the writings and teaching of famous New Thought teacher Marianne Williamson. She rose to fame with her 1992 book *A Return to Love* and her appearances on the Oprah Winfrey show. She was for several years the spiritual leader of Renaissance Unity Spiritual Fellowship, based in Warren, Michigan. Born in Houston in 1952 and raised Jewish, she turned toward Unity's esoteric Christian vision in 1977.

Williamson has been a professional speaker since 1983 and the founder of Project Angel Food. She is also president of the Global Renaissance Alliance, a worldwide network of peace activists. She works with figures such as Deepak Chopra, Barbara Marx Hubbard, and Neale Donald Walsch. She has a political and civic emphasis in her teaching, as in her book *A Healing for America*.

ACIM is also a central element in the teaching of Jon Mundy, a former Methodist pastor, and cofounder of Interfaith Fellowship in New York City.

A Course in Miracles

TYPOLOGY	Western esoteric
HOME PAGES	Foundation for Inner Peace (Judith Skutch Whitson)
	www.acim.org
	Foundation for *A Course in Miracles* (Ken Wapnick)
	www.facim.org
	Marianne Williamson,
	www.marianne.com
	www.renaissancealliance.org

Course in Miracles Society,
www.jcim.net
Northwest Foundation for "A Course in Miracles"
(Paul Tuttle), www.nwffacim.org
New Christian Church of Full Endeavor
www.newchristianchurch.com
Circle of Atonement (Robert Perry)
www.circleofa.com
Jon Mundy
www.miraclesmagazine.org

READING D. Patrick Miller, *The Complete Story of the Course* (Berkeley, CA: Fearless Books, 1997)

▸ The Dalai Lama and Tibetan Buddhism

(Special note: This entry adopts a first-person approach since I had the privilege of doing an extensive interview with His Holiness the Dalai Lama in August 2000.)

The Dalai Lama is the leading apostle of Buddhism in the world today, and the chief ambassador for the Tibetan version of Buddhism. After Billy Graham and the late John Paul II, he is probably the most recognized religious figure on our planet. Born as Lhamo Thondup in 1935 in northeast Tibet, he was chosen as the fourteenth Dalai Lama (Tibet's highest religious figure) at age two. He was enthroned in 1940 and became political leader of Tibet at age fifteen, just after Mao's armies began their takeover of Tibet. In exile since 1959, the Dalai Lama has become a world leader in ethics, politics, and religion.

My interview with the Dalai Lama took place at his headquarters in Dharamsala, India. He told me that he believes he is a reincarnation of a previous Dalai Lama, but he is not sure of the details. "According to some of my dreams, I have some very close connection with the thirteenth Dalai Lama as well as the fifth Dalai Lama." He said that he must not focus on his fame. "It does not matter whether people regard me as a very high being, almost like Buddha, or a counterrevolutionary. What matters is whether I remain a genuine Buddhist monk and accordingly make some contribution for the betterment of other sentient beings."

The Dalai Lama is no advocate of one world religion, as some New Age Buddhists seem to believe. He has consistently spoken against this in his public speeches. "So if one is always trying to look at things in terms of similarities and parallels, there is a danger of rolling everything up into one big entity," he writes in *The Good Heart*, his book about the teachings of Jesus. He adopts a more relativist view of religions, believing that Buddhism is best for him but that no religion is best for everyone.

In terms of his own faith, the Dalai Lama drew a parallel between emotional love for Buddha and Christian love for Jesus. He said that his reflection on Buddha's teaching and sacrifice has led him to tears at times. Does he thank Buddha for the good things in his life? "Frankly speaking, my own happiness is mainly due to my own good karma," he said. "It is a fundamental Buddhist belief that my own suffering is due to my mistakes. If some good things happen, that is mainly due to my own good actions, not something related to a direct connection with Buddha."

In my interview, I devoted considerable time in asking him about the identity and integrity of Jesus. The Dalai Lama seemed at ease with the questioning, even while admitting that this was possibly the toughest area for exploration between evangelical Christians and Buddhists. I reminded him of his belief that Jesus is "a fully enlightened being" and asked, "If Jesus is fully enlightened, wouldn't he be teaching the truth about himself? Therefore, if he is teaching the truth, then he is the Son of God, and there is a God, and Jesus is the Savior. If he is fully enlightened, he should teach the truth. If he is not teaching the truth, he is not that enlightened."

As the Dalai Lama felt the momentum of the question, he laughed more than at any other time in the interview. He obviously understood the argument, borrowed from C.S. Lewis' famous book *Mere Christianity*. "This is a very good question," he said. "This is very, very important, very important." Even in Buddha's case, he said, a distinction must always be made between teachings that "always remain valid" and others that "we have the liberty to reject." He argued that the Buddha knew people were not always ready for the higher truth because it "wouldn't suit, wouldn't help." Therefore, lesser truths are sometimes taught because of the person's ignorance or condition. This is known in Buddhist *dharma* as the doctrine of *uppayah*, or skillful means. The Dalai Lama then applied this to the question about Jesus.

"Jesus Christ also lived previous lives," he said. "So, you see, he reached a high state, either as a *Bodhisattva*, or an enlightened person, through Buddhist practice or something like that. Then, at a certain period, certain era, he appeared as a new master, and then because of circumstances, he taught certain views different from Buddhism, but he also taught the same religious values as I mentioned earlier: Be patient, tolerant, compassionate. This is, you see, the real message in order to become a better human being." He said that there was no lying involved since Jesus's motivation was to help people.

While the Dalai Lama's claim that Jesus is a fully enlightened being offers some common ground with Christian faith, he does not seem to grasp the difficulties inherent in his position. In the four Gospels the integrity of Jesus's moral teaching is intimately linked with the accuracy of his identity, not only as presented by the opponents and disciples of Jesus, but also as presented by Jesus himself. It is virtually impossible to picture an enlightened Jesus once a Buddhist perspective is used to evaluate his truth claims.

For example, Jesus praised Peter for his belief that Jesus is the Messiah, the Son of the living God. Jesus said God revealed this to the disciple. From a Buddhist perspective, there is no God to reveal anything. If there is no God, then Jesus is not the Son of God, and Peter's confession is false. What does this suggest about the integrity of Jesus as a teacher? Furthermore, why is it that humans in Jesus's day could not be given the same Buddhist message delivered by Gautama just a few centuries earlier in India?

Finally, claims that Jesus is really a Buddha in disguise is no compliment to Jesus or Buddha. How would Buddhists feel if Christians claimed that Gautama was really a Christian figure ahead of his time? Still, it is no small matter that the most famous Buddhist on earth has a high regard for Jesus Christ. When he was asked to compare himself with Jesus in an interview with the *New York Times* in 1993, the Dalai Lama refused to do so. However limited his grasp of the identity of Jesus, his recognition of the greatness of Jesus provides a hope that he will think more deeply about what it really means that Jesus is a great master and a fully enlightened being.

The Dalai Lama and Tibetan Buddhism

TYPOLOGY	Buddhist Tibetan
HOME PAGE	www.tibet.com
CRITIC PAGE	In the Shadow of the Dalai Lama
	www.trimondi.de

▶ Davidian Adventism

Most people connect Davidian Adventism with David Koresh's Branch Davidian movement and the fiery apocalypse that engulfed Koresh and most of his followers on April 19, 1993. However, the Koresh group must be distinguished from others who are part of the larger Davidian tradition. The Branch Davidians were started by Ben and Lois Roden in 1955 after the death of Victor Houteff, founder of the Davidian Seventh-Day Adventist Association. Houteff's wife, Florence, won a leadership battle against Ben Roden after her husband's demise. But she lost control of her own followers in the early 1960s, and Ben Roden purchased Mount Carmel after its financial collapse.

Some of Victor Houteff's followers set up a continuation of his work in Riverside, California, in 1961, under the leadership of M. J. Bingham. They moved to Exeter, Missouri, and are known as the Bashan Davidians. Bingham (b. February 22, 1905) died on August 1, 1988. His wife, Jemmy (b. December 3, 1928), now leads the movement. She met Bingham when he preached the message of the shepherd's rod in her native Guyana. They were married in 1955. The group owns twelve hundred acres at Bashan Hill in Exeter.

M. T. Jordan split from Bingham's group and started the Gilead Davidians in Canada. Don Adair moved from California to be with a Davidian group in Salem, South Carolina, and he is now their leader. Wanda Blum (formerly Adair's wife) and others split from the Salem group and eventually settled in northern California. Tony Hibbert, a Jamaican living in New York, also led a group of Davidians who split from the Adair movement, and they have their headquarters in Mountain Dale, New York. Some of the Mountain Dale members moved to Waco in 1991 and started a separate Davidian group.

The South Carolina movement is based in Tamassee. They use the title General Association of Davidian Seventh-Day Adventists. Adair goes by the title vice president because Victor Houteff is viewed as the last and final president. They have reprinted all forty books and pamphlets written by Houteff.

The New York Davidians are based in Mountain Dale, New York. They use the title General Association of Davidian Seventh-Day Adventists and make explicit reference to the works of Victor Houteff as well. Members of the group in Waco refer to themselves as Davidian Seventh-day Adventists. They bought the original Mount Carmel site that was sold by Lois Roden to Presbyterians.

All Davidian Adventist groups share many of the doctrines and practices of their Seventh-day Adventist heritage. Where they gain their unique identity, whether as a collective or as individual groups, is the ways in which they have reshaped these doctrines to adopt a different understanding of the church, eschatology, law, and Christian life. Their central unique claim has to do with the prophetic claims made about Victor Houteff. In the case of David Koresh, the apocalyptic element in Davidian Adventism was taken to an extreme. This became a factor in the events that led up to the standoff with government authorities in Waco in 1993.

Davidian Adventism

TYPOLOGY	Christian Protestant Adventist sectarian
FOUNDER	Victor Houteff (1885–1955)
HOME PAGES	General Association of Davidian Seventh-day Adventists
	Don Adair group (South Carolina)
	www.davidian.org
	The Shepherd's Rod (Mountain Dale, NY)
	www.shepherds-rod-message.org
	The Shepherd's Rod (Hendersonville, NC)
	www.shepherds-rod.org

▶ Doukhobors

The term *Doukhobors* means "spirit wrestlers" and was used as a pejorative by a Russian Orthodox archbishop in 1875 against a sectarian group that was resisting the Orthodox religious path. The Doukhobors believed that there was no need for priests or churches and that God can be found through direct spiritual contact. The group experienced intense persecution after they resisted military conscription. They destroyed their own firearms on June 29, 1895, as a signal of their belief in peace.

Russian authorities allowed more than seven thousand Doukhobors to move to Canada in 1899. The famous Russian novelist Leo Tolstoy aided them in their emigration. They arrived in Halifax, on Canada's east coast, on January 20 and then moved to Saskatchewan, where they settled in sixty-one villages. Peter Vasilievich Verigin, their leader, joined them in 1902. The commune lost their land over a legal dispute with the Canadian government in 1907, and many moved to southern British Columbia the next year. Verigin was killed in a train explosion in 1924. Assassination was suspected, but the case was never solved.

In 1938 those Doukhobors who wanted to maintain communal life organized into the Union of Spiritual Communities of Christ under the leadership of Peter P. Verigin. Most Canadian Doukhobors live in the area of Grand Forks, British Columbia, and in parts of Saskatchewan. The Doukhobors are now celebrated as part of the Canadian mosaic, though the government of Canada has frequently victimized them.

The Doukhobors have often been identified with the actions of a radical minority group known as the Sons of Freedom.[4] This group engaged in acts of terror in response to government persecution in the 1930s. They also were infamous for their nude marches in protest of government policies against them. They were centered in

Krestova, British Columbia. In 1950 S. S. Sorokin became their leader, and they changed their name to the Christian Community and Brotherhood of Reformed Doukhobors.

Doukhobors are usually pacifists and vegetarians, and they adopt a mystical approach to faith. They reject typical outward symbols of faith, including baptism, though they usually have bread, salt, and water at meetings as symbols of the basic elements of life. For them, the Bible gives way to the oral tradition of the movement, especially as expressed in hymns. Doukhobors place great stress on living in obedience to the teachings of Jesus.

Doukhobor life retains a deep connection to its Russian roots, in spite of centuries of persecution. One Doukhobor hymn reflects a bittersweet reflection upon their Canadian base:

> Many years we have sojourned, dear brethren,
> In a land that is foreign and cold,
> And your people still have no conception,
> Of the truth that we strive to uphold.
> Our life here is not for excesses,
> But for bringing of life from above;
> Let Humanity be as one family,
> On the basis of freedom and love.

Doukhobors

TYPOLOGY	Christian Orthodox sectarian
HOME PAGES	Voice of the Doukhobors
	www.iskra.ca
	Koozma J. Tarasoff site
	www.spirit-wrestlers.com
	Doukhobors Genealogy
	www.doukhobor.org
READING	Koozma J. Tarasoff, *Spirit Wrestlers: Doukhobor Pioneers' Strategies for Living* (Ottawa: Legas Publishing, 2002)

▸ Druids

The Druids were apparently seers, soothsayers, and a sort of intellectual class in pre-Christian society in Gaul (France), Britain, and Ireland. In the second century BC Julius Caesar reported on their role as judges and priests and on their proficiency in the physical sciences. They were believed to have magical powers and to offer human sacrifice. The Romans attempted to extinguish Druidism.

There have been three distinct eras of Druidism. First, there were classical Druids, a people of ancient times, arising from Neolithic cultures. Second, there were revival Druids, groups that emerged in the eighteenth and nineteenth centuries, pursuing their understanding of ancient practice, based on oral tradition. Last, there are modern Druids, who have been practicing since the 1930s, deriving their understanding of Druidism from the findings of history and archaeology and from their own intuition about what constitutes Druid ritual and outlook.

Today Druidism is practiced by several organizations. The Order of Bards, Ovates, and Druids (OBOD) traces its roots back to the eighteenth century. The order is based in East Sussex, U.K. The British Druid Order, founded in 1979, is also headquartered in East Sussex and is currently led by Greywolf. In the United States the Reformed Druids of North America (RDNA) began existence as an act of protest by students at Carleton College in Northfield, Minnesota. A college ruling about compulsory religious attendance led some students to start a Druid group in rebellion against the authorities. After the college reversed its policy, the group continued.

Isaac Bonewits, one of the most famous Druid leaders, became a priest in the RDNA in 1969 but left to form the ADF, or Ar nDraiocht Fein (Irish wording for "Our Own Druidism") in 1983. Bonewits thought that RDNA was not serious enough about the origins and spread of Druid life. He was the archdruid of ADF for ten years and is now archdruid emeritus.

A number of groups have emerged from these three movements.

The OBOD claims descent from the Ancient Druid Order (ADO), which OBOD leaders believe was founded in 1717. In 1964 the ADO continued under Thomas Maughan, and the OBOD emerged under Ross Nichols, who claimed to have worked with Gerald Gardner, the famous leader of British witchcraft. In 1988 OBOD leadership passed to Philip Carr-Gomm, who initiated a distance-learning program that has attracted eight thousand people.

On the question of historical roots for modern Druids, Carr-Gomm refers to the mystical path as the way to find Druid ideals. "The primary source can never be presented in literature, because it can only be found in places where we must set books aside—in places where both this world and the Otherworld are strongly present—by sacred springs and holy wells, by the seashore or in stone circles, beside great trees or strong mountains. When we open ourselves to these places, to the beauty and the splendor of the natural world, we discover the true source of inspiration for Druidry. It has always been said that the Druid tradition was an oral one, but a more accurate term would be aural, since we learn the most by listening: to our hearts, to others and to the natural world—to the sound of the rivers and the trees, the stars and the night sky."

Druids	
TYPOLOGY	Western esoteric
HOME PAGES	OBOD: Order of Bards, Ovates, and Druids
	http://druidry.org/
	Reformed Druids of North America
	www.geocities.com/mikerdna
	The British Druid Order
	www.druidorder.demon.co.uk
	Ar nDraiocht Fein
	www.adf.org
READING	Ronald Hutton, *The Pagan Religions of the Ancient British Isles* (Oxford: Blackwell, 2003)

▶ ECKANKAR

ECKANKAR is a Gnostic spiritual movement, now based in Minneapolis. Though it claims to be an ancient religion, its modern roots can be traced to the spiritual journey of Paul Twitchell. Twitchell founded ECKANKAR in 1965 but claimed that he was the 971st living Eck Master, suggesting a long history to the ECKist path. Twitchell died in 1971.

The mantle of leadership in ECKANKAR was passed to Darwin Gross on October 22, 1971. Gross later married Twitchell's widow and remained the leader in ECKANKAR until 1981. Gross was forced to resign his position and was succeeded in 1983 by Harold Klemp, the 972nd living Eck Master, after a nasty battle for leadership. Defenders of Gross claim he was a victim of "a well-planned illegal takeover by the Occult Dark Forces" that included Klemp and Peter Skelsky (ECKANKAR president). The dark side is also said to include the Spiritual Counterfeit Projects (SCP), a Christian cult-monitoring organization, and David Lane, whose research on ECKANKAR caused much of the turmoil through which the organization passed in the late 1970s.

Lane discovered in 1977 that Twitchell had covered up his associations with other spiritual traditions, including Swami Premananda's Hindu movement and the Church of Scientology. More seriously, Twitchell was connected for almost a decade (1955–63) with Kirpal Singh, a leader in the Radhasoami Sant Mat movement (whose teaching most closely resembles those of ECKANKAR). Lane discovered that significant portions of Twitchell's writings had been plagiarized from various sources, especially the writings of Julian Johnson, a disciple of Sawan Singh, one of the older Sant Mat leaders. Lane's research had a major impact on ECKANKAR and formed the heart of SCP's critique of the movement.[5]

As head of ECKANKAR, Darwin Gross ordered Eckists to trash

Lane's material and the SCP journal. Klemp, born in 1942, has made some acknowledgment of Twitchell's debt to his Radhasoami roots and admitted that Twitchell was not always careful in his recounting of his life story. While these admissions are noteworthy, Lane's research raises serious questions about Twitchell's credibility, given the extent of his plagiarism. Twitchell's reports on contacts with ancient Tibetan masters and travels in the eternal realms are hard to believe, given the duplicity about his life story.

ECKANKAR claims to be the "religion of the light and sound of God." Eckists believe that their living Eck Master is in supernatural communication with them, especially through dreams. ECKANKAR often chant on Hu, which they claim to be an ancient name of God. Eckists also believe in soul travel. Klemp tells a story of a new member who is given the pseudonym Melissa. The report on her highlights reliance on the current Eck Master, known as the Mahanta.

"She was moving in her true spiritual form, the Soul body. But suddenly doubt and fear filled her heart. A former Pentecostal, she immediately called out the name of Jesus. Things started to go in reverse. Where once she had moved forward, she was now traveling backward in the spiritual worlds. Quickly, she caught herself. Melissa told herself that she would put her complete faith and trust in the Mahanta. Again she moved forward."

ECKANKAR

TYPOLOGY	Sant Mat and Western esoteric
FOUNDER	Paul Twitchell (d. 1971)
CURRENT LEADER	Harold Klemp
HOME PAGE	www.eckankar.org
CRITICAL SITES	The Unauthorized Eckankar Page
	www.geocities.com/eckcult
	David Lane archives
	http://vclass.mtsac.edu:940/dlane/ekdebates.htm
	Ford Johnson data
	www.thetruth-seeker.com

▸ Elan Vital

Elan Vital is the spiritual movement led by Prem Pal Singh Rawat, also known as Guru Majaraj Ji, former head of the Divine Light Mission (DLM). The mission was started by Prem's father, Shri Hans Ji Maharaj. It is part of the Sant Mat tradition in the broader Sikh religion. Prem Rawat was born December 10, 1957, in Hardwar, India. He became head of DLM in 1966 after the death of his father.

In 1971 Majaraj Ji visited England and the United States, and the DLM became one of the best-known new religious movements in the West. Prem was hailed at the time as the "Lord of the Universe" and the "Perfect Master," and his followers ("premies") viewed him as being on the level of Buddha or Jesus. His three older brothers were said to embody the three major Hindu deities (Bal Bhagwan Ji as Vishnu, Raja Ji as Brahma, and Bhole Ji as Shiva). Prem's mother and brothers moved to the United States to be with Prem. The DLM was based in Denver, Colorado.

The movement experienced a financial crisis in 1973 when plans to fill the Houston Astrodome were not realized. A further crisis occurred the next year when Prem married Marolyn Johnson (renamed Durga Ji). This enraged his mother, and she returned to India with two of her sons. She claimed that Bal Bhagwan Ji was the rightful guru. In 1982 and 1983 DLM ashrams were closed. About the same time, Prem chose to be called simply Maharaji and the movement became known as Elan Vital.

Both in the DLM and in Elan Vital, the key motif has been to receive "Knowledge" from Prem. He teaches four meditation techniques, passed on to followers through instructional videos. The language about "Knowledge" and meditation was far more religious in Prem's earlier period as head of DLM. Prem basically ignores his previous teaching about his alleged status as an incarncation of God. However, his critics provide abundant evidence of his past claims to transcendence. In one 1971 talk he stated, "Everything depends on me. Not even a leaf moves a millimeter without my wish." Devotees sang of Prem in this fashion:

> The middle of the summer of seventy-one
> Few of us knew that the Lord had really come,
> But the Truth can't remain a secret for too long
> Cause He's gonna turn the whole world on, very quickly,
> He's gonna turn the whole world on.

Since 1997, significant opposition to Prem has appeared on the Internet. Critics seem mainly upset that he ignores his past life as Guru Maharaj Ji. They also argue that he lives a lavish lifestyle, inconsistent with his own teaching, and that he is immune to correction. The movement experienced internal torment in 2000 when it became known that one of Elan Vital's longtime instructors was a pedophile. The movement dismisses its critics as mentally unbalanced and hateful.

Elan Vital offers the four meditative modes of "Knowledge" free to those who are interested. The "Knowledge" offered by Prem is about self-knowledge and about the inner secrets of happiness. Though the movement has lost its earlier religious ethos, it continues to promote Prem as the sole person who can provide the techniques that lead to full self-realization.

Elan Vital

TYPOLOGY	Sant Mat and Western esoteric
FOUNDER	Prem Pal Singh Rawat
HOME PAGES	www.elanvital.org
	www.tprf.org
	www.maharaji.net
CRITICAL SITES	www.ex-premie.org
	www.prem-rawat-maharaji.info
	www.drek.us
	http://gurumaharaji.info
	www.geocities.com/maharajiwd/
READING	James V. Downton Jr., *Sacred Journeys: The Conversion of Young Americans to Divine Light Mission* (New York: Columbia University Press, 1979).

▶ Emergent Church

The term "emergent church" refers to a new movement among evangelical Christians that builds on a deep engagement with postmodern culture through appreciation of key components in a postmodern outlook. The emergent church is usually identified with Brian McLaren, author of *A Generous Orthodoxy* and identified as one of the top twenty-five leading evangelicals by *Time* magazine. Other emergent church leaders include Leonard Sweet, Robert Webber, Sally Morgenthaler, and Thomas Hohstadt. The movement receives its best intellectual support from Dallas Willard and the late Stan Grenz.

Robert Webber has pictured the emergent movement as a third alternative to traditional evangelicals and pragmatic evangelicals. The former term refers to an older evangelical paradigm that places emphasis on apologetics and sound doctrine. By "pragmatic," Webber means the seeker-sensitive paradigm, connected most famously with Bill Hybels and Rick Warren. Emergent leaders believe that the older models of evangelical Christianity fail either because of an outdated epistemology or because of a capitulation to a consumer view of religion.

The emergent church movement embraces paradox and balances competing realities. Leonard Sweet states that "our faith is ancient. Our faith is future. We're old-fashioned. We're new-fangled. We're orthodox. We're innovators. We're postmodern Christians." McLaren writes that he can be viewed as "Missional, evangelical, Post/Protestant, Liberal/Conservative, Mystical/Poetic, Biblical, Charismatic/Contemplative, fundamentalist/Calvinist, Anabaptist/Anglican, Methodist, catholic, Green, Incarnational, Depressed-Yet-Hopeful, Emergent, Unfinished."

Both Charles Colson and D. A. Carson have criticized the emergent church for being too sympathetic to postmodernism and too open to relativism. These concerns are worth keeping in mind but must not be overstated. The emergent church is far more concerned to address postmodernism and relativism than to embrace either or both uncritically. Robert Webber has noted, "A postmodern setting demands relationship, participation, community, symbol, servanthood and the like. The radical renorming of biblical priorities coupled with an absolute rejection of slick marketing, showy worship and phony verbal games precede the birth of an honest, genuine, authentic community passionately engaged with being the truth."

The emergent church places a great deal of emphasis upon worship in community. This arises out of an emphasis upon the relational and subjective element in Christian faith. McLaren and other emergent leaders are critical of the seeker-sensitive movement because of its alleged preoccupation with entertainment. Sally Morgenthaler argues, "The new worship paradigm contends that unbelievers can respond positively to a worship that has been made culturally accessible to them; it also proposes that unbelievers come to church, not primarily to investigate the 'claims of Christ,' but to investigate the 'Christ in us.'"

R. Albert Mohler Jr., president of Southern Baptist Theological Seminary, gave this indictment of McLaren: "Embracing the worldview of the postmodern age, he embraces relativism at the cost of clarity in matters of truth and intends to redefine Christianity for this new age, largely in terms of an eccentric mixture of elements he would take from virtually every theological position and variant." This is far too harsh and distorts McLaren. However, McLaren should be more aware of the epistemological complexities involved in his critique of traditional evangelicalism. He and other emergent leaders should also correct an implicit elitism that shows itself in the rhetoric in emergent church discourse. Of course, traditional evangelicalism has an explicit elitism that emergent leaders properly critique.[6]

Emergent Church

TYPOLOGY	Christian Protestant evangelical
WEB SITES	Brian McLaren
	www.anewkindofchristian.com

Leonard Sweet
www.leonardsweet.com

Thomas Hohstadt
www.futurechurch.net

Sally Morgenthaler
www.sacramentis.com

Dallas Willard
www.dallaswillard.org

Chad Hall
www.coolchurches.com

John C. O'Keefe
www.ginkworld.net

Karen Ward
www.emergingchurch.org

Mark and Jeanette Priddy
www.allelon.org

Emergent Village
www.emergentvillage.com

Next Wave
www.the-next-wave.org

The Ooze (Spencer Burke)
www.theooze.com

READING   Brian McLaren, *A Generous Orthodoxy* (Grand Rapids, MI: Zondervan, 2004)

D. A. Carson, *Becoming Conversant with the Emerging Church* (Grand Rapids, MI: Zondervan, 2005)

▶ Falun Gong (Falun Dafa)

Falun Gong is a controversial Chinese spiritual movement founded in 1992 by Li Hongzhi. It is also known as Falun Dafa. While Falun Gong is technically a term for the breathing exercises of the Falun Dafa, the two names are now used in a more popular sense to refer to Li's group.

Spiritual practice in Falun Gong is built around Qigong, a broad set of movements that include meditation, breathing, and physical exercises. Many who engage in Qigong activities do not think of themselves as engaging in religion but rather as practitioners of ancient techniques, rooted in Taoism, for cultivating physical and mental health. Qigong becomes religious as it is integrated into a larger context of teaching and community. Falun Gong members often deny being part of a religion, in part due to the connotation of that term in China, though it is hard to dispute the movement's religious nature when one studies the inner doctrine of the founder.

According to Li Hongzhi, he was born in the Jilin province of China on May 13, 1951. The Communist government of China claims that he was born on July 7, 1952, and had his birth certificate changed so that he could claim a parallel to Buddha's alleged birth date. Li Hongzhi, who now lives in the United States, states that Falun Gong has had up to 100 million followers in China. Since 1999 the movement has been systematically and severely repressed. For all practical purposes the movement has been destroyed in China.

On April 25, 1999, ten thousand Falun Gong members held a surprise rally in Beijing to protest some informal attacks on the movement. The Communist Party was embarrassed and threatened by the demonstration, and Jiang Zemin, the party's general secretary at the time, ordered retaliation. An official sanction against Falun Gong was announced on July 22, 1999. Since then, Falun Gong members have been arrested and tortured in China, as has been documented by human rights groups. Falun Gong has engaged in worldwide protests against the Chinese government.

The movement tends to downplay its esoteric aspects, as Samuel Luo, a prominent critic, has argued. Li claims the following: (1) he was taught in secret by well-known Taoist and Buddhist masters; (2) he could perform miracles by age eight, including going through walls; and (3) he arranged events in previous lifetimes so that his current teachers knew the truth to pass on to him. Li also believes that his followers are implanted with spiritual turning wheels in their stomachs that transmit supernatural energy and dispel bad energy. Li told *Time* magazine that aliens are the source of the modern computer.

Li claimed in a lecture on February 15, 2003: "I atoned for the sins of all sentient beings in the Three Realms (heaven, earth and the underworld). So think about it, as far as our students are concerned, it was as if I scooped you out of hell back then. I have truly borne for you the sins you committed over hundreds and thousands of years. And it doesn't stop at just that. Because of this, I will also save you and turn you into Gods. . . . Never, from the beginning of time, has any God dared to do this."

Li also argues that the Chinese suppression of Falun Gong was predicted centuries ago by Nostradamus, the famous psychic. However, the relevant passage reads nothing like one would expect for a prophecy about the attack on the Falun Gong in China. Here is the wording from Nostradamus's *Centuries* 10.72:

> *In the year 1999, seventh month,*
> *From the sky will come a great King of Terror,*
> *In order to bring back to life the great king of Angolmois,*
> *Before and after Mars reigns in the name of bringing*
> *   people happiness.*

Falun Gong

HOME PAGES	www.falundafa.org
	http://clearwisdom.net
	www.faluninfo.net
OTHER SITES	Human Rights Watch, http://hrw.org
	Samuel Luo, www.falungonginfo.org
	Barend J. ter Haar, www.let.leidenuniv.nl/bth/

▶ Family International

The Family International is the current name of the group known formerly as the Children of God, the Family of Love, and the Family. This controversial movement was started by David Berg in 1968 and has been the target of frequent police action, litigation, and media scrutiny worldwide. Berg is known affectionately in the movement as Dad, Father David, and Moses David.

David Brandt Berg was born in 1919. His mother was an evangelist. Berg married Jane Miller in 1944 and four years later became a minister in a Christian and Missionary Alliance church in Arizona. He was forced out in 1951. Berg moved with his wife and four children to Huntington Beach, California, in 1968. He reached out to the hippies of Southern California and soon had a small group of followers.

In 1969 Berg led his group out of California. They spent time traveling in the United States, settled for a while in Quebec, Canada, and then moved to Jordan's Soul Clinic in Texas in February 1970. By 1972 the group was under pressure from critics, and Berg issued a warning about judgment against America. He and his members dispersed to different nations. Berg and his family moved to London, England. He was joined by his mistress, Maria (birth name Karen Zerby), who was born in New Jersey in 1946.

Berg communicated with his followers through what were known as MO letters or MLs. ML 273 was issued in January 1974 and encouraged the membership to engage in sexual activity with strangers in order to win them to Jesus. This was known as "flirty fishing" and constituted one of the most notorious parts of Berg's ideology. The teaching was elaborated in 1976 in a string of MO letters known as "King Arthur's Nights."

The group had liberal sexual policies internally. Sexual activity was not restricted to a married couple. Some members made soft-core videos for Berg. Some members-only material contained

graphic language and illustrations related to Berg's sexual instruc-
tions. This open model of sexuality dominated the Family until MO
letter 1434, "Ban the Bomb" (March 1983), restricted sex to those
adults in one's own house group.[7]

The Family International faced its most intense scrutiny from the
media and the courts from 1988 through 1996. ABC covered the
abduction of children from a Family home in Thailand on its 20/20
program in 1988. Two years later the police raided a group home in
Barcelona. The Australian Family was raided in 1992, and the British
court system targeted the Family in 1993, in a trial that was to last
three years. The Argentine Family was raided in 1993. In all these situ-
ations concerns were raised about child abuse, particularly allegations of incest. However, little thought was given to the trauma that
the police actions made upon the children.

Berg died in 1994. Maria then married Peter Amsterdam and they
serve as leaders of the group. Maria and Peter instigated major policy
changes in Family practice, including warnings against physical, emotional, and sexual mistreatment of children. They also adopted a
more relaxed model of church leadership, expressed in the Family's
"Love Charter" that was released in 1995. These changes led the
British court to adopt a more open attitude to the Family in its rul-
ings about child custody.

The Family has always retained many of the beliefs central to
classical Christianity, though Berg had deficient understandings of
the Trinity, biblical authority, and the nature of the church. They
obviously departed from traditional Christian teaching in their radical sexual views. The group retains belief that it is morally right to
have sex with others in one's house group who are of the opposite
sex. They also teach that both males and females should think of
Jesus as a love partner while engaging in masturbation.

On January 8, 2005, Ricky Rodriguez, Maria's son, killed longtime Family member Angela Smith and then shot himself. Rodriguez
(known in the group as Davidito) taped a video before his death and
blamed the Family for the rage that led to the murder-suicide. He
was once championed as the future leader of the movement but left

it in 2001. Family leaders blame the media and the anticult movement for fueling Ricky's anger and violence.

Family International

TYPOLOGY	Christian Protestant sectarian
FOUNDER	David Berg (1919–94)
HOME PAGES	Main Home Page
	www.thefamily.org
	Family Lit Trunk (Family response to critic James Penn)
	www.geocities.com/familylittrunk
	Family Care Foundation
	www.familycare.org
	Aurora Productions
	www.auroraproductions.com
CRITIC SITES	Moving On
	www.movingon.org
	XFamily
	www.xfamily.org/
	ExFamily.org
	www.exfamily.org/
	New Day News
	www.newdaynews.com
	Data on Family Care Foundation
	www.angelfire.com/clone/charityalert
	Family Art Corner
	www.geocities.com/familyartcorner
READING	William Bainbridge, *The Endtime Family* (Albany: State University of New York Press, 2002)
	James D. Chancellor, *Life in the Family* (Syracuse: Syracuse University Press, 2000)
	Deborah Davis, *The Children of God* (Grand Rapids, MI: Zondervan, 1984)
	James R. Lewis and J. Gordon Melton, eds., *Sex, Slander, and Salvation* (Stanford, CA: Center for Academic Publication, 1994).
	J. Gordon Melton, *The Children of God* (Salt Lake City: Signature, 2004)
	David Van Zandt, *Living in the Children of God* (Princeton, NJ: Princeton University Press, 1991)
	Miriam Williams, *Heaven's Harlots* (New York: William Morrow, 1988)

▸ Freemasonry

Given that many Freemasons deny that their organization is religious, it may come as a surprise that Freemasonry is included in a book on religions. However, there are four reasons why we should consider Freemasonry in this context. First, the ethos and rites of the Masonic Lodge contain elements of a religious nature. Second, some Masons, historically and in the present, have viewed Masonry as a religious movement. Third, Freemasonry has exercised an enormous influence on Western esoteric religious life. Last, charges against Masonry are so pervasive that they impact study and proper understanding of the lodge and other esoteric movements.

Freemasonry is a fraternal order known for its secret rituals and the use of secret signs. The origins of Freemasonry are usually traced by scholars to the founding of the Grand Lodge in London in 1717, though there is evidence of Masonic ritual in Scotland in the preceding century. While most Masons follow the York Rite, the Scottish Rite, with its thirty-three degrees, is the subject of more speculation. Roman Catholic popes have condemned Masonry, and many Protestant denominations forbid membership in the lodge.

Three popular views about Freemasonry circulate among Christians. First, many conservative Christians believe that Masonry is the embodiment of evil. These people claim that Masons worship Satan, ignore crimes done by Masons, and engage in bloody and occult rituals. Second, more moderate Christians argue that Masonry is essentially religious, proposes a deistic view of God, and advances pluralism because it avoids explicit Christian commitment. Last, many Christians believe that the lodge is simply a fraternal order and, while mandating belief in God, is not a religion.

The wildest accusations against the lodge are fabrications by careless critics. For example, the charge that Masons worship Lucifer is based on a lie about Albert Pike, a leading nineteenth-century

Masonic scholar, who was falsely charged with worshipping Satan. While Masons are advised to care for fellow members, their oaths forbid them to break the law or harbor any criminal. The Grand Lodge removed all references to symbolic bloody oaths in Masonic initiations several years ago. In the last decade Masonic scholars have written devastating critiques of authors, such as Jim Shaw, who advocate extreme views about the lodge.

The charge that Masonry has occult connections and is a revival of ancient mystery religion has some truth to it. Pike recast many Masonic rituals by drawing parallels with what he knew of ancient Egyptian religions. Most Masons in his day and since have cared little about Pike's mystical musings. However, it would be helpful if modern Masons rewrote the language of various degrees in the Scottish rite to remove Pike's influence. The language is so esoteric that it is hard to imagine that many Masons realize what is being said in the rituals.

The history of Masonry reflects the deeper currents in changing religious ideology. Early Masonic writings manifested a more explicit Christian focus. Then, during the nineteenth century, an affinity for pluralism led some Masons to become more universal and inclusive in their teachings. With the rise of secularism in the twentieth century, and with a greater sensibility to specific religious claims, most Masons now insist that the lodge is not a church of any sort.

Freemasonry

TYPOLOGY	Western esoteric
HOME PAGES	Grand Lodge of London, www.grandlodge-england.org Masonic Quarterly magazine www.mqmagazine.co.uk Library and Museum http://freemasonry.london.museum
OTHER SITES	Quatuor Coronati Lodge No. 2076 www.quatuorcoronati.com Canonbury Masonic Research Cent www.canonbury.ac.uk Centre for Research into Freemasonry

86 FREEMASONRY

www.shef.ac.uk/~crf
Masonic Info
www.masonicinfo.com

READING
Arturo de Hoyos and S. Brent Morris, *Is It True What They Say About Freemasonry?* (Silver Spring, MD: Masonic Information Center, 1997)

Gary Leazer, *Fundamentalism and Freemasonry* (New York: Evans, 1995)

David Stevenson, *The Origins of Freemasonry: Scot land's Century, 1590–1710* (Cambridge: Cambridge University Press: 1990)

Steve Tsoukalas, *Masonic Rites and Wrongs* (Phillips burg, NJ: P&R, 1995)

▶ Fundamentalism

The term *fundamentalist* is often used to describe right-wing elements in any religion. This entry will use it in its classical sense as a reference to the reactionary movement within Protestantism that arose to protest liberalism in Christian thought. The twentieth-century conflict between liberals and fundamentalists is part of a larger story about the breakdown in confidence in classical Christian faith that spanned the previous three centuries.

The Reformation of the sixteenth century led, ironically, to a crisis in epistemology as initial doubts about Catholicism gave way to doubts about Christian faith itself. Skepticism about central Christian beliefs was muted in the seventeenth century but became explicit among Enlightenment figures in the next century. David Hume doubted miracles; Voltaire questioned biblical authority; and Immanuel Kant doubted the proofs for God's existence.

Doubts about classical Christian faith increased in the nineteenth century with Darwin's theory of evolution and with new arguments about the unity of religions. Further, the Bible was being subjected to rigorous analysis, not only in relation to Old Testament source criticism, but also in connection with evidence for the historical Jesus. All of the above formed the matrix for both the rise of liberal theology and conservative reaction by Catholics and Protestants.

Fundamentalists were strongly opposed to the various strands of skepticism and in particular were appalled that liberal theologians would deny the miraculous and abandon a literal understanding of major Christian doctrines. Early fundamentalist leaders affirmed the inerrancy of the Bible, the deity of Christ, the Virgin Birth, the substitutionary atonement, and the Second Coming. They defended these doctrines in a twelve-volume series known as *The Fundamentals*, released between 1910 and 1915.

The fight between liberals (or modernists) and fundamentalists split denominations and led to conflicts at institutions such as Princeton Theological Seminary. J. Gresham Machen left Princeton and founded Westminster Theological Seminary as a fundamentalist alternative. Harry Emerson Fosdick, one of the leading modernists, argued against fundamentalist intolerance in his 1922 sermon "Shall the Fundamentalists Win?"

After the Scopes trial in 1925, fundamentalists became increasingly withdrawn from mainstream life. This insularity led to adoption of an even more narrow perspective and a louder polemic about classical Christian doctrines and what seem to outsiders like secondary issues. Thus, fundamentalist preachers became preoccupied with issues such as dancing, card playing, movie attendance, and social drinking. Modern fundamentalists often endorse only the King James Version.

During World War II, a more irenic version of fundamentalism appeared and became known as evangelicalism. It has been principally identified with evangelist Billy Graham. Other early evangelical leaders included Harold Ockenga, Carl F. H. Henry (the first editor of *Christianity Today* magazine), and Charles Fuller (the founder of Fuller Theological Seminary). These evangelicals retained a conservative doctrinal framework but placed more emphasis upon academic learning, cultural engagement, and tolerance.

Fundamentalism	
TYPOLOGY	Christian Protestant
WEB SITES	David Cloud site, www.wayoflife.org
	The Sword of the Lord, www.swordofthelord.com
	Bob Jones University, www.bju.edu
READING	Joel Carpenter, *Revive Us Again* (New York: Oxford University Press, 1997)
	James Davison Hunter, *Evangelicalism: The Coming Generation* (Chicago: University of Chicago, 1987)
	George M. Marsden, *Fundamentalism and American Culture* (Oxford: Oxford University Press, 1980)
	Martin E. Marty, *The Irony of It All, 1893–1919*, vol. 1 of *Modern American Religion* (Chicago: University of Chicago Press, 1986)

▶ Hare Krishna (ISKCON)

The Hare Krishna movement is officially known as the International Society for Krishna Consciousness, or ISKCON. It is both a new religious movement and part of ancient Hinduism. Western awareness of the movement goes back five decades, to a time when Srila A.C. Bhaktivedanta Swami Prabhupada, the movement's founder and guru, brought the Hare Krishna faith to the United States. The movement is recognized most famously by its dancing in the streets, chanting of the Hare Krishna mantra, and by the saffron robes and shaved heads of male Krishna devotees.

Prabhupada was born on September 1, 1896, in Calcutta. He studied at Scottish Churches' College and was married in 1918, spending most of his life as a pharmacist and business manager. He was initiated as a disciple of Srila Bhaktisiddhanta Sarasvati Thakur in 1932. After years of preparation, Prabhupada set sail for the United States on August 13, 1965, in order to bring the message of Krishna consciousness to the West. He attracted a significant number of followers in Manhattan, and the movement spread quickly to other parts of the world. Prabhupada died November 14, 1977 in India.

ISKCON is modeled after the larger Vaisnava (or Vaishnava) tradition in Hinduism. It places emphasis upon bhakti-yoga, the ecstatic love of God. Hare Krishna devotees object strongly to the Advaitist position that God is impersonal. In ISKCON the believer does not become one with God in an ontological sense. Krishna is viewed as the Supreme Personality of the Godhead. Liberation is attained through the process of hearing and chanting about Krishna. Most ISKCON devotees still look to Prabhupada as their main guru and spiritual guide.

Prabhupada was known for his strict adherence to Hindu morals.

Unlike many Eastern gurus who came to the West, he did not use his status to seduce his followers sexually. He never entertained doubts about his belief system. He even denied that Neil Armstrong had landed on the moon, since the Hindu scriptures teach that the moon is both farther away than the sun and inhabited.

He accepted the Hindu scriptures literally, including the claim that earlier beings engaged in space travel. Based on this belief, Prabhupada wrote a booklet called *Easy Journey to Other Planets*. His commentaries take the stories of Hindu gods and goddesses as literal historic narratives. The guru believed that his understanding of Hinduism represented its purest form.

When Prabhupada died, eleven of his disciples assumed the mantle of leadership. These gurus were (1) Harikesa Swami, (2) Jayatirtha dasa Adhikari, (3) Hamsaduta Swami, (4) Hrdayananda Gosvami, (5) Ramesvara Swami, (6) Bhagavan dasa Adhikari, (7) Kirtanananda Swami, (8) Tamala Krsna Gosvami, (9) Satsvarupa dasa Gosvami, (10) Bhavananda Gosvami, and (11) Jayapataka Swami. The movement has experienced enormous turmoil since Prabhupada died, particularly in relation to Kirtanananda.

The ISKCON Governing Body (GBC) expelled Kirtanananda, and a West Virginia judge sentenced him to thirty years in prison for using murder, kidnapping, and fraud to protect an illegal, multimillion dollar enterprise. He entered prison in 1991 and was released in June of 2004. This crime story is covered in the books *Monkey on a Stick* and *Betrayal of the Spirit*.

In 2000 former members who were raised as children in ISKCON brought a lawsuit against the group because of neglect and abuse (emotional, physical, and sexual) experienced in the movement's schools. ISKCON reached an agreement in 2005 with the U.S. bankruptcy court system to create a multimillion-dollar fund for the victims. The internal chaos in ISKCON since the death of its founder has led to the exodus of most of the original disciples, including Stephen J. Gelberg, one of the major academics in the movement.

Hare Krishna (ISKCON)

FOUNDER	A . C. Bhaktivedanta Swami Prabhupada (1896–1977)
WEB SITES	www.iskcon.com
	www.prabhupada.com
	www.krishna.com
OTHER SITES	Surrealist.org (Nori J. Muster)
	http://surrealist.org/links/harekrishna.html
	ISKCON Revival Movement
	www.iskconirm.com
	Hare Krishna Links
	http://mitglied.lycos.de/gbc/isklinks.htm
	Chakra
	www.chakra.org
READING	Edwin Bryant and Maria Ekstrand, eds., *The Hare Krishna Movement: The Postcharismatic Fate of a Religious Transplant* (New York: Columbia University Press, 2004)
	John Hubner and Lindsey Grueson, *Monkey on a Stick: Murder, Madness, and the Hare Krishnas* (New York, Harcourt, Brace, Jovanovich, 1988)
	Nori Muster, *Betrayal of the Spirit* (Champaign, IL:, University of Illinois Press, 1997).
	Federico Squarcini and Eugenio Fizzotti, *Hare Krishna* (Salt Lake City: Signature, 2004)

▸ Heaven's Gate

Heaven's Gate represents one of the more tragic episodes in modern religion: the faith-motivated suicide of twenty-one women and eighteen men whose bodies were discovered on March 26, 1997, in a house in San Diego, California. Members of the California-based UFO group, led by Marshall Herff Applewhite, believed that suicide was simply about leaving behind the body ("container"), after which the soul would go to sleep until "replanted" in another "container." Eventually the soul would be "grafted" onto a being at the "level above human" on board a UFO spaceship. The timing of the suicides was triggered in part by the appearance of the Hale-Bopp comet.

Applewhite was among the thirty-nine who took their lives. They had taken applesauce or pudding mixed with drugs and then suffocated themselves with plastic bags over their heads. The victims ranged in age from midtwenties to seventy-two. When their bodies were discovered, they were all dressed in unisex clothing and wearing Nikes. Some of the men were castrated—an indicator of the antibody ideology of the group. The Web site of the group still announces, "Red Alert: Hale-Bopp Brings Closure to Heaven's Gate." Rio DiAngelo, a lone survivor who later killed himself, told the Associated Press in 2002: "What I've gained from this group is phenomenal," he said. "If he [Applewhite] is just a gay music teacher from Texas, how could he teach all these advanced ways of being that really work?"

Heaven's Gate was the creation of Applewhite and Bonnie Lu Nettles. The two started their apocalyptic group in 1975 in Houston, Texas, under the name Total Overcomers Anonymous. They had some public exposure in the early years but remained a small sect on the fringe of society. Nettles died in 1985 from cancer, and Applewhite continued to lead the few who had adopted his message.

Applewhite originally went by the nickname Bo and later was called Do (pronounced "Doe"). Nettles was known first as Peep, then as Ti.

Applewhite was born into a traditional Christian family, studied at Union Theological Seminary, and then pursued music and the performing arts. Nettles studied in the metaphysical tradition, had connections with Theosophy, and participated in channeling. When with Nettles, Applewhite experienced visions and paranormal events that they claimed included contact with space beings. Members viewed the two of them as "the Two"—a reference to the two prophets mentioned in Revelation 11. The group also viewed some biblical events as accounts of visits from UFOs.

The group believed that Jesus was a "Representative" sent by the beings of the Kingdom Level above Human to teach about entrance into the Kingdom of God. Humans who were inspired by demons killed "the Captain" (another term for Jesus), and his teachings were changed into "watered-down Country Club Religion." Applewhite and Nettles claimed to represent a new chance for humanity to hear what Jesus had taught two thousand years ago. Applewhite stated, "The same grace that was available at the end of the Representative's mission 2000 years ago is available now with our presence. If you quickly choose to take these steps toward separating from the world, and look to us for help, you will see our Father's Kingdom."

Heaven's Gate

TYPOLOGY	Western esoteric UFO religion
FOUNDERS	Marshall Applewhite and Bonnie Lu Nettles
HOME PAGE	www.heavensgate.com
READING	Wendy Gale Robinson, "Heaven's Gate: The End?" *Journal of Computer Mediated Communication* (http://jcmc.indiana.edu/vol3/issue3/robinson.html)

▶ Hinduism

The term *Hinduism* is now used of the dominant religious tradition in India, but Hindu history is actually a complex and contradictory story of many traditions. For example, Hindus have not had a consistent understanding of God throughout history. The earliest Hindu scriptures express belief in a host of gods and goddesses. Thus, the first Vedic material mentions the worship of Agni, Soma, Varuna, Indra, and other deities. Gradually this polytheism was replaced by a focus on the famous trinity of Hinduism: Brahma, Vishnu, Shiva.

The three major deities in Hindu tradition are believed to manifest themselves in many forms, including the much-beloved Krishna. Hindus also worship the feminine aspect of the divine in goddesses such as Durga and in the consorts of Vishnu, Shiva, and Krishna. There is also a long-standing adoration of Ganesh the elephant-headed god, Hanuman the monkey god, and many other deities peculiar to certain regions of India or specific traditions within Hinduism.

Western scholars have often overstated Hindu commitment to God as ultimately impersonal, a position known as *advaitism*. It is commonly argued that all Hindus believe in a pantheistic or monistic understanding of God. Of course, many Hindu gurus and philosophers defend this view as essential to Hinduism. However, there are still millions of Hindus who believe that God is ultimately personal. The Hare Krishna movement has made the personalist position widely known worldwide.

Hindu scholars distinguish those sacred writings believed to be direct revelations from God from those writings that serve as lesser vehicles of religious truth. The former category is known as *sruti* (Sanskrit for "what is heard"). This highest category of revelation is applied to the Vedas and the Upanishads. There are four famous Vedic collections: the Rigveda, the Samaveda, the Yajurveda, and the

Atharveda. The Vedas comprise the earliest scriptures for Hindus, while the Upanishads comprise a second phase of divine revelation.

Hindus give enormous weight to a second level of religious texts. The Bhagavad-Gita has gained particular honor and is often called the "Bible" of Hinduism, even though it is part of a longer epic poem. R. C. Zaehner, the famous scholar of Hinduism, stated that the Gita is "the most important, the most influential, and the most luminous of all the Hindu scriptures." The traditions of the gods and goddesses are recorded in the Puranas. Best known here are the stories about the pastimes of Lord Krishna. The Laws of Manu provide details on ritual and moral guidance.

Even though Hindus believe that this is a world of *maya*, or illusion, humans are responsible for their actions and beliefs. For many Hindus, enlightenment is achieved through realization that the self (atman) is God (Brahman). Hence the famous line "Atman is Brahman." Other Hindus speak of oneness with God without advocating the loss of self-identity. For all Hindus, salvation involves following the moral duties that apply to all humans and the particular responsibilities connected with individual stages in life. Hindus believe that we are caught in *samsara*, the cycle of birth, death, and afterlife. In this age of bondage (kali-yuga), Hindus hope for *moksha* (the term for liberation or salvation) by getting beyond the impact of negative karma.

The following items represent the chief concerns that Christians must raise about major elements of Hinduism.

1. The legends and stories about the gods and goddesses of Hinduism do not have the ring of historicity to them. Granted, the vast majority of Hindus believe that the stories about Krishna, Hanuman, Shiva, and other deities actually took place. However, there is no historical evidence for these legends. A. L. Basham, one of the world's greatest scholars of India and its religions, has stated that there is no proof at all of the historical reality of Krishna. The mythical nature of the Hindu deities is in contrast to the historical evidence for Jesus Christ.

2. The polytheistic nature of Hinduism is contradictory to the Bible's message of one God. Of course, Christians must note that Hindus usually believe that the thousands of deities in the Hindu

world are manifestations of one ultimate God. Nevertheless, biblical faith mandates worship only to the God and Father of the Lord Jesus Christ, and not to the many deities of the Hindu pantheon. The Bible also explicitly and repeatedly condemns the worship of idols.

3. The fatalistic law of karma undermines the biblical teaching on grace and mercy. Likewise, the theory of reincarnation is not taught in the Bible. Hinduism teaches that karma is absolute, while Christian faith teaches that God's mercy can override the wages of sin.

4. The caste system, which is clearly advocated by the ancient Hindu scriptures, denies the dignity and equality of all humans. In spite of India's laws about equality, the country remains divided along caste lines. Indian society still teaches that some people are untouchable. These individuals are known as Dalits, who are estimated to number more than 250 million in India. (About 60 percent of Indian Christians are from a Dalit background.)

5. Hindu leaders in India often protest that Christians try to convert Hindus to Jesus. However, Hindu gurus have frequently attempted to convert a Western audience to Hinduism. Religious freedom should include the right to change one's religious convictions. Tragically, Hindu extremists have resorted to violence against Christians in the last decade.

6. The Hindu appreciation for Jesus Christ is not matched by an acceptance of the Gospels' teaching that Jesus is the only Son of God, who died for our sins and rose to heavenly glory.

Hinduism	
WEB SITES	Hindu Gallery
	www.hindugallery.com
	Hindu Resources Online
	www.hindu.org
	Hindu Universe
	www.hindunet.org
	Hindu Website
	www.hinduwebsite.com
READING	Wesley Ariarajah, *Hindus and Christians* (Grand Rapids, MI: Eerdmans, 1991)

Jonah Blank, *Arrow of the Blue-Skinned God* (New York: Doubleday, 1992)

Elisabeth Bumiller, *May You Be the Mother of a Hundred Sons* (New York: Random House, 1990)

David Burnett, *The Spirit of Hinduism* (Tunbridge Wells, U.K.: Monarch, 1992).

Harold Coward, ed., *Hindu-Christian Dialogue* (Maryknoll, NY: Orbis, 1989)

Frederick Copleston, *Religion and the One* (London: Search, 1982)

Diana Eck, *Encountering God* (Boston: Beacon, 1993)

Franklin Edgerton, trans., *The Bhagavad Gita* (New York: Harper & Row, 1944)

Gavin Flood, *An Introduction to Hinduism* (Cambridge: Cambridge University Press, 1996)

Klaus Klostermaier, *A Concise Encyclopedia of Hinduism* (Oxford: Oneworld, 1998)

Julius Lipner, *Hindus* (London: Routledge, 1998)

Geoffrey Parrinder, *Avatar and Incarnation* (New York: Oxford University Press, 1970)

Sarvepalli Radhakrishnan, *Selected Writings* (New York: Dutton, 1970)

R. C. Zaehner, *Hinduism* (London: Oxford University Press, 1966)

▸ International Churches of Christ

The International Churches of Christ (ICOC) is a controversial movement founded by Kip McKean. The ICOC has roots in the older Church of Christ tradition, also known as the Stone-Campbell restoration movement. In the early nineteenth century several Christian leaders, upset at diverse Protestant movements, attempted to return to the original church of Christ described in the New Testament. The ICOC emerged from the stricter churches in the Stone-Campbell movement.

McKean was baptized in the Crossroads Church of Christ in Gainesville, Florida, in 1972. While leading the Lexington Church of Christ near Boston in 1979, he led thirty people to a more radical commitment to Christian life and evangelism. Out of this group emerged what became known as the Boston Church of Christ, also called the Boston movement. McKean pulled away from the larger Church of Christ tradition in 1987. The title International Churches of Christ was chosen in 1993.

The ICOC has been criticized for its exclusivist ideology, acting as if it is *the* body of Christ in the world. In addition, critics argue that the movement adopts a legalistic understanding of baptism, especially given the urgency with which members want outsiders to be baptized in order for their sins to be forgiven. The ICOC has also been sharply condemned for its authoritarian style, a possible reflection of Kip McKean's military background.

On November 11, 2001, it was announced that Kip and his wife, Elena, would take a sabbatical from their leadership roles. Earlier in the year their daughter Olivia had left the church. These two items brought discomfort to ICOC members, but there was more shock to come when Kip McKean announced on November 6, 2002, that he was resigning his position as World Missions Evangelist and top World Sector leader.

McKean stated in his resignation letter: "This hour is personally a time of tears. God through His Word, through circumstances and through true brothers has made it clear that my leadership in recent years has damaged both the Kingdom and my family. My most significant sin is arrogance—thinking I am always right, not listening to the counsel of my brothers, and not seeking discipling for my life, ministry and family. I have not followed Jesus's example of humility in leadership."

The ICOC experienced worldwide turmoil in the wake of McKean's departure. In February 2003 Henry Kriete, a leader in the London Church of Christ, wrote a stinging open letter about the systemic evil in the movement. Major ICOC leaders were forced to apologize for their duplication of the leadership style of McKean. The once united grouping of churches experienced fragmentation as different theologies and styles of church life were adopted.

On July 13, 2003, McKean wrote a fifty-page circular letter to all ICOC churches under the title "From Babylon to Zion." He described his spiritual downfall in detail and argued for the movement to return to its original vision. He announced that he had become the leader of the church in Portland, Oregon, and that he and his wife had found a new zeal for Christian work. "Rest assured, at this time Elena and I are totally committed to brotherhood and to evangelizing the world through the fellowship of the ICOC. 'Our highest joy' is Zion. (Psalm 137:6) Therefore, we solicit your prayers that the Spirit will guide us to begin to rebuild the wall, alongside each of you."

International Churches of Christ

TYPOLOGY	Christian Stone-Campbell restoration sectarian
FOUNDER	Kip McKean
HEADQUARTERS	Los Angeles
SCRIPTURE	Bible
CRITIC SITES	www.reveal.org
	www.rightcyberup.org
	http://icoc.blogspot.com
	www.tolc.org
	http://members.aol.com/djrtx/resource.htm

▸ Islam

In studying Islam, one faces limitations on the historically reliable evidence about the religion's founder, Muhammad. There is little of substance about Muhammad's early life in the Qur'an, and the situation is not much better for his life after departure to Medina. It is no wonder that every biographer has had to turn to traditional Islamic sources to construct a full-blown narrative. However, the search for the historical Muhammad beyond the Qur'an remains problematic for two additional reasons.

First, as Ignaz Goldziher and Joseph Schacht showed, the *hadith* (with its corresponding Muslim jurisprudence) are clearly anchored in the life situation of Muslims two centuries after the prophet. There are no historically objective grounds to separate the spurious from the authentic in the hundreds of thousands of traditions examined by Sunni or Shi'ite scholars.

Second, recourse to non-Qur'anic sources leads to a further complication. If the *sira, tafsir, hadith,* and *maghazi* material becomes primary in a biography, scholars are faced with difficult and sometimes embarrassing data about the prophet. Do angels really have wings? Did the prophet teach that females make up the majority in hell? What did Muhammad believe about the *djinn*? Did Muhammad teach that Allah turned Jews into pigs and apes? What was his attitude about the beating of wives?

A proper evangelical Christian response to Islam must be multifaceted in light of the breadth of Islamic history, the vast spread of Islam globally, the variety within Islam, and the tangled sociopolitical realities of the Middle East and other parts of the Muslim world. In other words, our analysis of Islam must not be simplistic. We should not, for example, say that Islam is or is not a "religion of peace," with no qualifications.

After the terrorist attacks of September 11, 2001, it bears repeating that Christian witness to Islam should focus more on the positive news about the Christian gospel and less about the weaknesses in Islam. Though remarks below contain negative assessments about Islam in general and Muhammad in particular, the most important thing that a Christian can do with a Muslim is to bear witness to the full message given in Jesus Christ.

Here are the most important issues in Christian response to Islam:

1. Since Islam claims to be built on Jesus as one sent from God, Muslim denial that Jesus is the Son of God represents an error at the very heart of Islam. Muhammad's failure to capture the essence of the New Testament teaching on Jesus shows how little he knew of the Gospel accounts. This error alone constitutes sufficient reason for abandoning any notion that Muhammad was a prophet of God. How could a prophet living after the time of Jesus be so misinformed about the identity of God's Messiah?

2. The Muslim denial that Jesus died on the cross is further illustration that Muhammad had no real sense of what constitutes the heart of Christianity. The Islamic notion that Jesus was replaced on the cross shows complete disregard for the Gospel records and for ancient historical testimony about his death. Muslims are forced to deny the Crucifixion on the basis of a few verses in a book written six hundred years after the death of Jesus, while denying hundreds of verses that attest to his death in books written at the time of Jesus.

3. On a broader level, Christians must remain skeptical about the Qur'an, given its abundant distortion of biblical stories and teachings, not simply in relation to Jesus, but also in connection with the whole range of scriptural data. Muhammad's knowledge of the Bible derived from his minimal contacts with Jews and Christians of his day and their reliance on extrabiblical traditions about the Jewish and Christian Scriptures.

Though the Qur'an contains many teachings in harmony with Christian faith and with Old Testament tradition, it is difficult to believe that it is a product of divine revelation, given its lack of order, its redundancy, and its increasing mean-spiritedness. It proves itself to be largely a product of Muhammad's thirst for prophetic status and unquestioned authority, especially in light of his growing use of the sword as a defense for his divine calling.

4. Christians must also express serious reservations about the prophet Muhammad, especially in contrast to Jesus Christ. This does not mean treating Muhammad as if he were the embodiment of evil. However, the following aspects of Muhammad's life are troubling: (a) his episodes of brutality, both in war and in dealing with some of his enemies; (b) his lack of tolerance toward critics and those who chose not to follow Islam; (c) his adoption of polygamy and arrogance toward his wives, especially by use of his prophetic status to crush dissent; (d) the consummation of his marriage to Aisha when she was very young; and (e) his marriage to Zaynab, his stepson's wife, while the stepson was still alive.

5. Christians must also reject central elements in the Islamic understanding of salvation. Islam has little concept of the New Testament doctrines of salvation by faith alone and grace alone, apart from the works of the law. Islam's emphasis upon law and obedience leads to uncertainty about assurance of salvation. Furthermore, the Qur'an puts such an emphasis upon the sovereignty of Allah's will in salvation that the ordinary Muslim cannot be certain of his or her eternal destiny.

6. The Islamic treatment of women must remain a matter of concern for Christians. Though Christian tradition has often abused women, this is no reason for ignoring the plight of many women in many Muslim countries. Generally, Muslim women in non-Western countries have little access to the freedoms taken for granted by Muslim females in the West.

7. The lack of human rights and freedom under Islam must also continue to be the object of Christian critique. The repression of non-Muslims, in one form or another, has been a constant reality in Muslim history. This is not to say that Muslim leaders forced Jews or

Christians to become Muslims; rather, Jews and Christians were generally treated as second-class citizens under Islamic caliphs.

Many Muslims have a distorted memory when it comes to the issue of the Crusades. They have every right to object to the wicked aspects of the Crusades carried about by the Church against Islam. However, the early Islamic empires were built on a crusade model, as Islamic armies overthrew Christian and Jewish peoples across North Africa, Palestine, and southern Europe.

Time Line of the Life of Muhammad	
c. 570	Birth in Mecca
575–	After the death of his mother, Muhammad is raised by his grandfather and uncle
595	Marriage to Khadijah, a traveling merchant
610	Muhammad claims to have divine revelations through mystical experience, forming the basis of the Qur'an
613	Muhammad begins to preach a monotheistic message and endures persecution
613	Muhammad deletes "Satanic verses" from the Qur'an because of false revelation that said worship of three idols was acceptable
619	After the death of Khadijah, Muhammad marries Sawdah, the first of his many other wives
620	Muhammad is taken by the angel Gabriel to Jerusalem and ascends to seventh heaven on a ladder (called the *miraj*)
622	Escape to Medina to avoid persecution in Mecca
624	Muhammad defeats Meccan enemies at the battle of Badr
627	Muhammad marries Zaynab, his cousin, who was previously married to the prophet's adopted son Zayd
627	Muhammad raids the Jewish clan of Qurayzah and orders the deaths of hundreds of Jewish men
628	Treaty signed with Meccan leaders at Hudaybiyyah
630	Muhammad conquers his enemies at Mecca and removes idols from city
632	Muhammad dies on June 8 after a period of ill health

Islam 101

The Five Pillars of Islam

1. *Shahadah* (Confession of Faith): "There is no God but Allah, and Muhammad is His messenger."
2. *Salat* (Prayer): All Muslims are to pray five times per day, facing Mecca, the holiest city.
3. *Zakat* (Tithing): Muslims must give financially to the poor and the needy. This involves giving at least 2.5 percent of their total wealth.
4. *Sawm* (Fasting): During the holy month of Ramadan, Muslims are to refrain from food, water, and sex from sunrise to sunset.
5. *Hajj* (Pilgrimage). As much as possible, at least once in a lifetime Muslims are to travel to Mecca to engage in rituals of prayer and worship at the central shrine in Islam's holiest city.

The Prophet

- Most Muslims believe that Muhammad was sinless.
- Muhammad is not viewed as divine.
- Most Muslims believe that the prophet was illiterate.
- The prophetic status of Muhammad is not to be questioned.
- Muhammad provides the greatest example for all aspects of life.
- The traditions about the prophet are known as *hadith*.
- The prophet was given permission by Allah to have twelve wives.

The Qur'an

- Muslims believe the Qur'an is the perfect Word of Allah.
- The Qur'an contains 114 chapters, or *surahs*.
- Muslims believe that the Qur'an was revealed to Muhammad by the archangel Gabriel.
- The Quranic material was composed from 610 through Muhammad's death in 632.
- The final compilation of the Qur'an was completed about 650.

Other Major Muslim Beliefs

- Islam started with Adam and not with Muhammad.
- Salvation is by the will of God through human obedience to God's law, or *shariah*.
- Though humans are imperfect, they are not fallen through original sin.
- Those chosen by God for salvation will enter heaven, or paradise.
- The damned will burn in eternal torment in hell.
- All countries and peoples should follow Islam and Islamic law.
- Muslims are to engage in *jihad*, which often means private spiritual struggle but also means defense of Muslim territory and military aggression.

- God will restore the world at the end of time through a coming human leader known as the *mahdi*.
- Muslim males can marry up to four wives.

Muslim Groups

- Almost 90 percent of Muslims belong to the Sunni tradition.
- Shi'ite Islam is popular in Iran and parts of Iraq, Lebanon, and Syria.
- Sufi Islam represents the mystical path in Islam.
- The Islam practiced in most Muslim countries is heavily influenced by local folk customs.

Muslim Views of Jesus

- Jesus was a prophet of God but not the Son of God.
- He was born of the Virgin Mary.
- He performed many miracles.
- He did not die on the cross.
- He did not rise from an empty tomb.
- He ascended to heaven after his death.
- He was a faithful Muslim, or follower of Allah.
- He predicted the ministry of Muhammad.

Time Line of Islam

632	Death of the prophet Muhammad
634	Death of Abu Bakr, the first *caliph*, or successor to Muhammad
637	Capture of Jerusalem by Muslim leaders
661	Assassination of Ali, the fourth *caliph*
680	Murder of Husain, grandson of the Prophet
690	Construction of the Dome of the Rock in Jerusalem
728	Death of Hasan al-Basri, early Sufi leader
732	Muslims defeated at the Battle of Tours
750	Rise of the Abbasid Dynasty, based in Baghdad
765	Split among Shi'ite Muslims over new leader
850	Death of al-Bukhari, specialist on Islamic *hadith*
940	Twelfth Shi'a Imam becomes the "hidden imam"
950	Death of Al-Farabi, the Muslim Aristotle
1037	Death of Ibn Sina (Avicenna), a great Islamic philosopher
1099	Crusaders capture Jerusalem
1111	Death of al-Ghazali, second to the Prophet as spiritual leader
1187	Saladin recaptures Jerusalem
1258	Mongols sack Baghdad
1300	Rise of Ottoman Empire

1315	Death of Raymond Lull, Christian missionary to Islam
1389	Ottomans defeat Balkan allies at Battle of Kosovo
1453	Ottomans capture Constantinople and rename it Istanbul.
1492	End of Muslim Spain
1517	Salim I conquers Egypt
1520	Rise of Sulayman the Magnificent, the Ottoman emperor
1563	Akbar gains power in India
1683	Vienna under siege by Muslim armies
1798	Napoleon in Egypt
1803	Wahhabi movement gains control in Saudi Arabia
1830	France occupies Algeria
1881	British take control of Egypt
1902	Qasim Amin pioneers feminism in Egypt
1910	Oil prospects in Persia
1924	Secularization of Turkey
1928	Muslim Brotherhood founded
1932	Political independence in Iraq
1947	Creation of Pakistan
1948	Founding of the state of Israel
1962	Algeria gains independence
1964	Formation of the Palestinian Liberation Organization
1965	Assassination of Malcolm X in New York City
1967	Six Day War between Israel and Egypt
1973	October War between Israel and Arabs
1977	Anwar Sadat makes peace with Israel
1979	Islamic revolution in Iran
1979	USSR invades Afghanistan
1982	Israeli invasion of Lebanon
1982	Assassination of Anwar Sadat
1987	Intifada begins in Palestine
1989	Iranian *fatwa* against Salman Rushdie for his *The Satanic Verses*
1991	Gulf War to liberate Kuwait
1993	Bombing of the World Trade Center
2000	Breakdown of Israel-Palestine peace talks
2001	September 11—attack on America
2001	Defeat of Taliban in Afghanistan
2002	Heightened suicide bombing in Israel
2002	Israeli government approves security wall
2003	USA attacks Iraq
2003	Increased anti-Semitic elements in Muslim thought
2004	Death of Arafat and renewal in hopes for peace

Islam

ISLAMIC WEB SITES	Al-Muhaddith, www.muhaddith.org Mamalist of Islamic Links, www.jannah.org/mamalist IslamiCity, www.islam.org Musalman: The Islamic Portal, www.musalman.com The Shi'a Homepage, www.shia.org
CHRISTIAN SITES	Answering Islam, www.answering-islam.org.uk Muslim-Christian Debate Web Site www.debate.org.uk Frontiers, www.frontiers.org.uk
ACADEMIC SITES	Islamic Studies (Professor Alan Godlas) www.arches.uga.edu/~godlas Middle East Forum, www.meforum.org Martin Kramer, www.martinkramer.o.3
READING	James A. Beverley, *Christ and Islam* (Joplin: College Press, 2001) George W. Braswell Jr., *Islam* (Nasvhille: Broadman & Holman, 1996) Kenneth Cragg, *The Call of the Minaret* (Maryknoll: Orbis, 1985) Norman Geisler and Abdul Saleed, *Answering Islam* (Grand Rapids: Baker, 2002) Martin Kramer, *Ivory Towers in the Sand* (Washington: Washington Institute for Near East Policy, 2001) Bernard Lewis, *Islam and the West* (New York: Oxford University Press, 1993) Rick Love, *Muslims, Magic, and the Kingdom of God* (Pasadena: William Carey, 2001) Fatima Mernissi, *The Veil and the Male Elite* (Boston: Addison-Wesley, 1991). Andrew Rippin, *Muslims* (New York: Routledge, 2000) Reinhard Schulze, *A Modern History of the Islamic World* (New York: New York University Press, 2000) Ibn Warraq, *Why I Am Not a Muslim* (Buffalo: Prometheus, 1995) Michael Cook, *Muhammad* (New York: Oxford University Press, 1983) Frank E. Peters, *Muhammad and the Origins of Islam* (State University of New York Press, 1994) Montgomery Watt, *Muhammad: Prophet and Statesman* (New York: Oxford University Press, 1961).
CD RESOURCE	*The World of Islam*, www.gmi.org

▶ Islamic Terrorism

The modern world has been consumed since September 11, 2001 with Osama bin Laden (b. 1957) and his version of Islam. Islamic terrorism is the military outcome of the growing radicalization in Islam since the early 1800s, both in response to the spread of Western colonialism and the demise of Muslim political supremacy. Today's Islamic terrorists are particularly angered over the Israeli-Palestinian conflict and the role of the United States in the Middle East.

Osama bin Laden traces his radicalism to the Wahhabism of Saudi Arabia, a movement that began with the reformer Muhammad ibn 'Abd al-Wahhab (1703–87). The Wahhabis advocated a puritanical and strict reading of Islamic law and belief. The Wahhabis threatened the interests of the Ottoman Turks and, in concert with the Saud dynasty, eventually gained control of Mecca and Medina, Islam's holiest cities.

A fundamentalist thrust in Islam emerged in Egypt as well, with the formation of the Muslim Brotherhood (also known as Al-Ikhwan al-Muslimun) in 1927. Tormented first by the presence of British rule and then by a tepid Muslim government, Brotherhood founder Hassan al-Banna and Sayyid Qutb, his chief intellectual heir, sought by any means, including violence, to restore true Islamic rule to Egypt.

The brotherhood started branches in Jordan and Syria, and militant groups in India, Iran, and Iraq imitated its radicalism. Muhammad Nawab-Safavi started his Fedayeen-e-Islami movement in Iran in the 1930s and told his followers: "Throw away your beads and get a gun: for beads keep you silent whilst guns silence the enemies of Islam." Abul A'la Maududi organized his militant Jamaat-e-Islami in the Punjab in 1941.

Western awareness of militant Islam came with the radical overthrow of the Shah of Iran in 1979 and the establishment of harsh Islamic rule under the Ayatollah Khomeini. Islamic terrorism came to the west with the bombing of the World Trade Center in 1993, the explosions at U.S. embassies in Africa, the attack on the USS *Cole* in

Yemen, and then the horrors of September 11. Recent terrorist bomb-
ings in Madrid and London have intensified concerns in the West
about militant Islam.

Islamic terrorists like bin Laden use the concept of *jihad* to defend
their actions. It is obvious that *jihad* in Islamic history carries the
meaning of military action as well as spiritual struggle. However,
thankfully most Muslims believe that nothing in the life of the
prophet Muhammad, the Qur'an, or Islamic law allows for the
wholesale and indiscriminate violence carried out by Al-Qaeda and
other Islamic terrorist groups.

Significant attention in debates about Islamic terrorism has been
given to the argument about a "Clash of Civilizations" between
Islam and the West. This view was advanced first by Harvard professor Samuel Huntington in a famous essay in *Foreign Affairs* (Summer
1993). Writing just after the first Gulf War, Huntington analyzed the
competing ideologies of our time.

On this, a number of Muslim intellectuals are calling for a new
and radical self-criticism within Islam. This point has been articulated
best by Kanan Makiya, author of *Republic of Fear* (on Saddam Hus-
sein's Iraq) and *Cruelty and Silence*. Makiya wrote in a London
Observer article: "Arabs and Muslims need today to face up to the fact
that their resentment at America has long since become unmoored
from any rational underpinnings it might once have had."

Islamic Terrorism	
WEBSITES	International Policy Institute for Counter-Terrorism www.ict.org.il
	Terrorism Research Centre, www.terrorism.com
READING	Peter L. Bergen, *Holy War Inc.* (New York: Free Press, 2001)
	Steve Coll, *Ghost Wars* (New York: Penguin, 2004)
	Samuel Huntington, *The Clash of Civilizations* (New York: Simon & Schuster, 1996)
	Roland Jacquard, *In the Name of Osama bin Laden* (Chapel Hill: Duke, 2002)
	Daniel Pipes, *Militant Islam Reaches America* (New York: Norton, 2003)

▶ Jehovah's Witnesses

Jehovah's Witnesses are well-known for their aggressive door-to-door evangelism, their stance against blood transfusion, and their prophecies of the end of the world. This group was started in 1879 under the leadership of Charles Taze Russell, who was born on February 16, 1852, in Old Allegheny, Pennsylvania. Russell's followers became known as Bible Students. After Russell's death in 1916, Joseph Franklin Rutherford won control of the movement. In 1931 the group adopted the name Jehovah's Witnesses. Since 1971, leadership has been invested in a group known as the Governing Body.

At the end of 2004 there were almost ninety-seven thousand congregations of Jehovah's Witnesses in the world. With headquarters in Brooklyn, New York, Witnesses believe they constitute the one true church of Jesus Christ. Witnesses teach that the Trinity doctrine is satanic, that Jesus was originally Michael the archangel, and that his Second Coming took place in 1914. Witnesses also believe that Jesus died on a stake and not on a cross. The group denies the physical resurrection of Jesus and the personal nature of the Holy Spirit. They believe that only 144,000 Witnesses will go to heaven. Jehovah's Witnesses are against Christmas and Easter celebrations, observance of birthdays, participation in the military, and saluting the flag of any nation.

Since Russell's day, Jehovah's Witnesses have been fixated on prophetic calculations. Their leaders, who claim to be prophets, can be viewed as false, given their penchant for error-laden apocalyptic pronouncements. The end of the world was predicted for 1914, 1918, 1925, the 1940s, and 1975. Sadly, generations of young Witnesses have skipped college because of Watchtower Society teaching that the earth was facing its demise. The Governing Body issued an apology in 1980 for the false predictions and confusions surrounding 1975.

Witness life is strictly controlled by the mother organization in Brooklyn. Members are forbidden to read material critical of the movement. At one time Witness leaders even stated that faithful disciples should believe what they are told even if they know it is untrue! Witnesses who disagree with Watchtower policy find themselves disciplined, sidelined, or excommunicated. The totalitarian spirit of the movement explains why members remain aloof about evidence of corruption and hypocrisy at headquarters and oblivious to doctrinal and scholarly blunders in Society teaching.

The most significant critic is Raymond Franz, a former member of the Governing Body. His memoir *Crisis of Conscience* is a powerful work against the legalism and hypocrisy of the Witness hierarchy. Franz is a nephew of longtime Society president Frederick W. Franz (1893–1992). The best scholarly study of the Witnesses is *Apocalypse Delayed*, the work of James Penton, a former member of the Society.

In 2000 William Bowen of Calvert City, Kentucky, discovered that one of his fellow elders in the local Kingdom Hall had been guilty of molesting a child many times. The Watchtower Society told Bowen that the person would be removed as an elder but that Bowen was not to report the person to the police. Bowen disobeyed the Society, resigned as an elder, and went public. He started silentlambs.org to provide a setting where victims of abuse can protest Witness cover-ups, thus serving as "a place for the lambs to roar." Bowen was kicked out of the Society in the summer of 2002.[8]

Jehovah's Witnesses

TYPOLOGY	Christian Protestant Adventist sectarian
HOME PAGE	www.watchtower.org
CRITIC SITES	Watchers of the Watch Tower World—Randall Watters www.freeminds.org
	Comments from the Friends—David Reed site www.cftf.com
	Watchtower Information www.watchtowerinformationservice.org
	Child Abuse and the Watchtower www.silentlambs.org
	Dissenting JWs on Blood Transfusion, www.ajwrb.org
READING	Raymond Franz, *Crisis of Conscience* (Atlanta: Commentary Press, 1983)
	M. James Penton, *Apocalypse Delayed* (Toronto: University of Toronto Press, 1985)

▶ Judaism

In regard to religion, the most significant fact to know about modern Jews is that about half are secular. The three most dominant religious groups within Judaism are the Orthodox, Conservative, and Reform.

1. *Orthodox Judaism.* This group usually includes the Hasidic movements. Hasidic Jews share much in common with the larger Orthodox world and usually resent being called Ultra-Orthodox. Orthodox Jews, including the Hasidim, place great emphasis upon the Torah since it provides the written law given to Moses on Mount Sinai. They also believe that Moses received the oral law from God. This oral law is contained in the Mishnah and the Talmud. Orthodox Jews believe that the Torah contains 613 *mitzvot*, or commandments. Orthodox rabbis are often trained at Yeshiva University.

Orthodox Judaism often places a great deal of emphasis on mystical writings. This is illustrated most famously in the study of the Kabbalah. This term comes from a Hebrew word for tradition and refers to a set of texts and ideas that originated in southern France and northern Spain in the thirteenth century. The most famous kabbalistic texts are *The Bahir* and *The Zohar*. Gershon Scholem is the great historian of the origins of the Kabbalah. Though the Kabbalah is a product of Jewish thought, kabbalistic texts are often crucial in ancient and modern Gnostic ideologies.

2. *Conservative Judaism.* Dr. Solomon Schechter was the leader behind the formation in America of the United Synagogue of Conservative Judaism in 1913, though the broader movement began in Germany in the mid-1800s, centering in the work of Zecharias Frankel (1801–75). Frankel was the founder of the Jewish Theological Seminary of Breslau in 1854. Conservative Judaism provides a middle ground between Orthodoxy and Reform Judaism. The Jewish Theological Seminary in America, a center of Conservative Judaism, was started in

1886. There are about eight hundred Conservative synagogues in the United States.

3. *Reform Judaism*. Reform Judaism grew out of the work of Rabbi Isaac Mayer Wise (1819–1900). Wise was trained in Europe but came to America in 1846 and sought to unify American Jews under a more liberal understanding of Jewish tradition. Reform Jews do not believe that either the Torah or the Talmud is explicit revelation of God. Reform Jews believe they have the right and duty to decide which laws apply to today's world. The principles of Reform Judaism were announced in the Pittsburgh Platform (1885), the Columbus Platform (1937), the Centenary Perspective (1976), and the recent Statement of Principles for Reform Judaism (1999).

There was considerable controversy among Reform Jews as the leadership moved to adopt the 1999 Statement of Principles. Rabbi Robert Seltzer stated in *Reformed Judaism* magazine, "We must guard against turning Reform Judaism into Conservative Judaism Lite." He was responding specifically to "Ten Principles for Reform Judaism," drafted by Rabbi Richard Levy in anticipation of the 1999 annual meeting in Pittsburgh.

There are more than nine hundred Reform synagogues in the United States, joined in the Union of American Hebrew Congregations. In 1875, Wise founded the Hebrew Union College in Cincinnati. The Hebrew Union College merged with the Jewish Institute of Religion (HUC-JIR) in 1959. HUC-JIR is the primary place for rabbinical training among Reform Jews, with locations in Cincinnati, New York, Los Angeles, and Jerusalem.

The following points outline a balanced Christian response to Judaism.

1. Christians must recognize the divisions within Judaism and among Jewish people, as noted above. Evangelicals often have a one-dimensional vision of Jews as practitioners of Orthodox Judaism. In fact, a large percentage of Jews in America and Israel are secular, and the majority of Jews in both countries do not follow the Orthodox life.

2. Christian response to Judaism must recognize the disgusting realities of anti-Semitism that have run through church history. It is difficult for Jews to hear the gospel, given the ways in which Jews have been persecuted and killed in the name of Jesus. The scars of anti-Semitism run deep in the Jewish psyche, not only in terms of history, but also in terms of continuing hatred and persecution.

3. Christians must resist any notion that Jews are "Christ killers." It is obvious that some Jewish leaders in the time of Jesus wanted Jesus dead. They deserve criticism for their blindness and hatred toward him and for their participation in plotting his demise, in conjunction with Roman leaders. However, this gives no credence to the long-standing diatribe against Jews in Christian tradition.

4. Given both historic and contemporary persecution of Jews, Christians should support the existence of the State of Israel. Affirmation of Israel does not demand uncritical acceptance of everything done by the Israeli government. Likewise, support of Israel does not have to be linked to dispensational eschatology. Yet it is hard to imagine an effective Christian witness to Jews paired to a belief that the Jewish people have no right to a homeland.

5. Some protest must be made when both secular and religious Jews mistreat Jews who have accepted Jesus as their Messiah. Orthodox Jews have a right to create their own boundaries in assessing what constitutes Judaism. Likewise, the larger Jewish community has a right to complain about misappropriation of symbols that usually refer to Orthodox Jewish religion. However, the reaction to messianic Jews sometimes goes far beyond legitimate debate and difference of opinion. It seems paradoxical that secular Jews are treated far better by religious Jews than are Jews who trust in Jesus.

6. Christian witness to Jews involves testimony about the person and work of Jesus—a topic often repugnant to Jewish people. However, in spite of anti-Semitism in the church, Christians can point to the grace represented in the death of Jesus, the power of his miracles, the courage in his actions, and the wisdom in his teachings. Christian confidence in Jesus the Jew as Messiah for both Jews and Gentiles must not diminish. What more would one want in a Messiah?

Time Line of Judaism Since AD 70

70	Destruction of Jerusalem and the Second Temple
73	Last stand of Jews at Masada
120–35	Rabbi Akiva leads in rabbinic Judaism
132–5	Bar Kokhba rebellion (Second Jewish Revolt)
200	Compilation of Mishnah
306	Council of Elvira forbids intermarriage with Jews
312/313	Emperor Constantine adopts Christianity
325	The Council of Nicea forbids Jews from converting pagans to Judaism
400	Commentary on the Mishnah edited
415	St. Cyril, the bishop of Alexandria, orders persecution of Jews
500	Ostrogoth king Theodoric conquers Italy and protects Jews
587	Recared of Spain adopts Catholicism and persecutes Jews
590	Pope Gregory the Great objects to forced baptism of Jews
626	Muhammad kills hundreds of members of a Jewish tribe
638	Jews are allowed to return to Jerusalem
691	The Dome of the Rock built in Jerusalem
691	First reports of Jews in England
732	The French defeat Muslim invaders at Tours
740	The Jewish kingdom of Khazar established
767	Karaite sect resists Talmudic traditions
807	Harun Ar-Rashid forces Jews to wear a yellow badge
969	Fatamid Muslim rule in Palestine
1066	Jews settle in England after the Norman conquest
1071	Seljuk occupation of Jerusalem
1078	Pope Gregory VII prohibits Jews from holding offices
1095	Henry IV of Germany grants a charter to Jews
1187	Saladin recaptures Jerusalem, allows Jews to return
1135	Birth of Maimonides (d. 1204)
1144	First known charge of Jewish ritual murder (Norwich, England)
1195	Maimonides completes *The Guide to the Perplexed*.
1204	First synagogue built in Vienna
1215	Fourth Lateran Council decrees Jews must wear a yellow sign
1229	King Henry III of England forces high taxation on Jews
1243	Accusations about Jewish desecration of the host in

	Germany
1254	French king Louis IX expels Jews from France
1285	Blood libel in Munich, Germany, results in the death of 68 Jews
1290	English King Edward I expels Jews from England
1322	Charles IV of France expels all French Jews
1389	Pope Boniface resists persecution of Jews
1415	Pope Benedict XIII bans Talmudic study
1420	Pope Martin V bans forcible conversion of Jews
1453	Fall of Constantinople (Istanbul) to Ottoman Muslims
1479	Jews expelled from Spain
1505	Birth of Solomon ben Moses, famous Kabbalist
1516	Jews relegated to ghetto in Venice
1543	Luther writes *About the Jews and Their Lies*
1553	Talmud publicly burned in Rome
1626	Birth of Shabbatai Zvi (d. 1676)
1632	Birth of Spinoza
1636	Rhode Island grants religious liberty to Jews
1654	Arrival of Jews in New York
1655	Jews readmitted to England by Oliver Cromwell
1700	Birth of the Baal Shem Tov (d. 1760)
1729	Birth of Moses Mendelssohn (d. 1786)
1781	Austria rescinds law forcing Jews to wear badges
1791	French Jews granted full citizenship
1819	Birth of Isaac Wise, American Reform leader (d. 1900)
1845	Birth of Baron Edmond James de Rothschild (d. 1934)
1858	Abduction of Edgar Mortara
1860	Birth of Theodor Herzl (d. 1904)
1873	Establishment of the Union of American Hebrew Congregations
1881	Start of mass migrations of Eastern European Jews
1886	Birth of David Ben-Gurion (d. 1973)
1894	Alfred Dreyfus Affair
1896	Theodor Herzl publishes *The Jewish State*
1897	First Jewish Zionist congress in Switzerland
1898	Birth of Golda Meir (d. 1978)
1913	Birth of Menachem Begin
1916	The Sykes-Picot Agreement divides up the Middle East
1917	The Balfour Declaration favors a Jewish Palestinian state.
1920	Haganah (Jewish defense organization) founded
1923	Kemal Ataturk overthrows Ottoman rule in Turkey
1929	Hebron Jews massacred by Arab militants
1929	Birth of Anne Frank (d. 1945)

1931	Jewish underground group Irgun formed
1933	Hitler becomes the German chancellor
1937	The Peel Commission recommends Holy Land partition
1938	Kristallnacht—destruction of German Jewish synagogues
1941	Lohamei Herut Yisrael (Lehi), or Stern Gang, formed
1943	Warsaw ghetto uprising
1948	Creation of the State of Israel

Orthodox Judaism 101

- Orthodox Jews believe in the one God, who has revealed himself to Israel.
- Orthodox Jews follow the 613 commands, or *mitzvot*, given in the Torah.
- Orthodox Jews follow an oral law they believe was given to Moses.
- Orthodox Jews obey the laws presented in the Mishnah.
- Orthodox Jews are guided by the Talmud.
- Orthodox Jews follow *gezeirah*, or rabbinic laws that provide "a fence around the Torah" to ensure that Jews do not accidentally break a mitzvah.
- Orthodox Jews obey the laws connected to Israel's holy days.
- Orthodox Jews rest on the Sabbath day.
- The Talmud forbids thirty-nine types of work on the Sabbath.
- Orthodox Jews obey the *Kashrut*, or Jewish dietary laws.
- Orthodox Jews have three formal prayer times every day.
- Women and men have separate seating in synagogue services.
- Orthodox Judaism forbids marriage to non-Jews.
- Orthodox Jews discourage, but do not forbid, Gentile conversion.
- Orthodox Jews are not to consider themselves better than non-Jews.
- A bar mitzvah is often held for Jewish boys at age thirteen to recognize their responsibility to obey Jewish law.
- Orthodox Jews can break Sabbath laws in order to save a life.
- Husband and wife are to obey the law of *niddah*, or separation during the wife's menstrual period.
- Orthodox Judaism condones certain forms of birth control, including the pill.
- Jewish law forbids homosexual acts.
- The Talmud allows Jewish men to divorce for any reason or no reason.
- The procedure for divorce is complex.
- In a divorce procedure, the wife receives a *get*, or document of release from the marriage.
- The rabbi can order a divorce if the husband breaks his duties to his wife.
- Abortion is commanded if a mother's life is at stake.

- Jewish law forbids cremation.
- The body of a dead person is to be cleaned and not left alone until burial.
- Open caskets are not permitted under Jewish law.

Judaism

General Web sites	World Jewish Congress
	http://www.wjc.org.il/
	Institute for Jewish Christian Studies
	www.icjs.org
	Judaism and Jewish Resources
	http://shamash.org/trb/judaism.html
	Eliezer Segal (University of Calgary)
	www.acs.ucalgary.ca/~elsegal
TRADITION SITES	Orthodox
	www.ou.org
	Conservative
	www.uscj.org
	Reform
	http://urj.org
	www.rj.org
ISRAEL/PALESTINE	www.academicinfo.net/mestpeace.html
	The American Israel Public Affairs Committee
	www.aipac.org
	Committee for Accuracy in Middle East Reporting in America, www.camera.org
	The Electronic Intifada, www.electronicintifada.net
	Ha'aretz
	www.haaretzdaily.com/
	Israel Ministry of Foreign Affairs
	www.mfa.gov.il/mfa
	The Jewish Virtual Library
	www.jewishvirtuallibrary.org
	Media Watch International
	www.honestreporting.com
	Middle East Forum
	www.meforum.org
	Middle East Media Research Institute
	www.memri.org
	Palestinian National Authority
	www.pna.gov.ps
	Tikkun
	www.tikkun.org
	Washington Report on Middle East Affairs

www.wrmea.com

READING   *On Judaism*

Hasia R. Diner, *The Jews of the United States* (Berkeley:
    University of California Press, 2004)

Hayim Halevy Donin, *To Be a Jew* (New York: Basic
    Books, 2001)

Martin Gilbert, *The Jews in the Twentieth Century*
    (Toronto: Key Porter, 2001)

D. D. Guttenplan, *The Holocaust on Trial* (New York:
    Norton, 2002)

Samuel Heilman, *Defenders of the Faith* (New York:
    Schocken, 1992)

Michael Marrus, *The Holocaust in History* (Toronto:
    Lester & Orpen Dennys, 1987)

Daniel C. Matt, *The Essential Kabbalah* (San Francisco:
    HarperSanFrancisco, 1996)

Jacob Neusner, *The Way of Torah* (Belmont:
    Wadsworth, 1997)

Gershom Scholem, *Origins of the Kabbalah* (Princeton,
    NJ: Princeton University Press, 1990)

On Israel and the Palestinian issue

Mitchell Bard, *Myths and Facts* (Chevy Chase, MD:
    AICE, 2002)

Thomas Friedman, *From Beirut to Jerusalem* (New
    York: Farrar, Straus, & Giroux, 1989)

David Grossman, *The Yellow Wind* (New York: Farrar,
    Straus, & Giroux, 1988)

Efrahim and Inari Karsh, *Empires of the Sand*
    (Cambridge: Harvard University Press, 1999)

Walter Laquer and Barry Rubin, eds., *The Israel-Arab
    Reader* (New York: Penguin, 2001)

Benny Morris, *Righteous Victims* (New York: Vintage,
    2001)

Michael Oren, *Six Days of War* (New York: Oxford
    University Press, 2002)

Tom Segev, *One Palestine, Complete* (New York: Henry
    Holt, 2000)

Avi Shlaim, *The Iron Wall* (New York: Norton, 2001)

On Christian response to Judaism

Michael Brown, *Answering Jewish Objections to Jesus*
    (Grand Rapids, MI: Baker, 2000–03), 3 vols.

▸ Kansas City Prophets

In 1988 John Wimber, leader of the Vineyard movement, developed a close association with Mike Bickle, then senior pastor of the Kansas City Fellowship (KCF). Bickle's ministry had become popular through its promotion of Bob Jones, John Paul Jackson, and Paul Cain, who became known as the Kansas City prophets. Wimber's fame launched Bickle and the KCF prophets into greater international prominence and controversy.

In 1990 the Kansas City Prophets, Wimber, and Jack Deere, a leading charismatic apologist, were accused by some Australian Christians of denying the sufficiency of Scripture and neglecting the cross of Christ. The Vineyard strongly denied the accusations. In May of the same year, Ernie Gruen, a leading Pentecostal pastor in Kansas, issued a two-hundred-page critique of KCF. He accused Bob Jones of engaging in wild speculation, false predictions, and bizarre visions. Gruen's report also argued that Bickle's fellowship had an elitist element, arising out of its focus on a new breed of super Christians.

The story of John Wimber's involvement with Bickle and the Kansas prophets was chronicled in David Pytches's 1991 work *Some Said It Thundered*. In late 1991 Bob Jones was disciplined for sexual misconduct and withdrew from ministry for several years. In 1992 Wimber became less focused on the prophetic. Bickle broke away from the Vineyard in 1996, in large part because of Wimber's negative reaction to John Arnott and the Toronto Blessing renewal.

Paul Cain, a native of Texas, is by far the most famous of the Kansas City prophets. Born in 1929 in Texas, he was raised Baptist and was a figure in healing revivals through the 1950s. He had some association with William Branham, one of the most famous healers. After 1959, Cain basically withdrew from public ministry until he connected with Mike Bickle in the mid-1980s. Cain maintained a worldwide itinerary from 1988 to 2004, often in association with Bickle,

Jack Deere, and Rick Joyner. In late 2004 these three announced that Cain had engaged in homosexual behavior and was an alcoholic. In 2005 Cain admitted his wrongdoings and asked for forgiveness.

Bickle now leads the International House of Prayer and the Friends of the Bridegroom ministry in Kansas City. John Paul Jackson founded Streams Ministries International in 1993, after working in Kansas City and then the Anaheim Vineyard. He is now based in New Hampshire. Bob Jones, a native of Arkansas, has regained his status as a major player in prophetic circles. He claims that a supernatural spirit being appeared to him on August 12, 2004, identified himself as the "Watcher," and prophesied a "new day" for the church.

Prophetic focus had become a staple among charismatics worldwide, due in some measure to the endorsement of Mike Bickle and John Wimber. While the Kansas City prophets do not deserve the nasty indictments against them, their prophecies are often mistaken if specific and are otherwise usually vague and highly speculative.[9]

Kansas City Prophets

TYPOLOGY	Christian Protestant charismatic
HOME PAGES	Mike Bickle
	www.fotb.com
	Paul Cain
	www.paulcain.org
	Bob Jones
	www.bobjones.org
	John Paul Jackson
	www.streamsministries.com
READING	James A. Beverley, *Holy Laughter and the Toronto Blessing* (Grand Rapids, MI: Zondervan, 1995)
	Mike Bickle, *Growing in the Prophetic* (Lake Mary, FL: Creation House, 1996)
	Jack Deere, *Surprised by the Power of the Holy Spirit* (Grand Rapids, MI: Zondervan, 1996)
	Hank Hanegraaff, *Counterfeit Revival* (Dallas: Word, 1997).
	John MacArthur, *Charismatic Chaos* (Grand Rapids, MI: Zondervan, 1992)
	David Pytches, *Some Said It Thundered* (Nashville: Thomas Nelson, 1991)

▸ Local Church (Witness Lee)

The Local Church is a controversial Christian movement rooted in the ministries of Watchman Nee (1903–72) and Witness Lee (1905–99). Nee was converted to Christ in 1920 and was impacted by both Methodism and the Plymouth Brethren tradition. Lee was born in northern China, was raised in a Christian home, and became a close associate of Watchman Nee in the 1930s. Lee moved to Taiwan in 1949. Watchman Nee and his Local Church movement were persecuted by Communist authorities in the early 1950s. Nee was sentenced to prison in 1956 and remained there till the end of his life.

The Local Church grew quickly under Witness Lee in Taiwan and other parts of Southeast Asia. Lee moved to the United States in 1962 and settled in Southern California. He carried on a regular teaching and preaching ministry until 1997, two years before his death. Living Stream Ministries (LSM) continues to publish his material, now available in more than fourteen languages and four hundred separate volumes. LSM also publishes *The Recovery Bible*, a title that reflects Local Church teaching that it is part of God's recovery of the original New Testament Church.

Controversy about Lee began in the mid 1970s when the Local Church in Berkeley was attacked by Jack Sparks, a leader in the Christian World Liberation Front (CWLF). The CWLF developed the Spiritual Counterfeits Project (SCP), an evangelical cult-monitoring group. Sparks wrote a chapter against the Local Church in his work *The Mindbenders* (1977), and Neil Duddy and the SCP attacked Lee's movement in *The God-Men* (1977, revised edition 1981). Nelson withdrew *The Mindbenders* from circulation in 1983 and published an apology in eighteen major U.S. newspapers. After a lengthy court case, the Local Church won a $12 million judgment in 1985 against SCP. SCP was forced into bankruptcy and reemerged under Chapter 11 protection.

In 1999 John Ankerberg and John Weldon included the Local Church in their *Encyclopedia of Cults and New Religions*. In 2001 leaders in the Local Church wrote the two authors and publisher to protest their inclusion in the book. They asked for a meeting to process the issue. Harvest House and the authors refused to meet with Local Church representatives and started legal proceedings against the Local Church in late 2002. In response, the Local Church started its own legal action against the publisher.

The Local Church is basically an evangelical Christian movement. Its relations with the broader evangelical community would be improved by addressing several weaknesses. First, the movement is inclined to elitism because of the way Witness Lee pictured the movement as a recovery of the Lord's church. Like so many other restorationists, he failed to see that the unity of the church is not solved by starting another group. Second, the rhetoric in Local Church literature about other Christian groups is too negative and is inconsistent with their otherwise open stance.[10] Finally, Local Church leaders are too reluctant to detect or admit errors in the teaching of Witness Lee.

Local Church (Witness Lee)	
TYPOLOGY	Christian Protestant evangelical
FOUNDERS	Watchman Nee and Witness Lee
WEB SITES	Living Stream Ministries
	www.lsm.org
	Contending for the Faith
	www.contendingforthefaith.com
	Affirmation and Critique
	www.affcrit.com
READING	Wing-Hung Lam, *Chinese Theology in Construction* (Pasadena: William Carey Library, 1983)

▶ Lubavitch

The Lubavitch movement, based in Brooklyn, New York, is one of the best-known groups in world Judaism. The group traces its roots to Europe in the eighteenth century but became famous through the work of Rabbi Menachem Mendel Schneerson, the seventh and last Lubavitcher rebbe. Rabbi Schneerson was born in 1902, was chosen as the rebbe in 1950, and died in 1994. His fame as a teacher, mystic, and leader inspired a worldwide following.

The Lubavitch are known for their aggressive evangelism, not to Gentiles, but to secular Jews. In 1972 Rabbi Schneerson announced the creation of *mitzvah tanks* to spread the message of the Lubavitch movement on the streets of New York. Lubavitchers would appeal to nonobservant Jewish men to come into the van (now the group uses refurbished mobile homes), put on *tefillin*, and say a short prayer. Jewish women were offered guides to the lighting of candles before the start of the Sabbath.

Schneerson was married in December 1928 in Warsaw to Rebbetzin Chaya Mushka, the daughter of the sixth Lubavitcher Rebbe. Schneerson's wife remained out of public attention throughout their fifty-nine years of marriage. She died on February 10, 1988, and fifteen thousand people joined in the procession to her burial, under police escort.

Rabbi Schneerson remained active as leader until he suffered a stroke on March 2, 1992, losing the ability to speak and becoming paralyzed on his right side. He died on June 12, 1994. His body was put to rest at the Ohel Chabad Lubavitch Cambria Heights, NY, next to the burial spot of his father-in-law, Rabbi Joseph Isaac Schneersohn, the sixth rebbe. *Ohel* is the term for a tent that is placed over the burial site of a holy person. Lubavitch come from all over the world to visit the *Ohel*. There is even a Web site (www.ohelchabad.org) that provides details about visiting or sending a letter to the rebbe.

Visitors are encouraged not to wear leather shoes. Men are to wear a hat, and women are to have a head covering. The usual practices are to write a letter to the rebbe before entering the *Ohel* and to leave by walking backward as a sign of respect.

There was considerable debate among Lubavitchers about who would follow Rabbi Schneerson after his death. In fact, some Lubavitch claimed that he would never die, even when he was on life support in a Manhattan hospital. Many Lubavitch believe that he is the long-awaited Messiah, and they expect him to return from the dead to bring God's full glory to the earth.

The Chabad-Lubavitch movement has an impressive Web presence, due largely to its first Internet leader, Rabbi Yosef Yitzchak Kazen, a native of Cleveland, Ohio. The Lubavitch world headquarters is at 770 Eastern Parkway, Brooklyn, NY 11213. In fact, most Lubavitch know the address simply as 770 because of the interest in visiting there to hear Rabbi Schneerson when he was teaching.

Lubavitch

TYPOLOGY	Judaism Orthodox Hasidic
FAMOUS LEADER	Menachem Mendel Schneerson (1902–94)
HEADQUARTERS	770 Eastern Parkway, Brooklyn, NY 11213
WEB SITES	www.lubavitch.com
	www.therebbe.org
	www.chabad.org

Lutheran churches trace their existence to the German Reformer Martin Luther, a monk who protested doctrinal errors and moral lapses in the popular Catholicism of his day. Luther is most famous for his ninety-five theses, a document that targeted the sale of indulgences in his area. This related to buying souls out of purgatory through payments to the Catholic Church. Luther's critique led to a trial before Catholic authorities and eventual excommunication in 1521. Luther stated at the Diet of Worms: "Unless I am convinced by Scripture and plain reason—I do not accept the authority of the popes and councils, for they have contradicted each other—my conscience is captive to the Word of God. I cannot and I will not recant anything, for to go against conscience is neither right nor safe. God help me. Amen."

The Augsburg Confession of 1530 is part of *The Book of Concord*, published in 1580, which also includes Luther's Small Catechism, his Large Catechism, and his Smalcald Articles (from 1537). In his writings Luther objected to celibacy, the worship of saints, and the doctrine of purgatory. Luther also became increasingly critical of the office of the pope. In his Smalcald Articles he states, "The Pope is the very Antichrist, who has exalted himself above, and opposed himself against Christ because he will not permit Christians to be saved without his power, which, nevertheless, is nothing, and is neither ordained nor commanded by God." His chief objection to the papacy arose out of his argument for salvation by grace alone through faith alone.

A large majority of Lutheran churches belong to the Lutheran World Federation (LWF), founded in 1947. In 2004 the LWF comprised 138 member churches, representing 65 million Lutherans from 77 countries. The Evangelical Lutheran Church in America (ELCA) is part of this federation. Membership in the ELCA is almost 5 million, making it the largest Lutheran church in the United States. The more conservative Lutheran Church–Missouri Synod has almost 2.5 million members, while the Wisconsin Evangelical Lutheran Synod, another conservative Lutheran group, has more than 400,000.

Lutherans have always held Luther in high esteem, and his writings play a significant part in the training of Lutheran ministers. However, in recent years Lutherans have also distanced themselves from darker sides of Luther's ideology, particularly his rantings against Jews. Luther grew increasingly intemperate about Jews, culminating in his 1543 work *Concerning the Jews and Their Lies*. His writings were cited by Hitler to justify Nazi policy. The Lutheran World Federation condemned Luther's anti-Semitism in 1984.

On October 31, 1999, the Lutheran World Federation and the Roman Catholic Church ratified a joint agreement on justification at an official ceremony in Augsburg, Germany. This ecumenical achievement was a result of three decades of scholarly engagement between Lutherans and Catholics. More conservative Lutherans, such as the Lutheran Church–Missouri Synod, refused to endorse the agreement, arguing that it represented a compromise of historic Lutheranism.

Lutherans	
TYPOLOGY	Christian Protestant
FOUNDER	Martin Luther (1484–1546)
WEB SITES	Confessional Evangelical Lutheran Conference
	www.celc.info
	International Lutheran Council
	www.ilc-online.org
	Lutheran World Federation
	www.lutheranworld.org
	Evangelical Lutheran Church in America
	www.elca.org
	Lutheran Church Missouri Synod
	www.lcms.org
	Wisconsin Evangelical Lutheran Synod
	www.wels.net
READING	Richard Cimino, ed., *Lutherans Today* (Grand Rapids, MI: Eerdmans, 2003)

▶ Methodists

The Methodist tradition in Protestantism traces to John Wesley (1703–91) and his brother Charles (1707–88), a hymn writer. The Wesleys were raised in the Church of England and attended Oxford University. After a failed ministry in America, John Wesley found himself spiritually depressed. This melancholy disappeared when he experienced conversion at an Anglican meeting in London on May 24, 1738. Here are his famous words about his transformation: "I felt my heart strangely warmed. I felt I did trust in Christ, Christ alone, for salvation; and an assurance was given me that he had taken away my sins."

John Wesley spent the rest of his life preaching the message of Christian grace. He severed relations with the Moravians, but he never left the Church of England, though his practices created strains within Anglican circles. Wesley's itinerant preaching grew because of the encouragement of George Whitfield, a popular revival preacher. Wesley sent Francis Asbury (1745–1816) to the Americas in 1771. Asbury, Thomas Coke, and others formed the Methodist Episcopal Church.

Methodists divided early along racial lines, with the formation of the African Methodist Episcopal Church in 1816. Later, in 1845, the larger Methodist movement split over the issue of slavery, and the Methodist Episcopal Church, South, was formed. This split was formally healed with reunion in 1939. The United Methodist Church, the largest American Methodist body, stands in this lineage and was officially founded in 1968.

John Wesley can also be considered the spiritual founder of churches in the Holiness tradition. Wesley's theology and ministry laid the roots for the Salvation Army, the Church of the Nazarene, the Church of God (Anderson, Indiana), the Wesleyan Church, and the Glenn Griffith churches, among others.

There are more than 120 distinct groups in the Methodist and Holiness traditions in North America. The great majority of

Methodist churches, both American and otherwise, belong to the World Methodist Council.

Methodist churches divide along liberal and conservative theological agendas. Like many denominations, mainline Methodist groups face a crisis over how to handle homosexuality and the ordination of gays. In March 2004 the Rev. Karen Dammann of Seattle was found not guilty of engaging in "practices incompatible with Christian teachings" even though she admitted to being a practicing homosexual. In December 2004 a United Methodist court in Pennsylvania removed Rev. Irene Elizabeth Stroud from ministry, citing her open lesbian relationship. That decision was reversed in April 2005 but both cases are the subjects of ongoing debates. The United Methodist Church has a policy against ordination of "self-avowed, practicing homosexuals."[11]

Holiness churches are more conservative theologically than is the United Methodist Church. Their divisions occur over different understandings of sanctification, the ordination of women, and what constitutes proper separation from the world. In many Holiness traditions, sanctification is viewed as a second work of grace distinct from justification. It is often viewed as a crisis experience, and the language of perfection is used about the believer.

Methodists	
TYPOLOGY	Christian Protestant
FOUNDER	John Wesley
HOME PAGES	World Methodist Council
	www.worldmethodistcouncil.org
	United Methodist Church
	www.umc.org
	African Methodist Episcopal Church
	www.ame-church.com
	Christian Methodist Episcopal Church
	www.c-m-e.org
	Church of the Nazarene
	www.nazarene.org
READING	Thomas Oden, *John Wesley's Scriptural Christianity* (Grand Rapids: Zondervan, 1994)

▶ Metropolitan Community Churches

The association of Metropolitan Community Churches dates back to October 6, 1968, when Troy Perry started a church based on a positive attitude toward homosexuality. The first meeting took place with twelve people in Perry's home in Huntington Park, California. Perry writes: "There wasn't a dry eye in the place. A hush fell over the place and everybody in that small living room was weeping silently. We all felt that we were a part of something great. God was preparing to move. We were to see God's handiwork, and that would be unbelievable." The MCC now has over 300 congregations spread across 22 countries.

Since the formation of the MCC other denominations have adopted a pro-gay view, including the United Church of Christ, and the United Church of Canada. The Anglican movement worldwide has experienced enormous friction because of the decision in 2003 by the Episcopal Church to ordain Gene Robinson, an openly gay pastor, as Bishop of New Hampshire. Virtually all mainline denominations have a lobby in favor of acceptance of gays, lesbians, bisexuals, and transgender persons. There are pro-gay groups for a range of religious groups and movements: Evangelicals Concerned is pro-gay while Dignity USA reaches Catholics and "A Common Bond" reaches Jehovah's Witnesses.

The MCC is quite conservative in its overall theology. Its Statement of Faith affirms the Trinity and adopts a high view of Scripture. This contrasts with some pro-gay churches which are quite radical in their Christology and explicitly repudiate the authority of Scripture. The MCC Web site states: "Lesbians and gay men face discrimination because of societal attitudes. Unfortunately, these attitudes are often taught by the church. Sadly, the Bible is often used as a weapon to 'bash' gays and lesbians. It is important to remember that such hurtful things are not a reflection of Christ, or the way God wants the church to be, or even what the Bible really says."

How should evangelical Christians respond to pro-gay churches like the MCC?

First, response must be rooted in love, especially since gays experience so much hate in both church and society. Evangelicals should be disturbed by antigay rhetoric that amounts to hate speech, as illustrated by Fred Phelps's infamous work at Westboro Baptist Church in Topeka, Kansas. Phelps warns against "the maudlin, kissy-pooh, feel-good, touchy-feely preachers of today's society."

Second, the position that homosexuality is wrong is based on the clear teaching of Scripture and is the dominant tradition in the history of Christian faith. Robert Gagnon has defended the traditional interpretation about Scriptural teaching in his exhaustive work *The Bible and Homosexual Practice*. Bruce Metzger, the famous Princeton New Testament scholar, wrote a stinging rebuke of his own denomination's task force on homosexuality because of its neglect of the plain reading of the Bible. Resistance to pro-gay theology is rooted in the Creation mandate of heterosexual marriage, in the prohibitions against same-sex acts in both Old and New Testaments, and in the teachings of the Church Fathers and leaders of the Reformation.

Metropolitan Community Churches	
TYPOLOGY	Christian Protestant pro-gay
FOUNDER	Troy Perry
HOME SITE	www.mcchurch.org
PRO-GAY SITES	Religious Archives Network
	www.lgbtran.org
	Whosoever Magazine (Online)
	www.whosoever.org
CRITICAL SITE	Evangelicals Concerned
	www.ecwr.org
	Exodus Global Alliance (Pat Lawrence)
	http://exodusglobalalliance.org
	Exodus International
	http://exodus.to

Sy Rogers
www.syrogers.com
Genesis Counseling (Joe Dallas)
www.genesiscounseling.org
National Association for Research and THERAPY
www.narth.com
www.robgagnon.net
P.A.T.H.
www.pathinfo.org

READING

Joe Dallas, *A Strong Delusion* (Eugene, OR: Harvest
House, 1996)
Robert Gagnon, *The Bible and Homosexual Practice*
(Nashville: Abingdon, 2001)
David Greenberg, *The Construction of Homosexuality*
(Chicago: University of Chicago Press, 1988)
Stanton Jones and Mark Yarhouse, *Homosexuality: The
Use of Scientific Research in the Church's Moral
Debate* (Downers Grove, IL: InterVarsity Press,
2000)
Elizabeth Moberly, *Homosexuality: A New Christian
View* (Cambridge, U.K. : James Clark, 1983)

▸ Mormonism

This entry on Mormonism is quite extensive for three reasons. First, Mormonism is one of the few modern religious movements that has experienced incredible growth. Second, proper critique of Mormonism is especially important in light of the new and controversial Mormon-evangelical dialogue. Third, some scholars believe that the Mormon Church is at a transition point in relation to its self-identity. Will it remain sectarian or will it change in order to be accepted as an orthodox Christian movement? On the latter point, it is very significant that J. Gordon Melton does not list Mormonism as part of the Christian tradition in his *Encylopedia of American Religions.*

Mormonism is usually identified with the Church of Jesus Christ of Latter-day Saints (LDS), based in Salt Lake City, Utah. It might seem hard to imagine why there could be any controversy over a church known for its Tabernacle Choir, pro-family ads, and clean-cut missionaries. However, much in the history of the LDS faith and belief system should lead to serious doubts about its authenticity as an orthodox Christian movement.

The story of Mormonism hinges on Joseph Smith Jr. He was born on December 23, 1805, in Sharon, Vermont, and moved with his family to Palmyra, New York, in 1816. Mormons believe that God the Father and Jesus came to Joseph in the spring of 1820 and told him to restore the one true church. This episode is called the First Vision story and constitutes one of the most important historic claims of Mormonism.

Smith also claimed that on September 21, 1823, an angel named Moroni told him of gold plates buried in the hill Cumorah (near Palmyra) that contain the full gospel. Joseph said he unearthed the gold plates in 1827 and translated the ancient writing on them into *The Book of Mormon,* which was published in 1830. That same year the Mormon Church was founded. Smith also claimed to receive direct revelations from God throughout his leadership as the first prophet of the church.

Mormons settled in Ohio, Missouri, and Illinois after the early years in New York State. They were persecuted heavily during their time in Missouri, in part because of their radical claims about taking ownership in Jackson County. Smith proclaimed that Independence, Missouri, would be the site of the New Jerusalem predicted in the book of Revelation.

During the early 1840s, there were both internal dissent and external criticism about Smith, particularly because of his practice of plural marriage—a practice that Smith denied. Joseph Smith and his brother Hyrum were killed by an anti-Mormon mob on June 27, 1844. Joseph was in jail in Carthage, Illinois, over charges of ordering the destruction of a newspaper called the *Nauvoo Expositor*, founded by a leading ex-Mormon, William Law. The newspaper circulated the view that Smith believed in many gods and practiced polygamy.

To understand the Mormon doctrinal framework, one must move beyond a surface reading of the LDS Articles of Faith, since Mormons have a unique interpretation of specific Christian terms. For example, Mormon affirmation of Father, Son, and Spirit does not mean commitment to a trinitarian understanding of God. Likewise, the Mormon understanding of eternal life is not rooted in an emphasis on grace alone through faith alone. Rather, eternal life is identified with following the rules and procedures of the Mormon Church.

Further, Mormon understanding of the Bible is skewed because of prior and ultimate trust in *The Book of Mormon* and the other Mormon scriptures (*Doctrine and Covenants* and *Pearl of Great Price*). Though Mormons give Jesus supremacy in their articles, the LDS understanding of the gospel of Jesus Christ is radically harmed by emphasis on the life and teachings of Joseph Smith.

Beyond these issues, other key items illustrate the degree of the Mormon departure from Christian orthodoxy. Mormons believe that there are many gods and that these gods formed and organized the universe. Mormons are also taught that the gods used to be men, who grew up to become gods. Worthy Mormon males can become gods someday. While some Mormon intellectuals claim that these notions about God are not official teaching, they are the views of the majority of the LDS faithful.

Mormonism also teaches that the eternal spirits who were not valiant in a heavenly battle between Jesus and Lucifer were sent to earth as humans and were cursed with a dark skin. The latter view led to the LDS church banning blacks from the priesthood until an alleged revelation reversed the ban in 1978. However, Mormons are still taught that dark skin is a sign of a prior curse in the eternal realm.

Mormons also argue that the natives of the Americas are descendents of Jews who came to the West hundreds of years before the time of Jesus. Mormons believe that Jesus, after his resurrection, made a special trip to visit the Americas, as documented in *The Book of Mormon*. The LDS also practice secret temple rituals, wear special endowment garments, and believe that there are two priesthoods for the Mormon male.

Though most Mormons are convinced that Mormonism is true, the average Mormon has little idea of the intellectual bankruptcy of much of the Mormon paradigm, particularly in relation to the integrity of Joseph Smith and his alleged revelations from heaven. Here are seven major realities Mormons should face.

1. *Changing revelation.* The original revelations of Joseph Smith are not what Mormons read today. This is not a picky complaint about minor translation problems. Changes have been made to the early revelations and to historical documents because of changing doctrinal views or to cover up immoral activity (polygamy) or intellectual blunder on the part of Joseph Smith.

There are significant differences between the first and later editions of *The Book of Mormon*. Also, the first revelations that appear in *The Book of Commandments* (1833) were drastically altered when given under the title *Doctrine and Covenants* (1835). The original history of the church was also changed to fit developing Mormon views and to hide unpleasant aspects of the life of Joseph Smith.

2. *An unstable church.* Some major doctrines of early Mormonism do not agree with the teachings of the current Latter-day Church.

This is most crucial when it comes to *The Book of Mormon* itself. Modern-day Mormons do not really believe some of its key teachings, simply because Smith changed his mind on some doctrines after its publication. One of the most serious issues involves the plurality of gods.

In *The Book of Mormon* there are repeated assertions that there is only one God, that he is a Spirit, and that he is eternal. For example, Moroni 8:18 states, "God is unchangeable from all eternity to all eternity." However, Smith later changed his mind about God's nature and announced, "We have imagined and supposed that God was God from all eternity. I will refute that idea and take away the veil." Thankfully, some Mormon leaders are now stressing a more traditional understanding of the eternal nature of God.

3. *Character of the founder.* One should be suspicious about the Mormon gospel, given the dishonesty, arrogance, and immorality of Joseph Smith. In 1826, after his alleged visits from heavenly messengers, Smith was arrested for "glass looking" (use of a magic device to find buried treasure). Wes Walters discovered the court document that implicates Joseph Smith in this unlawful scheme. It is hard to trust Smith's integrity on heavenly treasure (the so-called "golden plates" buried by the angel) when he was a deceiver and a law breaker by attempting to find earthly treasure on the property of gullible individuals.

Further, the lying and scheming behind Joseph Smith's plural marriage discredits him as a prophet of God. In the Mormon *History of the Church* Smith expresses astonishment that he is being accused of having seven wives and claims that he has only one wife. In fact, as Mormon historians admit, he was married to at least thirty-three women besides his original wife. Some of these women had living husbands at the time. The history of Mormon polygamy, particularly in the case of its founding prophet, is a story of deception and unbearable heartache.

4. *Discredited sources.* In 1835 Joseph Smith made one of his biggest blunders, one that gives some indication of his arrogance as well as the naiveté of his Mormon followers. In that year he came into pos-

session of some Egyptian documents, which he purchased from a merchant who was traveling through Mormon territory. Smith looked at one of the Egyptian documents and announced that it was really written by Abraham, Israel's ancient patriarch.

"The Book of Abraham" was accepted by Smith's followers and became part of *The Pearl of Great Price*, one of the four standard works of Mormonism. This episode shows both an ego ready to claim the ability to translate Egyptian and a group ready to accept anything the prophet stated. Since no Mormons at the time knew Egyptian, they could not correct the prophet. However, in the twentieth century, the documents that Joseph used were discovered and were translated by competent Egyptologists. They have nothing to do with Abraham and instead contain directions for the burial rites of Egyptian mummies.

5. *Problems with* The Book of Mormon. There are several reasons why the traditional LDS views of *The Book of Mormon* represent a house of cards.

First, there is no good reason to trust Joseph Smith's integrity. He is no reliable witness on earthly matters and should not be trusted on divine ones, as noted earlier.

Second, there is every indication that *The Book of Mormon* is a product of the nineteenth century. It deals with religious issues common to Smith's day, including debates over the proper name of the Christian church, the fate of the heathen, the proper mode of baptism, and so on.

Third, contrary to popular Mormon sentiment, there is no archaeological support for its version of what was going on in the Americas from 2200 BC through AD 400. Archaeologists do not use it as a field guide for the study of the geography and history of the Americas. The Smithsonian Institution in Washington regularly sends out notices that *The Book of Mormon* is not used by its workers. Likewise, anthropologists repudiate the common Mormon view that American natives are descendants of Jews who migrated to the Western hemisphere.

Fourth, *The Book of Mormon* copies the King James Version of the

Bible (1611), even with the latter's use of italics. Why is the King James language being quoted in documents that were allegedly written more than a thousand years earlier? The easiest answer is that Joseph Smith neglected to think of all the ways *The Book of Mormon* would give signals that it was a product of his own time.

Finally, historians have tracked down other books that likely influenced Smith in his authorship of *The Book of Mormon*. Of particular importance here is *View of the Hebrews*, written by Ethan Smith and published in New York in 1823 and reprinted in 1825. Many of the concepts of *The Book of Mormon* duplicate Ethan Smith's earlier work. In fact, Mormon historian B. H. Roberts had an enormous crisis of faith because of his close study of the parallels between the two works.

6. *Imaginary visions.* Mormonism's integrity rests on the credibility of the First Vision story of Joseph Smith. In his personal history, Smith writes about his search for the true church when he was a teenager. "So, in accordance with this, my determination to ask of God, I retired to the woods to make the attempt. It was on the morning of a beautiful, clear day, early in the spring of eighteen hundred and twenty."

Smith writes, "I saw a pillar of light exactly over my head, above the brightness of the sun, which descended gradually until it fell upon me. When the light rested upon me I saw two Personages, whose brightness and glory defy all description, standing above me in the air. One of them spake unto me, calling me by name and said, pointing to the other—'This is My Beloved Son. Hear Him!'"

The teenager then asked which church to join. "I was answered that I must join none of them, for they were all wrong; and the Personage who addressed me said that all their creeds were an abomination in his sight; that those professors were all corrupt; that: 'they draw near to me with their lips, but their hearts are far from me, they teach for doctrines the commandments of men, having a form of godliness, but they deny the power thereof.'"

Though most Mormons believe this account without reservation, there is good evidence to suggest that it is a product of Smith's imagination.

First, the notion that every other church was wrong is impossible to reconcile with the promise of Jesus that the gates of hell would not prevail against the church. The claim of wholesale apostasy in all Christian churches is simply a fabrication of Joseph Smith. It speaks more of his pride and arrogance than it does about the state of churches in the United States or other parts of the world.

Second, it is particularly telling that Smith failed to remember the year of this alleged encounter. He states that he sought God's help when there was a revival going on in his area. That revival has been shown by Wes Walters to have taken place in 1824, four years after Smith's date for the First Vision. How is it possible that Smith could forget the year of his face-to-face encounter with God the Father and Jesus Christ, his Son?

Further, Smith's First Vision account, which appears in *The Pearl of Great Price*, is contradicted by three other accounts from him. In other words, Smith could not keep his own story straight about the pivotal event of his life. The four accounts from him disagree on when the vision occurred, where the vision occurred, why the vision occurred, and who appeared to Joseph.

7. *Problems with "inner testimony."* Most Mormons do not know details about the case against the teachings and integrity of Joseph Smith. If pressed on the matter, many will simply refuse to face these hard issues that impact their faith. Further, Mormons are constantly trained to answer all objections by reference to the inner testimony of the Holy Spirit that Joseph Smith is a prophet of God and that Mormonism is true.

This feeling-oriented defense of belief is rooted in a classic reference in *The Book of Mormon*. In Moroni 10:4–5, we read:

And when ye shall receive these things, I would exhort you that ye would ask God, the Eternal Father, in the name of Christ, if these things are not true; and if ye shall ask with a sincere heart, with real intent, having faith in Christ, he will manifest the truth of it unto you, by the power of the Holy Ghost. And by the power of the Holy Ghost ye may know the truth of all things.

This subjective defense lacks credibility, given the strength of the objective evidence about the intellectual, moral, and spiritual failures of Mormon leader Joseph Smith. Mormons urge others to ask God to show them by inner light that Smith is a prophet of God. This approach is impossible to take when one faces the evidence that proves Joseph Smith is no reliable guide to truth.

While Mormonism is not totally wrong, the central views that are unique to Mormonism are false. Joseph Smith did not restore the gospel of Jesus. Rather, he distorted the Bible's plain teaching, denied clear Christian doctrines, and added untrue and harmful beliefs, thereby discrediting himself and all those who follow his message. Mormons should reexamine their faith and have the courage to return to the Christian faith adequately described in the New Testament.

Time Line of Mormonism

1805	Birth of Joseph Smith on December 23 in Sharon, Vermont
1812	Solomon Spalding writes a manuscript about discovery of the record of earlier civilization in a hill
1816	The Smith family moves to Palmyra, New York
1820	The Smith family engages in "money digging"—use of magic objects to find buried treasure
1820	Smith receives the First Vision from God the Father and Jesus
1823	Ethan Smith publishes *Views of the Hebrews* in New York (second edition in 1825)
1823	On September 21 and 22, the angel Moroni tells Smith of gold plates containing *The Book of Mormon*
1824	Major revival in upper New York State
1826	Smith tried and maybe arrested for "glass looking" on March 20
1827	Smith marries Emma Hale (age twenty-two) on January 27
1827	Smith gets gold plates from the angel Moroni at the hill Cumorah
1828	In February, Martin Harris takes a copy of characters from gold plates to Professor Charles Anthon at Columbia University
1828	Harris loses 116 pages of transcripts of the gold plates in June

1829	John the Baptist confers Aaronic priesthood on Joseph Smith and Oliver Cowdery in Harmony, Pennsylvania, on May 15
1829	Peter, James, and John confer Melchizedek priesthood on Smith and Cowdery
1829	Translation of *The Book of Mormon* completed
1830	*The Book of Mormon* printed on March 26
1830	The church organized on April 6
1831	Smith and wife move to Kirtland, Ohio, in January and February
1831	Some Mormons move to Independence, Missouri
1831	Smith receives revelation on July 20 that the Zion site is to be in Independence, Missouri
1832	Brigham Young joins the church on April 14
1832	Smith arrives in Missouri on April 24
1833	Smith completes translation of the New Testament on February 2
1833	Word of wisdom revelation given to Smith on February 27
1833	Mormons subject to mob attacks in Missouri
1833	*Book of Commandments* published
1834	Eber D Howe's *Mormonism Unveiled* published
1835	*Doctrine and Covenants* accepted as scripture
1835	Smith acquires Egyptian texts and translates them
1836	Jesus appears to Smith and Cowdery in Kirtland Temple, along with Moses, Elias, and Elijah, on April 3
1836	Smith reportedly has affair with Fanny Alger
1837	Smith and Rigdon start Kirtland Safety Society Anti-Banking Company
1838	Smith starts writing *History of the Church*
1838	Military group known as Danites formed in June
1838	Mormons attacked by mobs in Missouri
1839	Smith and others travel to Washington, DC
1840	Smith announces baptism for the dead publicly
1841	Smith marries Louisa Beaman, aged twenty-six
1842	Smith starts teaching on the plurality of gods
1842	Smith joins a Masonic lodge and in May introduces temple ceremonies similar to Masonic ones
1843	Smith starts to translate Kinderhook plates
1843	Smith dictated revelation on plural marriage on July 12
1844	Smith announces candidacy for president
1844	*Nauvoo Expositor* charges Smith with polygamy
1844	Smith killed on June 27 in gun battle while a prisoner in Carthage

1844	Sidney Rigdon excommunicated on September 8
1846	On February 4 Mormons begin trek to Utah
1847	Brigham Young and the first group of pioneers enter Salt Lake Valley
1848	Crops saved by flock of seagulls eating crickets
1850	*Deseret News* begins publication in Salt Lake City
1852	First public announcement of doctrine of polygamy
1856	Brigham Young gives blood atonement speech
1857	Mountain Meadows Massacre (120 Arkansas travelers killed in Utah)
1877	John D. Lee executed for leadership in massacre
1880	John Taylor becomes president of the church
1880	*The Pearl of Great Price* accepted as scripture
1889	Wilford Woodruff becomes president
1890	Manifesto about suspension of polygamy
1893	Salt Lake City Temple dedicated
1898	Lorenzo Snow becomes president
1901	Joseph F. Smith becomes president
1918	President Smith receives vision of redemption of the dead
1918	Heber J. Grant becomes president
1945	George Albert Smith becomes president
1951	David O. McKay becomes president
1961	Metropolitan Museum in New York presents LDS church with papyri fragments once owned by Smith
1964	Jerald and Sandra Tanner publish *Mormonism: Shadow and Reality*
1970	Joseph Fielding Smith becomes president
1972	Harold B. Lee becomes president
1973	Spencer W. Kimball becomes president
1976	Two revelations added to Mormon canon (become D&C 137–8 in 1981)
1978	Revelation accepted on September 30 that lifts ban on priesthood to blacks
1981	New editions of Mormon scriptures published
1985	Mark Hofmann sells forged documents to church leaders and plants bombs in two locations in Salt Lake to kill suspected critics
1985	Ezra Taft Benson becomes president
1994	Howard Hunter becomes president
1995	Gordon B. Hinckley becomes president
1995	"The Family: A Proclamation to the World" published
1997	Membership reaches 10 million in November
2002	Winter Olympics in Salt Lake City
2003	Elizabeth Smart rescued from polygamist Brian David Mitchell

2004	DNA evidence contradicts Mormon claim of link between Native Americans and Jews
2004	Ravi Zacharias preaches in Mormon Tabernacle
2004	Grant Palmer, LDS scholar, excommunicated
2005	LDS church celebrates bicentennial of birth of Joseph Smith

Mormonism

TYPOLOGY	Christian Protestant restorationist sectarian
FOUNDER	Joseph Smith (1805–44)
HOME PAGE	www.lds.org
CRITIC SITES	Utah Lighthouse Ministry, www.utlm.org
	Mormonism Research Ministry (Bill McKeever) www.mrm.org
	Mormon Central (Michael Marquardt) www.xmission.com/~research/central
	Recovery from Mormonism, www.exmormon.org
	Watchman Fellowship, www.watchman.org
	Institute for Religious Research, www.irr.org
	Al Case, www.lds-mormon.com
READING	Richard Abanes, *One Nation under Gods* (New York: Four Walls Eight Windows, 2002)
	Will Bagley, *Blood of the Prophets: Brigham Young and the Massacre at Mountain Meadows* (Norman, OK: University of Oklahoma Press, 2002)
	Francis J. Beckwith, Carl Mosser, and Paul Owen, eds., *The New Mormon Challenge* (Grand Rapids, MI: Zondervan, 2002)
	Fawn M. Brodie, *No Man Knows My History* (New York: Knopf, 1977)
	Michael Marquardt and Wesley Walters, *Inventing Mormonism* (Salt Lake City: Signature, 1994)
	Bill McKeever and Eric Johnson, *Mormonism 101* (Grand Rapids, MI: Baker, 2000)
	Richard and Joan Ostling, *Mormon America* (San Francisco: HarperSanFrancisco, 1999)
	Grant Palmer, *An Insider's View of Mormon Origins* (Salt Lake City: Signature, 2002)
	Simon Southerton, *Losing a Lost Tribe* (Salt Lake City: Signature, 2004)
	Jerald and Sandra Tanner, *The Changing World of Mormonism* (Chicago: Moody, 1980)
	Dan Vogel, *Joseph Smith: The Making of a Prophet* (Salt Lake City: Signature, 2004)

▶ MSIA: Movement of Spiritual Inner Awareness

John-Roger, a former Mormon, founded the Church of the Movement of Spiritual Inner Awareness (MSIA) in 1968, legally in 1971. He was born Roger Hinkins on September 24, 1934, in Utah. He claims to have been visited by two trance-channelers when he had a near-death experience in 1963. Newly aware of his "spiritual personality" named John, he created the name John-Roger "in recognition of his transformed self." John-Roger (often referred to as J-R) devoted himself to writing and teaching full-time, first devising a series of six seminars and eventually developing the *Soul Awareness Discourses*, a series of 144 monthly lessons designed to be completed in a twelve-year study. John-Roger has written about fifty books, including *Spiritual Warrior* and *When Are You Coming Home?*

MSIA teaches that John-Roger was the "Mystical Traveler" from 1963 through 1988. The Mystical Traveler holds, or "anchors," the Traveler Consciousness on the planet at a particular time. In 1988 the mantle passed to John Morton, who is the spiritual director of MSIA. Morton has studied with John-Roger since 1975. They describe the Mystical Traveler Consciousness as a "way shower into the higher, spiritual levels." MSIA teaches that Jesus was human and a Mystical Traveler, according Him an elevated status they describe as "similar to being President of Earth." According to the group, "the Christ Consciousness is the spiritual line of energy undergirding MSIA."

Controversy has surrounded MSIA. At one time it was accused of basically being a duplication of ECKANKAR. MSIA leaders dismissed parallels with that movement as arising from shared truth rather than as being intentional and unacknowledged borrowing. MSIA was the focus of intense media scrutiny in 1994 when Michael Huffington was running for the U.S. Senate. *Time* magazine referenced the involvement of his wife, well-known journalist Arianna Huffington, with MSIA and noted that the American Family Foundation, a cult-watching group, had labeled the group as "destructive." John-Roger coauthored the *New York Times* best seller *Life 101*, published in 1991, with his follower Peter McWilliams. After McWilliams left the group, he wrote a bitter memoir called *Life 102: What to Do When Your Guru Sues You* (Los Angeles: Prelude Press, 1994). McWilliams died of cancer in 2000 but reached reconciliation with the movement before his death.

MSIA describes its purpose as "to teach Soul Transcendence, which is becoming aware of yourself as a Soul and as one with God, not as a theory but as a living reality. Your Soul is the highest aspect of yourself, where you and God are one. MSIA provides a variety of tools and techniques that allow you to experience your Soul and, therefore, your own Divinity." MSIA incorporates elements of Sant Mat, Christianity, Buddhism, and Taoism.

Followers are encouraged to release themselves from earthly attachments. The soul has been trapped in "the material world" that is suffering, and everyone is doomed "to continue a cycle of death, rebirth and reincarnation." They refer to their practices as "spiritual exercises." These involve meditation, controlled breathing, and sacred chants for gaining greater health, achieving mental clarity, and increasing energy.

MSIA: Movement of Spiritual Inner Awareness

TYPOLOGY	Western esoteric
FOUNDER	John-Roger (born Roger Hinkins)
CURRENT LEADER	John Morton
HOME PAGES	www.msia.org
	www.john-roger.org
	www.ndh.org
READING	James Lewis, *Seeking the Light* (Los Angeles: Mandeville Press, 1998)

▶ Nation of Islam

The rise of the Black Muslim movement is one of the most fascinating aspects of Islam in the United States. Its roots lie in a resurgence of black nationalism at the turn of the twentieth century, represented most significantly in the work of Marcus Garvey (1887–1940), a central figure in the Rastafarian movement, and Noble Drew Ali (1886–1929), founder of the Moorish Science Temple, another black nationalist group.

Black Nationalism took its formative shape through the influence of Fard Muhammad, who started preaching the Black Muslim message in Detroit in July 1930 and founded the Nation of Islam (NOI). Although he disappeared after four years, he influenced a man named Elijah Muhammad, who heard Fard speak in 1930. Elijah Muhammad, born in 1897, accepted Fard's message about the supremacy of the black race and the devilish nature of the white race.

Elijah Muhammad moved to Chicago in 1932 and led the NOI movement until his death in 1975. He was a controversial leader, not only because of his racist views, but also due to his extramarital affairs, which shocked his NOI followers, including Malcolm X. Malcolm X, born as Malcolm Little in 1925, converted to Islam in 1948, joined the NOI in 1953, and became a leader in the movement.

In April 1963 Malcolm X confronted Elijah about his adultery, and the leader tried to rationalize his behavior. That led to some estrangement between the two, heightened by comments made by Malcolm X about President Kennedy's assassination in November. Malcolm X left the Nation of Islam in early 1964 and was killed by three of its radical members on February 21, 1965.

The role of Malcolm X was then picked up by Louis Farrakhan (b. May 11, 1933), who became Elijah's national minister in 1965 and minister of the movement's mosque in Harlem. After Elijah's death ten years later, Farrakhan had increasing disagreements with Wallace Deen Muhammad, Elijah's son and successor. From 1975 through 1985, Wallace steered the Nation of Islam on a more moderate course, shut his NOI down in 1985, and emerged as a major Sunni leader in the United States.

These changes did not sit well with Farrakhan, who declared in November of 1977 that he was recreating the Nation of Islam on the more radical teachings of Elijah Muhammad. In the last quarter of a century, Farrakhan has become one of the most powerful and controversial black leaders in America. On October 6, 1995, he led the Million Man March for blacks in Washington. His power in the black community remains regardless of Farrakhan's wild accusations about whites (particularly Jews) and the exotic theories in NOI ideology, including extravagant claims about visits to a man-made planet.[12]

It has been argued in the last decade that Farrakhan has grown more moderate in his ideology. This is disputed by the Anti-Defamation League (ADL), which provides quotations from his speeches to illustrate continuing anti-Semitism. The ADL gives this statement from Farrakhan on the Holocaust: "German Jews financed Hitler right here in America. International bankers financed Hitler and poor Jews died while big Jews were at the root of what you call the Holocaust. Little Jews died while big Jews made money." In spite of such language, the Nation of Islam denies that its leader is racist or anti-Semitic.

Nation of Islam	
TYPOLOGY	Islam sectarian
HOME PAGES	www.noi.org
	www.finalcall.com
CRITIC PAGE	Anti-Defamation League (ADL)
	www.adl.org
READING	Mattias Gardell, *In the Name of Elijah Muhammad* (Durham, NC: Duke University Press, 1996)
	Garry Wills, "A Tale of Three Leaders," *New York Review of Books* (September 19, 1996)

▸ New Age

The term *New Age* is the popular designation for what scholars now refer to as Western esotericism. There is no one New Age movement in any strict sense, since New Age religion represents a diverse collection of groups and individuals, with various and competing emphases in beliefs and practices. Consciousness of a New Age spirituality emerged in the early 1970s and peaked with the televising of Shirley MacLaine's *Out on a Limb* in 1987. While elements in the Western esoteric tradition date back to the time of Plato, it is only in the last three decades that there has been widespread belief that humanity has reached a true Age of Aquarius.

Twelve common themes emerge in the study of the hundreds of New Age groups and the major leaders of Western esotericism.

1. *There are many paths to God and the divine realm.* New Age writers regularly affirm the unity of religions and a common mystical experience behind all religious paths. It is often argued that there is one God and that God can be experienced through many paths and understood in a vast number of ways.

2. *Human beings are divine.* It is no secret that New Age writers have little patience for the Christian doctrine of original sin. Rather, New Agers emphasize the "God within," our "God consciousness," or the inherent divinity of all humanity. The New Age teaching that humans are divine is in keeping with its roots in Eastern religion and philosophy.

3. *Human beings have the potential to achieve higher consciousness and divine perfection.* This theme, which flows out of the affirmation of human divinity, is at the heart of New Age ideology of all types. This theme expresses itself in utopian language about human possibility and in teaching about the soon dawning of complete transformation in society.

4. *Reincarnation and karma provide the best explanation about the past*

and future of human beings. This popular New Age idea shows the pervasive influence of Eastern religion, particularly Hindu teaching. New Age teachers place emphasis on the positive aspects of reincarnation rather than giving reports about the negative aspects of karma.

5. *Psychic claims are often true, and the occult world provides important paths and tools to achieve higher consciousness.* New Age religion is largely sympathetic to paranormal and psychic views. This explains why New Age groups and teachers show up at psychic fairs. (New Age followers do not interpret the occult to mean approval of anything satanic or demonic.)

6. *Science, in its truest vision and best exponents, conforms to New Age teaching.* The New Age interest in science is best expressed in the writings of Fritjof Capra, author of *The Tao of Physics,* and Robert Pirsig, who wrote *Zen and the Art of Motorcycle Maintenance.*

7. *Alternate and holistic medicine is a helpful corrective to the West's obsession with traditional Western medicine.* New Agers claims that modern medicine is rooted in a truncated view of science and medicine, failing to capture the holistic nature of humans (as body *and* spirit) and thereby reducing medicine to mere technology.

8. *The task of the New Age is to bring peace to planet earth and achieve harmony among all people and tribes and nations.* Though the New Age tends to be individualistic, the major New Age voices have argued for a radical investment in working for peace. The "Aquarian Conspiracy" that Marilyn Ferguson describes is not a secret conspiracy of evil New Age manipulators taking control of the world. It is, rather, an open conspiracy of people working together to transform the political, educational, and social order to improve planet earth.

9. *Morality is relative, and religious absolutes are often harmful.* The New Age takes particular offense at moral and religious absolutism. The power of moral relativism is illustrated by Shirley MacLaine's defense of her affair with a married British politician by saying that they used to be lovers in a previous life.

10. *This is a new age for humanity, and incredible transformation immediately awaits our world.* New Agers are usually highly optimistic

about the present and future possibilities of the planet, in large part because so many New Age leaders and groups believe that the spirit world has pointed in various ways to our time as the moment for radical planetary change for the good.

11. *An energy pervades the universe that is beyond the physical and that unites all things and provides the source for inner healing, human potential, and planetary change.* Various New Age health practices and most New Age philosophies affirm the reality of a cosmic energy that can be tapped into to achieve divine potential.

12. *Eternal spirit masters and teachers have been presenting the New Age message to humanity for thousands of years.* This theme illustrates the point that the New Age message is actually not new, according to New Age thinkers. The masters and teachers have given their revelations to previous ages, through various spirit guides and teachers, including Jesus of Nazareth.

While New Agers always speak highly of Jesus, the New Age view of Jesus leaves a lot to be desired. In Western esotericism Jesus is viewed as distinct from the Christ. He is said to be a vessel for the Christ and is not the only Christ figure. The Christ now works apart from Jesus of Nazareth. In the New Age world, there is virtually no focus on the death of Christ as atonement for sin. Likewise, the Second Coming of Christ is not about Jesus. In New Age circles Jesus is never considered to be the only Son of God or to be the one way to eternal life.

New Agers are drawn to the fanciful and unhistorical pictures of Jesus found in New Age works such as *The Unknown Life of Jesus, The Aquarian Gospel of Jesus the Christ, A Course in Miracles*, and *The Urantia Book.* Jesus is viewed on a level with other spiritual masters, and his name is often invoked in drawing attention to particular New Age groups and leaders. In the final analysis, the New Age understanding of Jesus has little concern about the core Christian affirmations about Jesus that have been believed for centuries by all Christian traditions. New Age leaders pay little more than lip service to the central elements of the New Testament about Jesus.

While there are positive elements to New Age spirituality, particularly in its social concerns, it is ultimately a non-Christian vision.

Given this, Christians should help those attracted to Western esoteric themes to see the historical Jesus as the face of God and "the Truth" for all time. Effective Christian witness to New Agers demands abandonment of paranoid and nasty interpretations of Western esotericism, involving allegations of satanic conspiracies and one-world apocalyptic images. New Age spirituality offers a soft version of religion. This makes it imperative that Christian response to the New Age movement be offered in the same love and grace that dominated the life and teaching of Jesus, the one and only Christ sent from God.

New Age

TYPOLOGY	Western esotericism
SCHOLARLY SITES	Esoterica (Online Journal)
	www.esoteric.msu.edu
	Association for the Study of Esotericism
	www.aseweb.org
	Alternative Spiritualities and New Age Studies
	www.asanas.org.uk
	The Alchemy Web Site (Adam McLean)
	www.levity.com/alchemy
READING	Russell Chandler, *Understanding the New Age* (Dallas: Word, 1988)
	Antoine Faivre, *Access to Western Esotericism* (Albany: State University of New York Press, 1994)
	Wouter J. Hanegraaff, ed., *Dictionary of Gnosis and Western Esotericism* (Leiden: Brill, 2005)
	Wouter J. Hanegraaff, *New Age Religion and Western Culture* (Albany: State University of New York Press, 1998)
	Douglas Groothuis, *Unmasking the New Age* (Downers Grove: InterVarsity, 1986)
	James Lewis and J. Gordon Melton, eds., *Perspectives on the New Age* (Albany: State University of New York Press, 1992)
	J. Gordon Melton, *New Age Encyclopedia* (Detroit: Gale, 1990)
	Elliot Miller, *A Crash Course on the New Age* (Grand Rapids, MI: Baker, 1989)
	John A. Saliba, *Christian Responses to the New Age Movement* (London: Cassell, 1999)

▶ New Apostolic Reformation

Cindy Jacobs, a prominent prophet in the charismatic world, declared several years ago that God would use C. Peter Wagner to "change the face of Christianity" and that "it will be like unto what Martin Luther did." Wagner is now based in Colorado Springs and is president of Global Harvest Ministries and chancellor of the Wagner Leadership Institute. More significantly, he claims to be the apostle of the New Apostolic Reformation (NAR). NAR leaders argue that its churches are "the fastest growing in all areas of the world."

Wagner also leads the International Coalition of Apostles (ICA) and the New Apostolic Roundtable. He is in partnership with many prominent pastors, including Ted Haggard, president of the U.S. National Association of Evangelicals. Pastors Mel Mullen (Red Deer, Alberta), Naomi Dowdy (Singapore), and Harold Caballeros (Guatemala) are also Wagner's partners. Beyond Jacob's endorsement, Wagner's apostolic authority is blessed by prophets Paul Cain, Rick Joyner, and Bill Hamon.

For more than two decades, C. Peter Wagner has been at the center of controversy in Christian circles. In 1982 he and John Wimber, the leader of the Vineyard movement, began teaching a course called "Signs, Wonders, and Church Growth" at Fuller Seminary in Pasadena, California. The hands-on course created a furor of protest because of its charismatic orientation. Wagner was later connected to the controversial Kansas City Prophets led by Mike Bickle.

The New Apostolic Reformation has already gained fierce critics. Wagner and his fellow apostles are on the list of some cult-watch groups. One site even suggests that NAR leaders engage in mind control and are motivated by financial greed. Others contend that Wagner is setting the scene for the Antichrist and that he is a dupe of the Latter Rain, a Pentecostal movement that originated in North Battleford, Saskatchewan, in 1948. Milder critics express caution about his spiritual mapping theories and accuse him of naïveté about healings and prophecy.[13]

The nastiest interpretations of Wagner merit attention only because of their popularity. Painting him as a pawn in the hands of Satan and the end times is profoundly misleading. Wagner and his colleagues are deeply committed to intercessory prayer. He and his wife, Doris, served for fifteen years as missionaries in Bolivia. On the money angle, it is important to note that both Global Harvest Ministries and the Wagner Leadership Institute belong to the Evangelical Council for Financial Accountability.

There is virtually nothing unique to Wagner's proposals, except his claim that he is the lead apostle in a new apostolic movement. The major characteristics of Wagner's movement represent a variation on old-fashioned Pentecostalism or new-fashioned charismatic Christianity. For the sake of argument, assume that God wants to restore apostles. Do Wagner and his roundtable members deserve the title? Sure, but only if *apostle* is used of those in positions of crucial leadership across the church. This honors the breadth of the universal church and deflates the self-referential elitism in Wagner's group.

New Apostolic Reformation

TYPOLOGY	Christian Protestant charismatic
LEADER	C. Peter Wagner
HOME PAGE	Global Harvest
	www.globalharvest.org
READING	C. Peter Wagner, *The New Apostolic Churches* (Ventura, CA: Regal, 1998)

▸ New Thought

The term *New Thought* refers to the metaphysical tradition associated with Phineas Parkhurst Quimby (1802–66) and his ideological heirs. Quimby, one of the original figures in the theory of mind over matter, was influenced by Mesmerism and hypnotism. He opened an office in Portland, Maine, in 1859. Though he started no church, he had an impact, either directly or indirectly, on numerous religious leaders, including the following: Warren Felt Evans (1817–89); Julius Dresser (1838–93); Horatio Dresser (1866–1954); Mary Baker Eddy (1821–1910), the founder of Christian Science; Emma Curtis Hopkins (1853–1925); Charles and Myrtle Fillmore; and Ernest Holmes (1877–1960), the founder of Religious Science.

There has been considerable debate over Mary Baker Eddy's debt to Quimby in her works, including *Science and Health with Keys to the Scriptures*, published in 1875. In the 1890s Julius Dresser and his wife accused Eddy of stealing Quimby's basic ideas. It is fair to say both that Mrs. Eddy downplayed her debt to Quimby and that she departed from his theology and healing in significant ways.

Emma Curtis Hopkins is often called the founder of New Thought. She was born in Connecticut in 1849 (and not in 1853, as often stated). She was one of the early students of Mary Baker Eddy and became editor of the *Christian Science Journal* in 1884. After a falling-out with Mrs. Eddy, Hopkins moved to Chicago and started her own work, though she spent her last years in New York City. She is often praised for the prominent role women played in her ministry and teaching.

The best-known contemporary groups associated with New Thought are the International Divine Science Association, the Unity School of Christianity, Religious Science International, the United Church of Religious Science, and Seicho-No-Ie, a Japanese movement started in 1930 by Masaharu Taniguchi. Of these groups, the Unity School is the largest in America. It was founded by Charles and Myrtle Fillmore.

Charles Fillmore was born in Minnesota on August 22, 1854. In 1876 he moved to Texas and met his future wife, Mary Myrtle Page, a teacher, who was born in 1845 in Ohio. Charles and Myrtle were married in 1881 and moved to Kansas City, Missouri, in 1884. In 1886 Myrtle was impacted by the teaching of E. B. Weeks, a follower of Emma Curtis Hopkins. Myrtle came away from the meetings with Weeks with an affirmation: "I am a child of God and therefore I do not inherit sickness." Over the next two years, Myrtle achieved a new level of healing from a constant threat of tuberculosis.

Charles became even more convinced of the New Thought healing paradigm after he heard Hopkins in Chicago. He and Myrtle started the magazine *Modern Thought* (later renamed *Unity Magazine*) in 1889, and they incorporated the Unity School of Practical Christianity in 1903. Charles wrote *Christian Healing* in 1909 and started radio broadcasts in 1922. Myrtle, called the "mother of Unity," died in 1931. Two years later Charles married Cora Dedrick and also wrote *The Metaphysical Bible Dictionary*. Charles retired that same year but continued to travel and teach until shortly before his death in 1948.

New Thought	
TYPOLOGY	Western esoteric
FOUNDER	Emma Curtis Hopkins
WEB SITES	New Thought Alliance
	http://newthoughtalliance.org
	New Thought Movement Homepage
	http://websyte.com/alan/#7
	Unity School of Christianity (Charles and Myrtle Fillmore)
	www.unityworldhq.org
	United Church of Religious Science (Ernest Holmes)
	www.religiousscience.org
	Seicho-No-Ie (Masaharu Taniguchi)
	www.snitruth.org
	Quimby Web site
	www.ppquimby.com
READING	Gail Harley, *Emma Curtis Hopkins* (Syracuse: Syracuse University Press, 2002)
	Neal Vahle, *The Unity Movement* (Philadelphia: Temple Foundation Press, 2002)

▸ Nichiren Shoshu and Soka Gakkai

Nichiren Shoshu derives from the life and teachings of Nichiren Daishonin and Nikko Shonin. Nichiren Shoshu was born on February 16, 1222, in Japan. His followers believe he achieved enlightenment in 1253 at the age of thirty-two. He accused the dominant Japanese Buddhist groups of being corrupt and asserted that his movement would be the one source of safety for the nation. Nichiren Daishonin died on October 13, 1882. Nichiren Shoshu followers believe that he appointed Nikko Shonin as his successor instead of five other prominent disciples. In 1290 Nikko Shonin founded the Head Temple (Taisekiji) at the base of Mount Fuji.

The movement focuses on the Lotus Sutra, one of the most sacred texts in Buddhism. Followers believe that three elements form the core of authentic spiritual practice. The first involves the worship of the *Gohonzon*, the ritual drawing of the name of the Lotus Sutra and various Buddhist deities. The second relates to the *Daimoku*, the title of the Lotus Sutra. Devotees chant the phrase *Nam Myoho Renge Kyo* (Salutation to the Lotus Sutra). The third element centers on ordination, or *kaidan*.

Before and during the Second World War, the Japanese government persecuted the Nichiren Shoshu movement for its lack of support for the militarization of the society. After the Allied victory, Nichiren Shoshu became influential through Soka Gakkai, its lay organization. However, in 1991, Nikken Abe, the sixty-seventh head priest of Nichiren Shohu, excommunicated Soka Gakkai. This led to an international battle between Nichiren Shoshu and Soka Gakkai, involving allegations of crimes against leaders of both movements. Even the Great Reception Hall and the Great Main Temple were destroyed under the orders of the head priest. These had been built through the leadership of Soka Gakkai and so were not allowed to stand.

Soka Gakkai was originally known as Soka Kyoiku Gakkai, founded in 1930 by Tsunesaburo Makiguchi (1871–1944) and his protégé, Josei Toda (1900–58). Makiguchi and Toda were imprisoned by Japanese authorities during World War II. Makiguchi died in prison. Toda led the movement after his release from prison until his death in 1958. Daisaku Ikeda (b. 1928) became president of Soka Gakkai in 1960 and then head of Soka Gakkai International (SGI) in 1975.

In 1987 Ikeda founded Soka University of America. Ikeda continued to lead Soka Gakkai after its excommunication from the larger Nichiren Shoshu tradition in 1991. SGI has done reasonably well in both Europe (with about thirty-nine thousand members) and the United States (with a similar number of active members). Social scientific studies of Soka Gakkai converts show that they are drawn to the movement through both the alleged power of the *Gohonzon* and the practical nature of Buddhism for everyday life.

Nichiren Shoshu and Soka Gakkai	
TYPOLOGY	Buddhism
WEB SITES	www.nichirenshoshu.or.jp
	www.nst.org
	www.cebunet.com/nst (Craig Bratcher)
	Soka Gakkai Web sites
	www.sokagakkai.info
	www.sgi.org
	www.sgi-usa.org
READING	Richard Causton, *Nichiren Shoshu Buddhism* (London: London River, 1988)
	Karel Dobbelaere, *Soka Gakkai* (Salt Lake City: Signature, 2001)
	David Machacek and Bryan Wilson, *Global Citizens: The Soka Gakkai Movement in the World* (New York: Oxford University Press, 2000)
	David A. Snow, *Shakubuku: A Study of the Nichiren Shoshu Buddhist Movement in America* (New York: Garland, 1993)

▶ Nuwaubian Nation

This esoteric group, based most recently in Eatonton, Georgia, is the creation of Dwight York, who goes by several other names, including Malachi Z. York. The movement has been subject to intense scrutiny since the arrest of York in 2002 on child-sex charges. He pleaded guilty to more than seventy sex charges on January 24, 2003. However, he petitioned the court on June 30, 2003, for abandonment of this plea. In late 2004 the courts refused a new trial, and York has been sentenced to 135 years in prison.

Two hundred FBI agents and eighty sheriff's deputies raided Nuwaubian headquarters on May 8, 2002, and took York and his "main wife," Kathy Johnson, into custody. Their arrests were the culmination of a four-year investigation into allegations of sexual abuse against children. Johnson pleaded guilty in April 2003 to knowing a felony was taking place and doing nothing.

York started a mission known as Ansaar Pure Sufi in 1967 in Brooklyn, New York, and he referred to himself as Imaam Isa. The group later identified themselves as Nubians and then took the title of Nubian Islaamic Hebrews. Orthodox Muslims viewed the group and its leader as heretical, but York accused them of mistranslating the Qur'an.

In 1993 the group purchased more than four hundred acres near Eatonton, Georgia. York referred to the state as the "Mecca of Nubians," and they developed an Egyptian theme on the property, including the building of small pyramids. Ex-members state that York lived in splendor while they endured cramped and squalid housing.[14]

While in Georgia, York continued to claim that they were a Sufi group but also said that they were the Ancient Mystic Order of Melchizedek. York is also known as Nayya Malachizodok El and Chief Black Eagle. He speaks confidently of the power of his writings to his followers: "You can't be fooled by any religious doctrines of any kind. No, not now a days! You have your first tool, this Holy Tablet, not someone else's interpretation. Your own scripture that will dispel all the lies causing all falsehood to perish. Making the truth come to light."

Nuwaubians believe that they are descended from Egyptians who walked to America before the continental separation and that they are the true Native Americans. The group teaches that blacks are the superior race. York's followers also claim that he is from another planet and that he is the incarnation of God.

One unofficial Nuwaubian Web site gives elaborate details about extraterrestrials that now live on planet earth. One species is said to be the Deros, a group of obese cave dwellers with low intelligence, led by Yabahaan. The Deros have elephantlike noses and are hatched from eggs that are from four to six feet in diameter. The site claims that some obese humans are descended from the Deros.

Before York's arrest in 2002, Nuwaubians came into frequent conflict with local officials for building permit and zoning violations. The sect accused county officials of racism, and both Jesse Jackson and Al Sharpton visited the group to support their concerns.

There has been speculation that York's daughter, Hagar York-El, might lead the group.

Nuwaubian Nation	
TYPOLOGY	Western esoteric
FOUNDER	Malachi Z. York
WEB SITES	www.unnm.com
	www.nuwaubiaholylandofthenuwaubians.com
	www.geocities.com/Area51/Corridor/4978
	www.geocities.com/Area51/Corridor/4978/unnm.html
	www.factology.com
	http://users.netropolis.net/moorish

▸ Orthodox Christianity

In 1990 Franky Schaeffer left the evangelical fold and joined the Greek Orthodox Church. Franky, son of well-known writer Francis Schaeffer, has not kept his conversion a secret. In a string of articles, books, and videos, he has become an apostle for Eastern Orthodoxy. In one book he accuses evangelicals of "dancing alone"—alone with the Bible, alone in personal conversion, with no regard for tradition, proper liturgy, and legitimate ecclesiastical authority.

Schaeffer may be the loudest convert, but he is not alone. Frederica Mathewes-Green, a regular contributor to *Christianity Today* magazine, penned *Facing East,* in which she reports on her "pilgrim's journey into the mysteries of Orthodoxy." In *Becoming Orthodox* Peter Gillquist, a former Campus Crusade for Christ leader, tells the story of two thousand American evangelicals who have joined this ancient church.

There are about 300 million Orthodox believers worldwide. The Orthodox believe that they are the "one, holy, catholic, and apostolic church" spoken of in the Apostles' Creed. About fifteen different churches unite under the banner of Orthodoxy, the best known being the Russian and Greek Orthodox churches, though pride of place goes to the churches of Constantinople, Alexandria, Antioch, and Jerusalem because of their ancient roots.

The Orthodox are committed to various early creeds (i.e., those creeds that defind essential Christian truth), to the teachings of the seven ecumenical councils, and to an affirmation of apostolic succession from Saint Peter to (the several Orthodox patriarchs including) His All-Holiness Bartholomew, the head of the Church of Constantinople and Ecumenical Patriarch to all Orthodox Communions. The Orthodox believe that Roman Catholics left the one Church in 1054, with the famous schism over papal supremacy and other doctrines. This split was sealed in blood when Roman Catholic armies on the

Fourth Crusade sacked Constantinople in 1204, leading to a three-day rampage of murder, rape, and theft that defies comprehension.

Certain distinctives in Orthodox liturgy may be jarring to evangelicals. Like Roman Catholics, the Orthodox place a great deal of emphasis upon Mary, pray to the saints, and pray for the dead—practices that seem foreign to the traditions of the New Testament (though Protestant neglect of Mary is also unbiblical). The Orthodox use of icons can be celebrated by anyone who has appreciation for art and beauty in worship. The judgment that iconography is idolatry is far too harsh, given the Christ-centered nature of Orthodox liturgy.

However, evangelicals have every right to object to the historic Orthodox insistence on the use of icons in worship. Daniel Clendenin asks the Orthodox to consider their undue emphasis on the use of icons. "Does it really serve any useful purpose, given this murky theological history of the icon, to continue to insist with the Council of 787 that Christians who reject icons are evil, pernicious, and subversive heretics?"

Of more concern is the Orthodox understanding of salvation, at least at some points. Thankfully, Christ is the only source of salvation in Orthodoxy, even though the Orthodox venerate Mary and the saints. Likewise, evangelicals can applaud Orthodox recognition that redemption is rooted in grace alone. That is, Orthodox doctrine explicitly condemns salvation by works.

However, the Orthodox focus on the deification of humanity (theosis), emphasis upon the sacraments, and reservations about justification by faith alone should give pause. It is not that they have a magical view of baptism, nor do they believe in salvation by works, but their emphases here can dull the sense of need for personal trust in the work of Christ and assurance of salvation in Christ. These concerns led a task force at Biola University to conclude that at crucial points evangelical doctrine and Orthodox theology are incompatible.

While Clendenin has a more positive assessment of evangelical and Orthodox unity, he also objects to the view that the Orthodox Church is the one, holy, catholic, and apostolic Church. "I believe that it is reasonable, even compelling, to affirm that we see the Spirit

working all across the world to inaugurate God's kingdom, far outside the narrow confines of Orthodoxy."

Orthodox Christianity 101

- The Orthodox Church affirms the doctrine of the Trinity.
- The Orthodox Church is the visible expression of the body of Christ.
- Orthodox Christians unite under the patriarch of Constantinople.
- Orthodoxy affirms the seven ecumenical councils.
- Orthodoxy values both Scripture and tradition.
- For the Orthodox, justification involves faith and obedience to God.
- In Orthodoxy, Church life is exercised through seven sacraments.
- Infants are to be baptized into the Church.
- Baptism and the Eucharist provide spiritual life to believers.
- The Bible is to be understood through Orthodox tradition.
- The Orthodox Church honors and venerates the saints, including Mary.
- Saint Peter was the first among equals in Church leadership.
- Praying for the dead is part of Christian life.
- Mary was a perpetual virgin.
- Mary was kept free from sin.
- Mary was assumed into heaven.
- Icons are to be venerated as part of divine liturgy.
- The Holy Spirit proceeds from the Father alone.
- Christians outside Orthodoxy should return to the mother Church.
- The goal of the Christian life is deification, or becoming one with God.

Orthodox Christianity

TYPOLOGY	Christian
LEADER	Ecumenical Patriarch of Constantinople
ORTHODOX SITES	Ecumenical Patriarchate
	www.patriarchate.org
	Patriarchate of Alexandria
	www.greekorthodox-alexandria.org
	Patriarchate of Antioch
	www.antiochpat.org
	Patriarchate of Jerusalem
	www.jerusalem-patriarchate.org
	Patriarchate of Moscow
	www.mospat.ru
	Patriarchate of Serbia
	spc.org.yu
	Patriarchate of Romania

www.patriarhia.ro
Patriarchate of Bulgaria
bulch.tripod.com/boc/
Patriarchate of Georgia
www.patriarchate.ge/
Church of Greece
www.ecclesia.gr
Church of Albania
www.orthodoxalbania.org
Church of Poland
www.orthodox.pl
Church of Czech - Slovakia
www.pravoslav.gts.cz
Church of Finland
www.ort.fi
Church of Estonia, www.orthodoxa.org
Orthodox Church of America, www.oca.org
Orthodox Church of Canada
www.orthodoxchurchofcanada.org

OTHER SITES   Orthodox World Links, www.theologic.com/links
Orthodox Faith, www.orthodoxfaith.com
Orthodox Net, www.orthodoxnet.com
Orthodoxy in America
http://orthodoxyinamerica.org
Pokrov: Dealing with Victims of Abuse
www.pokrov.org

READING   Victoria Clark, *Why Angels Fall* (New York: St. Martin's, 2000)
Daniel B. Clendenin, *Eastern Orthodox Christianity* (Grand Rapids, MI: Baker, 2003)
Daniel B. Clendenin, ed., *Eastern Orthodox Theology* (Grand Rapids, MI: Baker, 2003)
Donald Fairbairn, *Eastern Orthodoxy through Western Eyes* (Louisville: Westminster John Knox Press, 2002)
Frederica Mathewes-Green, *At the Corner of East and Now* (New York: Tarcher/Putnam, 2000)
Robert L. Saucy, John Coe, and Alan Gomes, Task Report on "Eastern Orthodox Teachings In Comparison with the Doctrinal Position of Biola University" (May 1998)
James Stamoolis, ed., *Three Views on Eastern Orthodoxy and Evangelicalism* (Grand Rapids, MI: Zondervan, 2004)
Timothy Ware, *The Orthodox Church* (Baltimore: Penguin, 1964).

▸ Osho (Rajneesh)

Osho was one of the most controversial Hindu gurus of the twentieth century, known especially for owning more than ninety Rolls-
Royces when he was living in America in the early 1980s. He was
born Rajneesh Chandra Mohan in central India in 1931 and claimed
enlightenment on March 21, 1953, while he was a philosophy student.
He received an M.A. degree in 1956 and was a professor from 1957
through 1966 at the University of Jabalpur.

In 1966 he began to focus on public communication of his spiritual message. He moved to Mumbai (formerly Bombay) in 1970 and
started to invite people into discipleship under him. During this time,
he was known as Bhagwan Shree Rajneesh and became one of the
most popular gurus for Westerners flocking to India in search of
enlightenment. From 1974 to 1981, Osho led his own ashram in Pune,
India, and then moved to the United States in 1981.

Osho's followers purchased a sixty-four-thousand-acre ranch in
Oregon that became known as Rajneeshpuram. Osho resided there
until 1985, when the commune broke up in disarray after several leaders (including Ma Anand Sheela, Osho's personal secretary) were
found guilty of criminal acts involving food poisoning, arson, and
wiretapping. Ma was sentenced to prison for her involvement.

On October 28, 1985, Osho was arrested at gunpoint in Charlotte,
North Carolina, and spent twelve days in jail. Some of his followers
claim that he was poisoned while in custody in Oklahoma on his
return to Oregon. His critics contend that he was addicted to Valium
and nitrous oxide. Even some of his close followers acknowledge his
frequent use of nitrous oxide (more commonly known as laughing
gas).[15] Osho was deported from the United States in November after
pleading guilty to immigration fraud and paying a fine of $400,000.

His 1986 world tour was marred by frequent denial of entry into
various countries or by expulsion soon after his arrival. He returned

to his ashram in India in January 1987. He adopted the name of Osho in 1989. His longtime girlfriend, Vivek, committed suicide shortly before Osho died in January 1990. Following Hindu custom, his body was cremated.

Osho is still viewed by many devotees as the perfect embodiment of enlightenment. Other disciples, notably Christopher Calder, claim that he was both enlightened and corrupt. Since his death, he has become the guru for a whole new generation of followers. Osho Commune International maintains the spiritual community in Pune, India.

On the tombstone of this religious leader is engraved "Osho Never Born Never Died Only Visited this Planet Earth between December 11, 1931–January 19, 1990."

Osho (Rajneesh)

TYPOLOGY	Hindu
HEADQUARTERS	Pune, India
WEB SITES	www.osho.com
	www.oshoworld.com
	Friends of Osho
	www.sannyas.net
	Sannyasworld
	www.sannyasworld.com
READING	Satya Bharti Franklin, *The Promise of Paradise* (New York: Station Hill Press, 1992)
	Judith M. Fox, *Osho Rajneesh* (Salt Lake City: Signature, 2000)

▶ Pentecostalism

The New Testament emphasis upon the Holy Spirit lies at the heart of the worldwide Pentecostal movement. Pentecostals usually trace their modern roots to the ministry of Charles Parham (1873–1929), founder of Bethel Bible School in Topeka, Kansas. On January 1, 1901, Agnes Ozman, one of his students, spoke in tongues. Parham himself, and about half the student body, also spoke in tongues during the next several days. Parham spread the Pentecostal message through his Apostolic Faith movement.

In 1905 William J. Seymour (1870–1922), a black Holiness preacher, met Parham in Texas and adopted his theology. In 1906 Seymour began work at the Azusa Street Mission in Los Angeles. The church (based at 312 Azusa Street) experienced a three-year revival from 1906 through 1909. This launched Pentecostal doctrine and practice to the entire world. Seymour's congregation rebuffed a takeover by Parham in late 1906. After the revival subsided, Seymour gradually lost influence in wider Pentecostal circles. He died on September 28, 1922.

Pentecostals emphasize the sign-gifts of the Holy Spirit, which include speaking in tongues, the gift of discerning of spirits, prophecy, and divine healing. Speaking in tongues is viewed as the initial sign of the baptism of the Holy Spirit. The early Pentecostals often believed that those who spoke in tongues were actually speaking in foreign languages, just like the early Christians in Acts 2. Pentecostals now hold that most tongues-speaking involves divinely inspired utterances that lie outside ordinary human language.

Pentecostalism is often defined through its famous healers, including Kathryn Kuhlman (1907–76), William Branham (1909–65), A. A. Allen (1911–70), Oral Roberts (1918–), Benny Hinn (1952–), and Rodney Howard-Browne (1961–). Other significant Pentecostal leaders include Thomas Ball Barratt (1862–1940), Aimee Semple McPherson (1890–1944), David du Plessis (1905–87), Demos Shakarian (1913–93), Pat Robertson (1930–), and David Yong-gi Cho (1936–).

The combined charismatic-Pentecostal movements represent the fastest-growing spiritual tradition in many countries. The largest trinitarian Pentecostal groups in the United States are the Assemblies of God and the Church of God (Cleveland). The tradition has been prone to splits. Melton's *Encyclopedia of American Religions* identifies more than four hundred different Pentecostal and charismatic groups. The earliest Pentecostals divided along racial lines during the Azusa Street revival. The most significant doctrinal division in Pentecostal history occurred in 1913 and 1914 over teaching that Jesus is the Father, Son, and Holy Spirit. This is known as Jesus-Only, or Oneness, Pentecostalism. The largest Oneness body is the United Pentecostal Church, formed in 1945.

As David Barrett and Todd Johnson show in their ongoing research on global religious trends, the sweep of Pentecostalism and charismatic Christianity is one of the most astounding developments in the Christian story since 1900. The continuing popularity and growth in this tradition makes it imperative that evangelicals urge Pentecostal leaders to address certain obvious concerns. This includes correction of anti-intellectual tendencies in Pentecostal rhetoric, abandonment of simplistic understandings of the Spirit, and curtailing of exaggerated claims related to healing, visions, and prophecies. There is no contradiction between obedience to the biblical precept "quench not the Spirit" and the command to "test the spirits."

Pentecostalism	
TYPOLOGY	Christian Protestant
SCRIPTURE	Bible
WEB SITES	Assemblies of God, http://ag.org
	Church of God in Christ, Inc. (Memphis, Tennessee)
	www.cogic.org
	Church of God (Cleveland, Tennessee)
	www.chofgod.org
	Rodney Howard-Browne
	www.revival.com
	Brownsville Revival, www.brownsville-revival.org
READING	Stanley M. Burgess, ed., *The New International Dictionary of Pentecostal Charismatic Movements* (Grand Rapids, MI: Zondervan, 2002)

The Peoples Temple will forever be associated with the mass suicide and murders of more than nine hundred of its members on November 18, 1978, in the jungles of Guyana. The killings in Jonestown immediately framed popular discourse about so-called cult groups, and its founder, the Reverend Jim Jones, has become the archetype of a cult leader.

James Warren Jones was born in 1931. His group, known originally as Wings of Deliverance, started in Indianapolis in 1955. In 1959 the group became part of the Disciples of Christ. Jones and a small cadre spent a few years in Brazil in the early 1960s and then moved to northern California in 1965. The group had a significant outreach to the poor in both San Francisco and Los Angeles. Jones was a dynamic preacher, but he was also increasingly paranoid and controlling. His early Christian vision gave way to a Marxist and anarchistic utopianism.

In 1976 the Peoples Temple leased almost four thousand acres from the government of Guyana. Jones and the majority of his followers moved there the next year. By then Jones had attracted a vocal opposition in California, particularly from a group known as the Concerned Relatives. They charged Jones and the top leadership of Peoples Temple with financial mismanagement and fake healings and even with conducting suicide drills. The Concerned Relatives also engaged in a custody battle over John Victor Stoen, a boy in the group.

The warning of a potential massacre, as well as a complaint about suicide drills, was raised by Jonestown escapee Deborah Layton in her affidavit to the United States government in June 1978, six months before the massacre. This and other allegations led Congressman Leo Ryan on a fact-finding mission to Jonestown in November. While Ryan and others were waiting at an airstrip to fly back home, several young men from the compound opened fire on them. Ryan and four others (three members of the media and one defector) were killed.

Others were wounded. Shortly after the assault, Jones led his followers in a mass suicide ritual known as the White Night. A total of 913 persons died at the compound. Larry Layton, Deborah's brother, was imprisoned for his role in the shootings at the airport, though he did not kill anyone.

Several factors make the tragedy of Jonestown more complex than discourse about cultic religion usually involves. First, Jones was an ordained minister in the Disciples of Christ, a mainstream Protestant denomination. Second, he was widely supported in the political and civic worlds of California. He was recognized as a passionate supporter of social justice—a fact often ignored in later discussions about him. Third, the group did experience intense opposition, fueling Jones's paranoia and leading his hardcore followers to adopt his apocalyptic response to criticism.

None of these caveats absolve Jones and his top leaders of their responsibility. Most writers on the Peoples Temple recognize that Jones's pathology was the ultimate explanation for the events of November 18, 1978. The vast majority of new religions survive the death of the founder. This is not so with the religion built by Jim Jones.

Peoples Temple	
TYPOLOGY	Christian utopian sectarian
WEB SITES	Alternative Considerations of Jonestown and Peoples Temple
	(Rebecca Moore and Fielding M. McGehee III)
	http://jonestown.sdsu.edu
	Deborah Layton, www.peoplestemple.com
READING	John Hall, *Gone from the Promised Land* (New Brunswick: Transaction, 2004)
	Deborah Layton, *Seductive Poison* (New York: Doubleday, 1998)
	Rebecca Moore, *A Sympathetic History of Jonestown* (Lewiston, NY: Edwin Mellen, 1985)
	Tim Reiterman and John Jacobs, *Raven* (New York: Dutton, 1982)

▶ Plymouth Brethren

Plymouth Brethren is the designation for those who follow in the heritage of John Nelson Darby (1800–82), a Bible teacher who separated from the Church of Ireland in 1827. While Darby did not start this fellowship of independent Christians, he was their most famous leader. The Plymouth Brethren are known for their detailed study of Scripture. Sadly, their biblical acumen has often been overshadowed by their frequent schisms, particularly among the Exclusive Brethren, who followed Darby's isolationism. The less sectarian heirs of Darby are known as Open Brethren. F. F. Bruce, well-known evangelical scholar, was part of this tradition.

The darkest hours in Exclusive Brethren history came in the later years of the ministry of James Taylor Jr, who became head of the group in 1959. His leadership was marked by legalism and ruthless sectarianism. His career ended in scandal because of alleged sexual misconduct at a meeting in Aberdeen, Scotland, in July 1970. His control over his group was such, however, that he was able to oust or silence most critics and command total trust as the "Elect Vessel" of the Lord for his worldwide following. The "Jims" (the nickname for those who followed the Taylorites) excused his vulgar language in worship, excessive drinking, overt sexual behavior, and ruthless treatment of any who dared question him. The scandal in Aberdeen was reported in newspapers in the United Kingdom and North America.

The Plymouth Brethren movement impacted wider conservative Christian circles in its focus on eschatology. Darby laid the groundwork for the widespread adoption of premillennialism that has become the dominant paradigm in evangelical prophetic writing. He laid great stress on the view that Christ will return before the Tribulation to take believers to heaven. This Rapture theory is part of the prophetic outlook adopted in the popular Left Behind novels, authored by Tim LaHaye and Jerry Jenkins.

Darby also had a high view of the authority of Scripture, including the view that the Bible is without error. Generally, the Plymouth Brethren accept the literal interpretation of Scripture. The inerrancy position and literal interpretation of Scripture became major elements in the fundamentalist movement of the early twentieth century.

One interesting difference between fundamentalists and some Plymouth Brethren groups involves the use of alcohol. Fundamentalists have often advocated total abstinence, while Plymouth Brethren leaders have often supported wine drinking on the basis of Jesus's changing water into wine at the wedding mentioned in John 2.

It is difficult to track contemporary Plymouth Brethren life, since the various groups often maintain a low public profile. The more exclusive groups have no major Web presence and are not interested in academic study of their history and ideology. Ex-members of the Exclusive tradition often describe their past religious life as "cultic" and "destructive."[16]

Plymouth Brethren

TYPOLOGY	Christian Protestant fundamentalist
EARLY LEADER	J. N. Darby
WEB SITES	www.johndarby.org
	www.peebs.net
	www.brethrenonline.org
	www.mybrethren.org

▶ Polygamous Mormonism

The mainline Church of Jesus Christ of Latter-day Saints (LDS) officially abandoned polygamy in 1890, though some leaders secretly continued the practice into the early part of the twentieth century.
Polygamist Mormon groups formed in the 1920s in Utah and Arizona,
tracing their ideology to Joseph Smith and also to an alleged 1886 revelation by Joseph and Jesus Christ to LDS president John Taylor.

The largest contemporary polygamous group is the Fundamentalist Church of Jesus Christ of Latter Day Saints (FLDS). Warren Jeffs
became the leader of the group in 2002 after the death of Rulon T.
Jeffs, his father. The FLDS is based in the twin cities of Colorado City,
Arizona, and Hilldale, Utah, in an area once known as Short Creek. In
1953 the group was raided by law enforcement as part of a crackdown
on polygamy. Today the group has followers in Bountiful, British
Columbia, led by Bishop James Oler. Former Canadian leader Winston
Blackmore was ousted by Warren Jeffs, and this has produced enormous friction among polygamous Mormons in Bountiful. The FLDS
has also opened the YFZ (Yearning for Zion) Ranch in Eldorado, Texas.

Other polygamous groups include the True and Living Church,
based in Manti, Utah, and led by James D. Harmston, and the Latter-
day Church of Christ (the Kingston Clan). The second largest polygamist group is the Apostolic United Brethren, now under the
leadership of Owen Allred. This group was led by Rulon Allred (b.
1906) until his murder in 1977. Allred's death was carried out by two
female followers of Ervil LeBaron, founder of the Church of the
Lamb of God, another polygamous group. Ervil had his brother Joel
killed on August 20, 1972. Joel started the polygamous Church of the
Firstborn of the Fullness of Times in 1955, and he excommunicated
Ervil in 1971. Ervil died in prison in 1981.

Interest in Mormon polygamy increased dramatically after the
kidnapping of Elizabeth Smart, who was taken from her home on

June 5, 2002. She was rescued from Brian David Mitchell, her abductor, on March 12, 2003. Mitchell, who had worked as a handyman at the Smart home, views himself as Immanuel, God's messenger. He and his wife, Wanda Eileen Barzee, were charged with aggravated sexual assault, kidnapping, and burglary. Mitchell wanted Elizabeth to become one of seven divinely chosen wives.

Mitchell's views are documented in "The Book of Immanuel David Isaiah," a handwritten twenty-seven-page collection of "revelations." At one point it is said of Wanda, "Therefore, Hephzibah Eladah Isaiah, thou art called and chosen to be a helpmeet unto my servant Immanuel David Isaiah, and to be his wise counselor and best friend, and to be submissive and obedient unto thy husband in all righteousness."

Patricia Hearst appeared on *Larry King Live* and argued that Elizabeth Smart was a victim of brainwashing and that her situation paralleled Hearst's kidnapping by the Symbionese Liberation Front. She had this message for Smart: "You have been so abused and so robbed of your free will and so frightened that you believe any lie that your abductor has told you. You think that either you will be killed if you reach out to get help or . . . your family will be killed."

Polygamous Mormonism

TYPOLOGY	Christian sectarian Mormon
WEB SITES	The Center for Public Education
	www.polygamyinfo.com
	Help the Child Brides
	http://helpthechildbrides.com
	Mary Mackert
	www.xpolygamist.com
	Tapestry against Polygamy
	www.polygamy.org
READING	Martha Sonntag Bradley, *Kidnapped from That Land* (Salt Lake City: University of Utah Press, 1996)
	Jon Krakauer, *Under the Banner of Heaven* (New York: Doubleday, 2003)
	Richard Van Wagoner, *Mormon Polygamy* (Salt Lake City: Signature, 1989)

▶ Presbyterian-Reformed

Reformed and Presbyterian churches trace their roots to John Calvin (1509–64), the Protestant leader. He was born in France and studied at the University of Paris. Raised Catholic, Calvin was influenced by Renaissance humanism and the ideology of Erasmus (d. 1536), the influential Dutch thinker. Calvin's conversion to Protestantism resulted from his ongoing study of the Bible and his experience of Catholic suppression of Protestant movements in France. Calvin left France in 1533 and settled in Basel, Switzerland. He released the first edition of his *Institutes of the Christian Religion* in 1536, the same year he moved to Geneva. After a brief exile in Strasbourg (1538–41), Calvin spent the rest of his life in Geneva.

Calvin's theology and understanding of church government became a dominant force in the spreading Protestant movement. His heritage is found largely in the Reformed and Presbyterian Church traditions, but Calvinistic theology has had a significant impact on Anglican and Baptist history. Calvin is most famous for his teaching on predestination. He was criticized by other Reformers for his complicity in the execution of Servetus (d. 1553), a Spanish radical who advanced an unorthodox interpretation of the Trinity. Though Calvin's teaching had an affinity with Luther's thought, the two most famous Protestants never met.

Calvin's ideas formed the doctrinal framework for the Scots Confession (1560), the Belgic Confession (1561), the Heidelberg Catechism (1563), the Canons of Dordt (1619), and the Westminster Confession (1646). It also had a significant impact on the London Baptist Confession of Faith (1689). Though these statements reflect Calvin's theology to a great degree, his *Institutes* and biblical commentaries provide a far broader and richer interpretation of Christian doctrine and life. For example, the first section of the *Institutes* places great emphasis upon the leading of the Holy Spirit in the discovery of Christian truth.

The Reformed tradition took particular hold in Switzerland, France, Scotland, the Netherlands, and Hungary in the sixteenth and seventeenth centuries, though the Huguenots in France suffered heavy persecution. Many Huguenots, including the father of Paul Revere, fled to the British colonies in America. Reformed and Presbyterian churches in Britain and the Netherlands have had the most impact in spreading Calvinistic Christianity to the United States and other parts of the world, particularly South Africa and Korea.

The Presbyterian and Reformed strains of Christianity remain a powerful presence in the world. The Reformed Ecumenical Council unites 10 million members from thirty-nine Presbyterian and Reformed denominations from twenty-five countries. The International Conference of Reformed Churches is a smaller conservative union that includes the Orthodox Presbyterian Church (OPC). The OPC, led by J. Gresham Machen, was formed in 1934 in reaction to liberalism at Princeton Theological Seminary. The World Alliance of Reformed Churches represents the largest ecumenical grouping, with more than two hundred churches representing 75 million believers from more than one hundred countries. The World Alliance includes the Presbyterian Church (USA), the United Church of Christ, and the United Church of Canada.

Presbyterian-Reformed

TYPOLOGY	Protestant
FOUNDER	John Calvin
HOME PAGES	International Conference of Reformed Churches www.icronline.com
	World Alliance of Reformed Churches www.warc.ch
READING	Donald K. McKim, ed. *The Cambridge Companion to John Calvin* (Cambridge: Cambridge University Press, 2004)
	Victor Shepherd, *The Nature and Function of Faith in the Theology of John Calvin* (Vancouver, British Columbia: Regent College Publishing, 1983)

▶ Priory of Sion

Christians are now obligated to deal with widespread belief in a secret religious society known as the Priory of Sion. The phenomenal best seller *The Da Vinci Code* maintains as "Fact" the following claim: "The secret society of the Priory of Sion was founded in 1099, after the First Crusade. In 1975, parchments referred to as 'Dossiers Secrets' were discovered at the Bibliothèque Nationale, which mention the names of certain members of the Priory, including Sir Isaac Newton, Botticelli, Victor Hugo and Leonardo Da Vinci."

The Da Vinci Code also claims that the Order of the Knights Templar was a creation of the Priory of Sion. Under the guise of protecting Jerusalem during the Crusades, the Templars' actual job, according to the novel, was to look for ancient documents buried beneath the temple. One of the major discoveries was the diary of Mary Magdalene (again according to the novel).

Further, it is argued that a modern French priest named Father Berenger Saunière discovered secret treasure and ancient parchments near his church in the village of Rennes-le-Château, in southwest France. The village is now a celebrated destination of priory enthusiasts and has become widely known in occult circles. There are dozens of books about the "mysteries" of Rennes-le-Château and the "strange" wealth of Father Saunière.

Critics of Saunière contend that he was removed from his role as parish priest because he engaged in "trafficking in masses." Before Vatican II, Roman Catholic priests were allowed to accept money for performing masses. However, Church officials discovered that Saunière engaged in a form of fraud through false advertising about masses for the living and the dead. Father Saunière died in 1917, but he remains the subject of endless speculation.

Dan Brown's theories about the Priory of Sion are worthless. Brown did not examine the credibility of Pierre Plantard, the original source behind contemporary legends about the Priory of Sion. Plantard's views influenced the authors of *Holy Blood, Holy Grail*, published in 1982, and this book shaped Dan Brown. Plantard's lies were exposed in 1993 by a French court when Plantard was forced to admit to his scam about the Priory of Sion.

Dan Brown is careless in his rhetoric about alleged ancient documents about the priory. As noted earlier, the novel states: "In 1975, parchments referred to as 'Dossiers Secrets' were discovered at the Bibliothèque Nationale." The famous French Library did *not* discover any parchments about the priory in 1975 or any other year. *Les Dossiers Secrets* are *not* parchments discovered in 1975; rather, that is the title of material published in the previous decade.

Plantard formed an association known as the Priory of Sion in 1956. However, it was not a secret society but rather dealt with local political and social issues. It was only in 1961 that Plantard claimed the Priory of Sion was an ancient society. This second version of the priory gained popularity after the publication of Gérard de Sède's *L'Or deRennes* in 1967. Plantard invented another version of the priory story in 1984. At one point Plantard even claimed he was a descendant of Jesus Christ. Yet he renounced everything in 1993.

The Priory of Sion is a modern fiction now viewed as an ancient society. *The Da Vinci Code* has caused great harm to the gospel, not only because of its fictions about secret societies, but also because of its careless arguments that Jesus and Mary Magdalene were married, that Jesus was not the Son of God, and that the Bible is the creation of the emperor Constantine.

Priory of Sion

TYPOLOGY	Western esoteric
CREATOR	Pierre Plantard (1920–2000)
CRITICAL SITE	Paul Smith research archive
	http://priory-of-sion.com
READING	James A. Beverley, *Counterfeit Code* (Pickering: Bay Ridge, 2005)
	Bart D. Ehrman, *Truth and Fiction in The Da Vinci Code* (New York: Oxford University Press, 2005)

▶ Protestants

Protestant is the designation given to those groups that trace their identity back to the sixteenth century and the work of Martin Luther, John Calvin, and the leaders of the Anabaptist movement. The term Protestant rose out of the fact that Luther protested what he regarded as errors and abuses in the Roman Catholic Church of his time. The essentials of Protestant Christianity are often identified as belief in Scripture alone, grace alone, faith alone, and Christ alone. However, these major theological points do not hide the obvious divisions within Protestantism.

Protestants now make up the second largest body of Christians in the world, next to the Roman Catholic communion. While Roman Catholic leaders warned in the sixteenth century about the dangerous precedent set by Luther in splitting the Church, they had no idea how fragmented Protestantism would become. It is easy to be overwhelmed by the number of Protestant groups both in North America and worldwide. J. Gordon Melton has documented more than a thousand distinct Protestant groups in the United States alone. On the world scene, David Barrett and Todd Johnson list thousands of denominations in their World Christian Database.

In order to understand the various Protestant groups, it is helpful to interpret them in terms of larger families within the Protestant tradition. Most of the specific groups fall under fourteen major denominational or family traditions. These traditions are best approached in terms of chronology, since earlier Protestant traditions form the matrix for ongoing developments.

Four family traditions emerged in the sixteenth century: Lutheran, Reformed and Presbyterian, Free Church / Anabaptist, and Anglican. Baptists started in the seventeenth century. The Pietiest / Methodist grouping began in the eighteenth. The nineteenth century witnessed the emergence of the Churches of Christ (Stone-Campbell Restoration), the Adventist family, and the Holiness churches. Five more

Protestant families started in the twentieth century: Pentecostalism, fundamentalism, evangelicalism, the charismatic church, and the emergent church.

These family traditions are not exhaustive of all Protestant groups. However, these traditions or denominations provide the framework to understand various sectarian or cultic movements that seem, at first sight, to be unique and distinct from the larger Protestant world. For example, the Jehovah's Witnesses are clearly rooted in the Adventist family, even though the movement claims to be the only true Christian church. Likewise, the Mormon Church is a product of the larger restorationist movement that swept the United States in the nineteenth century. The Family International (formerly the Children of God) gained some of its dynamic from the broad currents of charismatic, fundamentalist, and evangelical church life of the 1960s.

Many charismatic and emergent church leaders would not want to be listed in what looks like a group of denominations. Yet, while it is not popular to be viewed as a denomination, every significant renewal movement or independent group of churches takes on the realities of denominational life by virtue of the necessities of organization, bureaucracy, promotion, and shared identity.

All the Protestant families noted have been impacted by the broad philosophical and theological currents that have dominated Western Christianity in the last five centuries. Each denomination or family has its own particular reading in relation to the Enlightenment, liberal theology, evangelicalism, postmodernism, and so on. Trends in philosophy and theology create divisions within and across the various Protestant families. This means, for example, that a moderate Southern Baptist might find more unity with a liberal Presbyterian than with a conservative in the Southern Baptist Convention.

Protestants

TYPOLOGY	Christian
READING	J. Gordon Melton, *Encyclopedia of American Religions* (Detroit: Gale, 2002)
	Hans J. Hillerbrand, ed., *The Protestant Reformation* (New York: Harper & Row, 1969)

▶ Purpose-Driven/Seeker-Sensitive Churches

Purpose-Driven and Seeker-Sensitive churches arise out of two of the largest churches in America. The Seeker-Sensitive movement is traced to the Willow Creek Church near Chicago, founded by Bill Hybels, a counselor to former President Bill Clinton during the Monica Lewinsky scandal. The Purpose-Driven movement has its roots in the ministry of Rick Warren, founding pastor of the Saddleback Community Church in Southern California. Warren is known most famously for his two bestselling works *The Purpose Driven Church* and *The Purpose Driven Life*. The latter has sold over 25 million copies.

The Willow Creek church started in October 1975, using rented space from a movie theater. After considerable growth over two years, the church purchased ninety acres of land in South Barrington in 1977, now the site of the main church sanctary and headquarters. The local Willow Creek church operates at three other sites in Illinois, with over 20,000 members, while the Willow Creek Association reaches over 10,000 different churches in thirty-five countries.

The Saddleback Valley Community Church had its first service at Easter in 1980. Rick Warren and his wife, Kay, moved to Orange County the previous December with plans to launch a church that reached the nonchurched. Their first Bible study had seven in attendance. Now over 20,000 people attend church services each weekend, and over 350,000 pastors and church leaders have been trained in Purpose-Driven seminars. Warren has been called America's most influential pastor.

Both Warren and Hybels receive significant criticism. Emergent Church leaders suggest that they have been seduced by a commercial mindset that leads to church as a form of entertainment. Fundamentalist Christians are even harsher on them, including the outrageous allegation that an occult spirit is behind *The Purpose Driven Life*. More commonly, both Warren and Hybels are charged with pragmatism, spiritual shallowness, and offering a man-centered, New Age-style religion. They are also frequently criticized for their connection with Robert Schuller, the founder of California's Crystal Cathedral.

These negative allegations are largely based on superficial and unfair analysis of both leaders and their respective movements. The statements of faith of both Saddleback and Willow Creek are thoroughly orthodox. Both Warren and Hybels have based their entire ministry model on reaching the unsaved, a fact that seems lost on most critics. They both openly acknowledge Jesus Christ as the only Savior, a fact that thoroughly discredits any suggestion that they are New Age. Warren was completely candid about his Christ-centered faith in a May 2005 forum in Key West, Florida, with some of America's leading journalists.

Warren and Hybels acknowledge learning some practical techniques from Robert Schuller. However, Hybels and Warren do not duplicate Schuller's emphasis on positive thinking, and they are far more guarded in their writings. Of course, critics of Schuller often fail to note that the Crystal Cathedral has a thoroughly orthodox Statement of Faith. It includes these affirmations: "Man is by nature sinful and cannot make himself good. He can only be made righteous by accepting God's forgiveness for sin through Jesus' sacrifice on the cross."

Richard Abanes has provided a superb response to critics of the purpose-driven model on his Web site and in his book *Rick Warren and the Purpose That Drives Him*. He deals with the accusations of Warren Smith, Ken Silver, Paul Proctor, Ingrid Schlueter, Todd Wilken, and the Lighthouse Trails Research Project, among others. Abanes's work is also a corrective to the flawed biography on Warren written by George Muir.

Purpose-Driven and Seeker-Sensitive Churches	
FOUNDERS	Rick Warren (Saddleback) and Bill Hybels (Willow Creek)
WEB SITES	Rick Warren and Saddleback, www.saddleback.com
	www.purposedrivenlife.com
	Willow Creek Church, www.willowcreek.org
	Willow Creek Association, www.willowcreekcom
	Richard Abanes site, www.abanes.com
READING	Richard Abanes, *Rick Warren and the Purpose That Drives Him* (Eugene, OR: Harvest House, 2005)

▸ Quakers

Quakers is the popular term for the Society of Friends, the spiritual movement that traces its roots to George Fox, a dissenting Christian leader of seventeenth-century England. Fox was born at Drayton-in-the-Clay, England, in 1624. He was raised in the Church of England but developed an independent spirit about certain traditions in both society and church life.

Fox was known for his focus on inward spirituality and enlightenment by the Holy Spirit. He refused to use the word "church" about buildings. He found little theological or spiritual help from either orthodox Christian pastors or various sectarian groups, including the Ranters. This deprivation led him to write, "When all my hopes in them and in all men were gone, so that I had nothing outwardly to help me, nor could tell what to do, then, oh, then, I heard a voice which said, 'There is one, even Christ Jesus, that can speak to thy condition'; and when I heard it my heart did leap for joy."

Fox's public ministry began in 1648. He was imprisoned in Derby in 1650. A judge referred to Fox and his followers as "Quakers" because of their emphasis on trembling before God's Word. In 1653 Fox was arrested and taken to London, where he met with Oliver Cromwell. Cromwell was impressed by Fox's spirituality and met with him two other times. Fox was jailed at least six times between 1654 and 1674, usually for refusing to take oaths or for disturbing the religious order. Fox married Margaret Fell in 1669 and traveled to America in 1671. He died in 1691.

Quakers prefer to call themselves Friends. They number about 350,000, located in seventy countries of the world. The three major Quaker groupings are the Friends General Conference (FGC), the Friends United Meeting (FUM), and the Evangelical Friends International (EFI). The Friends World Committee for Consultation (FWCC), based in London, serves as a larger unifying body. The EFI, with strong influence from the Holiness movement, claims an explicit Christ-centered emphasis, based in affirmation of Scripture. The broader Quaker tradition is more liberal and sympathetic toward other religions. This perspective is defended in Chuck Fager's book *Without Apology* (Kimo, 1996).

Quakers are famous for their silence in worship, though they also have meetings in which sermons are given. Friends put great emphasis upon the equality of believers. This accounts for the absence of clergy and also explains why anyone may speak a word in worship based upon the leading of the Spirit. Quakers stress the "inner light" and do not participate in the Lord's Supper or practice any form of baptism. Friends are known for their social protest of war and were one of the first groups to speak out against the slave trade in America.

The most famous Quaker in American history is William Penn (1644–1718), the founder of the state of Pennsylvania. Susan B. Anthony (1820–1906), one of the pioneers of the women's suffrage movement, was also a Quaker. Richard J. Foster, author of *Celebration of Discipline*, is a Quaker, though he writes mainly for broad evangelical Christian audiences.

Quakers

TYPOLOGY	Christian Protestant
HOME PAGES	Friends General Conference
	www.fgcquaker.org
	Friends United Meeting
	www.fum.org
	Evangelical Friends International
	www.evangelical-friends.org
	Friends World Committee for Consultation
	http://fwccworld.org
GENERAL SITE	www.quaker.org
READING	Hugh Barbour and J. William Frost, *The Quakers* (New York: Greenwood, 1988)

▸ Raelians

The Raelian movment is a modern-day esoteric UFO religion, led by a Frenchman named Rael. Raelians received worldwide attention when they announced that the first cloned baby was born on December 26, 2002. The subsequent media hunt for "Clone Baby Eve" (with DNA proof to be provided) paused in January 2003 after a whirlwind of political protest and legal threats.

The Raelian movement traces its origin to December 13, 1973, when French journalist Claude Vorilhon (now Rael) claims he was contacted by an extraterrestrial named Yahweh Elohim. Rael describes Elohim as about four feet tall, with long, dark hair, almond-shaped eyes, and olive skin. He is said to have told Rael, "We were the ones who made all life on earth; you mistook us for gods; we were at the origin of your main religions. Now that you are mature enough to understand this, we would like to enter official contact through an embassy." The alien creature is said to have emerged from a UFO near Clermont-Ferrand in central France.

Raelians believe humans were not created by God or random evolution but by a team of superscientists who used DNA to create humans in their image. Humanity's fall is related to forbidden scientific knowledge being passed on to some early humans. Rael's mission is to provide the true message to the world and create an embassy in Jerusalem that can serve as a landing base for the extraterrestrials. Rael first advanced his message through an organization known as MADECH, founded in 1974.

Rael claims that the extraterrestrials took him to their planet on October 7, 1975.

He states that he had sexual encounters with six female robots while he was there and was also introduced to cloning. The movement developed a CLONAID program and believes that human cloning represents the path to gaining eternal life.

According to Rael, who believes he is the Messiah, the space creatures taught the same message to Moses, Buddha, Muhammad, and Jesus. However, that revelation got scrambled and distorted through history. For example, Jews and Christians believe that Elohim is one of the names of God in Genesis when actually it should be translated "those who came from the sky"—a clear reference to the UFO aliens.

The group's scientific pursuits on cloning have been taken seriously by some outside observers. CLONAID CEO Brigitte Boisselier has a double doctorate in chemistry and worked for twelve years in a respected French chemical firm before moving to Quebec to work with Rael. Boisselier announced the birth of "Eve" at a Florida news conference on December 27, 2002. The group got 30 million hits on their Web site as a result.

The scientist said the baby weighed seven pounds and was created through the use of DNA from the skin cells of the mother, an American citizen. U.S. journalist Michael Guillen was supposed to be given proof of the cloning, but Rael stopped the verification procedures in early January 2003.

Raelians	
TYPOLOGY	Western esoteric UFO religion
FOUNDER	Claude Vorilhon (b. 1946), now known as Rael
HEADQUARTERS	Montreal, Quebec
HOME PAGE	www.rael.org
UFO CRITIC SITE	UFO Skeptic—Philip Klass
	www.csicop.org/klassfiles
GROUP LITERATURE	*The Message Given by Extra-Terrestrials*
READING	Susan Palmer, *Aliens Adored* (Piscataway, NJ: Rutgers University Press, 2004)

▶ Ramtha School of Enlightenment

The Ramtha School of Enlightenment features the work of JZ Knight, one of the most influential and well-known New Agers. A native of New Mexico, she was born Judith Darlene Hampton on March 16, 1946. Knight claims that her roots in poverty gave her inner strength to resist conformity. "I wasn't the pretty little girl that was born into the Leave it to Beaver family that had to do everything right and belong to all the right clubs and do all the right things and read all the right books and wear all the right clothes. I was just one of a lot of kids that a poor woman had, and she was trying to keep her family together. That freedom allowed me to learn, and it allowed me to develop an interior strength."

Knight states that in February 1977 she was contacted by a 35,000-year-old warrior from the eternal realm. "Beloved woman, I am Ramtha the Enlightened One, and I have come to help you over the ditch. It is called the ditch of limitation. I am here, and we are going to do grand work together." Knight claims that Ramtha once lived in the northern part of the lost continent of Atlantis. Knight channeled Ramtha for the first time in November 1978. She achieved fame and wealth in the 1980s, particularly after being endorsed by Shirley MacLaine and Linda Evans.

Knight has been criticized over the years for the high cost of her public teaching and private channeling sessions. Additionally, there was some controversy over JZ advising followers to put money into Arabian horses. JZ later reimbursed some disgruntled investors. She has also been attacked by the anticult movement for breaking up families who were divided over moving to Knight's new headquarters in Yelm, Washington.

She married Jeff Knight, her third husband, in 1984. She claimed that Ramtha told Jeff that he was married to JZ in a previous life and that they were soul mates. Their marriage ended in a bitter court battle. Jeff claimed that he was under undue influence from Ramtha when he and JZ initially agreed on the divorce settlement. The courts dismissed allegations of brainwashing in relation to Ramtha's School of Englightenment. Jeff, who was bisexual, died in 1994.

Knight claims that various scientists have performed tests proving that she is not faking her experiences with Ramtha. In 1997 an Austrian court ruled that JZ is the proper holder of copyright over material from Ramtha. The case involved a dispute with Julie Ravel, a Berlin woman, who claimed to be the proper agent of Ramtha. Ramtha is alleged to have said through JZ that "the world does not need another guru. The world does not need another priest. The world does not need another preacher. The world does not need another spiritual interpretation of the stars. What the world needs is truth."

Ramtha School of Englightenment

TYPOLOGY	Western esoteric
FOUNDER	JZ Knight
HOME PAGE	www.ramtha.com
READING	JZ Knight, *A State of Mind* (New York: Warner, 1987)
	J. Gordon Melton, *Finding Enlightenment* (Hillsboro, OR: Beyond Words, 1998)

▶ Rastafarianism

Rastafarianism is a religious and political movement that emerged in Jamaica in the third decade of the twentieth century. Early Rastafarian leaders such as Leonard Howell and Joseph Nathaniel Hibbert drew their original inspiration from the radical teachings of Black Nationalist prophet Marcus Garvey (1887–1940). Most people know Rastafarianism through reggae or the dreadlock hairstyle of its followers. Bob Marley and Burning Spear have been the movement's most famous ambassadors. The religion is also known for its ritual use of marijuana, or ganja.

The term Rastafarianism comes from the name of Ras Tafari, who became Emperor Haile Selassie I of Ethiopia in 1930. Early Rastafarians looked to him as a messianic figure to lead blacks out of oppression. Rastas placed great import on the titles given to Haile Selassie. He was called "King of Kings, Lord of Lords, Conquering Lion of the Tribe of Judah, Defender of the Faith and Light of the World." Haile Selassie was also said to be the 225th descendant of King David.

These factors led early Rastafarians to proclaim that the emperor was divine, even though he had formal ties with the Ethiopian Orthodox Church. The emperor was disconcerted by Rastafarian worship of him when he visited Jamaica in 1966. While the emperor was alive, Rastafarians believed he would bring Africans back to their homeland. With his death in 1975, that affirmation is taken in a less literal sense. Rastafarians often identify Haile Selassie as Jesus Christ.

There has been little rigidity in Rastafarian doctrine and lifestyle, particularly in the last several decades. Most followers believe that blacks, the true descendants of the Hebrews, were sent into slavery and exile because of disobedience to Jah, or Jehovah. Rastafarians claim that whites have kept them in Babylon. Some Rastas defend the use of ganja with Bible references. Other Rastas protest the use of the Christian Bible as a tool of the white race. Many Rastas use a version of the Bible known as the Holy Piby, compiled by Robert Athlyi Rogers of Anguilla from 1913 through 1917. Generally, Rastafarian culture is patriarchal, though women have increasing leadership roles outside the home. This is documented in Barry Chevannes's ethnographic fieldwork in Jamaica.

There is no one organization or person that speaks for all Rastafarians. The better known groups are the Twelve Tribes of Israel, the House of Bobo, and the Nyahbinghi Order. The order states in its anthem: "To advance, to advance with truths and rights, To advance, to advance with love and light. With righteousness leading. I n I Hail to Rastafari I n I King, Imanity is pleading, One Jah for I n I." ("I n I" is a common Rastafarian phrase that reflects unity with Jah.)

Some Rastas have argued that the popularization of Rasta music and culture has led to an accommodation with the larger white culture once so widely vilified.

Rastafarianism	
TYPOLOGY	Christian Black Nationalist
WEB SITES	Nyahbinghi Order
	www.nyahbinghi.org
	House of Bobo
	http://houseofbobo.com
	Ras Adam Simeon site
	http://web.syr.edu/~affellem
	Rasta Times
	www.rastafaritimes.com
	Rastafari Speaks
	www.rastafarispeaks.com
READING	Leonard Barrett, *The Rastafarians* (Boston: Beacon, 1997)
	Barry Chevannes, *Rastafari* (Syracuse: Syracuse University Press, 1994)
	William David Spencer, *Dread Jesus* (London: SPCK, 1999)

▶ Roman Catholicism

The Roman tradition has done much to preserve central teachings of the gospel. Evangelicals ought to celebrate their agreement with Catholics on every essential doctrine and in all areas where we can unite on moral and social issues. Evangelicals share with orthodox Catholics [as with Eastern Orthodoxy] a confession of the triune nature of God, the supremacy of Jesus Christ as the only Savior and Lord, the authority of the Bible, the necessity of evangelism, and the hope of eternal life with God.

Alongside gratitude for all aspects of true unity with Catholics must also come evangelical openness to learn from Rome where the Catholic tradition has something to teach Protestants in general and evangelicals in particular. Roman Catholics have had a higher appreciation for church unity, in stark contrast to the fragmentation that has dominated Protestant history. Likewise, however deep are our differences over doctrines related to Mary, the Catholic appreciation for her is a rebuke to Protestant neglect. Also, there is in Catholic worship a sense of awe and majesty that ought to be recaptured by evangelicals.

Evangelicals have rightly challenged the Roman Catholic tradition at these important points: (a) the church as Roman, (b) the doctrine of papal infallibility, (c) aspects of the doctrine of salvation, (d) certain teachings about Mary, (e) aspects of the emphasis upon a celibate priesthood, and (f) disharmony between Catholic traditions and biblical revelation.

1. *Where is the church of Jesus Christ?* Throughout its history, the Roman Catholic Church has tended to identify itself as *the* Christian church. (This does not mean all Catholics have thought that all Protestants or Orthodox were going to hell.) While Vatican II resisted the temptation to say that the church of Jesus is the same as the Catholic Church, the bishops in Rome made it clear that the Roman Church is the mother church.

The identification of the church of Jesus with the Roman Church is marred at every point where the history of Catholicism shows flagrant disregard for both truth and goodness. Evangelicals often forget that orthodox Catholicism teaches not only the infallibility of the pope but also the infallibility of the Church. It is difficult to reconcile the notion of the Church's infallibility with the dark stains that have blotted Roman history.

When Pope John Paul II startled the world with his Lenten apology in the spring of 2000, he spoke with humility about the sins of Catholics past and present. "The children of the Church know the experience of sin, whose shadows are cast over her, obscuring her beauty. For this reason the Church does not cease to implore God's forgiveness for the sins of her members." How can Catholics affirm Church infallibility, given the sin of its members?

This becomes especially problematic when the sins involve popes and archbishops and, more important, structural and ideological defects that were or are part of the institutional life of the Vatican. In this regard, the sordid aspect of the Crusades and the innocent lives lost at the hands of Roman inquisitors should make any Catholic realize that the church of Jesus cannot be equated so easily with Rome.

2. *Is the pope infallible?* Evangelical objection to papal infallibility should not be about whether Peter was in Rome. The issue of infallibility is also not about whether God could have made all popes infallible. On this, evangelicals should grant the obvious: all things are possible with God. The crux of the debate is simply whether in fact the popes have been infallible.

On this, the record of papal history is clear: popes have made flagrant and serious errors in their teachings in regard to both faith and morals. For example, (a) Pope Honorius I was condemned by a council of the Church for teaching heresy about the will of Christ, (b) three popes erred in their condemnation of the views of Galileo, (c) many popes throughout history have advocated views that have furthered anti-Semitism, and (d) many popes have taught views that have created false views of women and sexuality.

Though Catholic orthodoxy does not teach that the popes are sinless, it is hard to have respect for the doctrine of papal infallibility in the case of popes who have shown themselves capable of great evil. Must Catholics extend this notion of infallibility to popes who bribed their way into office, who killed and raped? Should infallibility be imagined of Pope Alexander VI, a monster of iniquity, who had the Florentine preacher Savonarola tortured? What shall we say of the infallibility of popes who called for crusades, inquisitions, and persecutions, whether of Muslims, Jews, witches, gypsies, Protestants, atheists, or fellow Catholics?

3. *How are we saved?* Thankfully, the Catholic-Lutheran dialogue has led to remarkable unity on many issues connected with justification. However, evangelicals have every right to continue to question whether the Roman sacramental scheme has made salvation something different from the picture given in Scripture. For example, does the emphasis upon infant baptism lull Catholics into a false sense of security about their status as members of the body of Christ? Has emphasis away from forensic justification led many Catholics to believe in works righteousness? Has the focus on Mary and on the priesthood led some Catholics to forget the centrality of Christ?

Further, Catholic leaders should pay attention to the fact that so many lay Church members are out of touch with biblical themes of faith and grace. Why is it that so many Catholics believe that salvation is by works? These questions are asked out of hope that Catholics may arrive at a more profound awareness of the simplicity of the salvation offered in Christ.

4. *Who is Mary?* The unique Catholic views about Mary depend almost solely on acceptance of papal infallibility and the veracity of Roman (and Eastern Orthodox) tradition. The view that Mary was sinless and that she was assumed into heaven is a giant leap from the important fact that she was faithful to Jesus in his hour of death. Beyond this, a plain reading of biblical material about Mary would not lead one to imagine that she was born sinless or that she was a perpetual virgin. Likewise, the growing adulation of Mary throughout Catholic history is out of proportion even with her significant calling as the mother of Jesus.

5. *Are traditions biblical?* An attention to tradition can be an important part of the proper handling of the Bible, and so the Catholic focus on tradition is not wrong in itself. However, the Church's emphasis upon tradition, when combined with the doctrine of infallibility, has created a setting in which doctrines, ideas, and practices that are not in full harmony with Scripture could develop.

The examples of the unfortunate effects of tradition in Catholicism are many. Catholic traditions about purgatory and indulgences come immediately to mind. Further, the long tradition of priestly celibacy has led to some dark moments in both the past and the present, not only in terms of the abuse of children, but also in regard to the way in which many women feel like second-class citizens in their Church. Also, Catholic traditions have often been mixed with pagan customs in ways that detract from the main teachings of the gospel.

Roman Catholicism 101

- There in one God in the Trinity of Father, Son, and Spirit.
- The Bible is the infallible Word of God.
- Laity are to read and obey the Bible.
- Jesus Christ is the only Savior and mediator.
- Sacred tradition and Scripture should receive equal reverence.
- Sacred Scripture contains the Apocrypha.
- Catholic doctrine is supported by Scripture and/or Sacred tradition.
- The Church of Jesus Christ "subsists in the Catholic Church."
- The pope is infallible when he declares dogma on issues of faith and morals.
- The pope has "full, supreme and universal power over the whole Church."
- The pope teaches in unity with Church councils.
- The Church includes the "separated brethren," who should return to the mother church.
- Salvation is not by works.
- Baptism (in fact or intent) is necessary for salvation.
- Infant baptism brings one into the body of Christ.
- Transubstantiation is the true view of the Eucharist.
- Penance (confession and conversion from sin) is necessary for salvation.
- The priesthood is for males only.
- Celibacy is the normal requirement for priests.
- It is right to pray for the dead.
- It is right to pray to the saints, especially Mary.
- Mary is subordinate to Jesus Christ.

- Mary is the "Mother of God."
- Mary can be called mediatrix.
- The Immaculate Conception of Mary is truth.
- Mary was a perpetual virgin.
- Mary was assumed into heaven.
- Mary is "pre-eminent, wholly unique" among Christians.
- Catholic orthodoxy is biblical Christianity.
- The whole body of Christ "cannot err in belief."
- Penance is to be offered in the confessional at least once a year.
- It is the sacred duty of Christians to evangelize the world.
- The devil is real.
- The teaching of purgatory is a true doctrine.
- Heaven and hell are eternal.

Time Line of Roman Catholicism

91	Pope Clement I leads Christians in Rome
189	Victor I becomes the 14th pope
251	Cyprian argues for the primacy of Rome
258	Sixtus II, the 24th pope, is martyred by imperial forces
270	Antony of Egypt becomes first hermit of the Church
311	Donatist schism in North Africa
313	Constantine's Edict of Toleration grants religious liberty
325	The Council of Nicea defines orthodoxy
365	Athanasius defends the doctrine of the Trinity
385	Bishop Ambrose of Milan resists the Roman emperor
387	Conversion of Augustine of Hippo
397	John Chrysostom becomes bishop of Constantinople.
405	Latin Vulgate completed by Jerome
410	The Goths sack Rome
416	The Council of Carthage condemns Pelagianism
431	The Council of Ephesus approves *theotokos* as a title for Mary
432	Saint Patrick returns to Ireland as missionary
440	Leo the Great becomes pope
451	The Council of Chalcedon affirms the Nicene view of Jesus
525	Benedict of Nursia establishes a monastery in Monte Cassino
550	African bishops condemn Pope Vigilius
553	Second Council of Constantinople
590	Gregory the Great begins papal rule
625	Honorius I becomes pope
632	Death of Muhammad

664	The Synod of Whitby accepts the authority of Rome for the English church
681	Third Council of Constantinople
725	Beginning of controversy over icons
731	The Venerable Bede writes *Ecclesiastical History*
732	Charles Martel defeats Muslims at Tours
787	Icons approved at Second Council of Nicea
800	Charlemagne crowned emperor
851	Martyrdom of Christians at Cordova by Muslims
863	Serbs evangelized by Cyril and Methodius
877	Death of philosopher Scotus Erigena in Ireland
909	Monastery founded at Cluny
1054	The Great Schism between East and West
1093	Anselm becomes archbishop of Canterbury
1095	Start of First Crusade by Pope Urban II
1115	Bernard of Clairvaux starts a monastery
1116	Peter Abelard teaches at Paris
1170	Archbishop Thomas Becket murdered
1173	Peter Waldo initiates reform
1187	Saladin captures Jerusalem
1209	Francis of Assisi chooses the monastic life
1215	The Fourth Lateran Council affirms papal supremacy
1273	Thomas Aquinas completes his *Summa theologia*
1302	Boniface VIII proclaims universal papal supremacy
1321	Dante writes *The Divine Comedy*
1378	Beginning of Great Schism in papacy, lasting to 1417
1380	Wycliffe works on Bible translation into English
1415	John Hus is burned at the stake by the Council of Constance
1418	*Imitatio Christi* surfaces, attributed to Thomas à Kempis.
1447	Nicholas V becomes pope
1453	Ottoman Turks take control of Constantinople
1456	Johann Gutenberg prints the first Bible
1478	Start of Spanish Inquisition
1492	Beginning of rule of Alexander VI, infamous pope
1498	Savonarola, leading Dominican preacher, is burned at the stake
1509	Erasmus protests abuses in Rome
1512	Michelangelo finishes painting the Sistine Chapel
1517	Martin Luther posts his ninety-five theses
1521	Luther is excommunicated
1534	Founding of the Jesuits by Ignatius
1536	John Calvin publishes *Institutes of the Christian Religion*
1557	Start of the Index of Forbidden Books

1601	Matteo Ricci travels to China as a Catholic missionary
1633	Condemnation of Galileo
1648	The Peace of Westphalia ends the Thirty Years' War
1704	Pope Clement XI condemns Chinese rites
1773	Pope Clement XIV suppresses Jesuits
1800	Pius VII becomes pope
1854	Pius IX affirms the Immaculate Conception of Mary
1859	Charles Darwin publishes *Origin of Species*
1864	Pope Pius IX publishes "Syllabus of Errors"
1870	Papal infallibility affirmed by Vatican I and Pius IX
1878	Leo XIII becomes pope
1896	Rome condemns Anglican orders
1903	Pius X becomes pope
1917	Vision of Mary by three children at Fatima
1919	Patriarch of Constantinople approves ecumenical relations
1938	Beginning of Nazi persecution of Jews
1950	Bodily Assumption of Mary into heaven affirmed by Pius XII
1960	Charismatic renewal impacts Catholicism
1962	Second Vatican Council starts under John XXIII
1966	Archbishop Ramsey meets Paul VI in Rome
1968	Pope Paul VI condemns the birth control pill
1978	John Paul II becomes pope
1979	Hans Küng removed as Catholic theologian
1980	Oscar Romero assassinated in El Salvador
1983	Revised *Code of Canon Law*
1992	*Catechism of the Catholic Church* released
1999	Agreement on justification between Lutherans and Catholics
2000	Vatican issues Lenten apology
2002	Crisis in American Catholicism over sex abuse scandals
2005	Death of John Paul II and election of Benedict XVI

Roman Catholicism

TYPOLOGY	Christian
CATHOLIC SITES	The Holy See
	www.vatican.va
	Catholic Answers
	www.catholic.com
	New Advent
	www.newadvent.org
	Zenit News

www.zenit.org
Dave Armstrong site
http://ic.net/~erasmus

CRITIC SITES   Alpha & Omega Ministries (James White)
www.aomin.org

READING   Boston Globe Investigative Staff, *Betrayal* (Boston:
Little, Brown, & Co., 2002)

Norman Geisler & Ralph MacKenzie, *Roman Catholics
and Evangelicals* (Grand Rapids: Baker, 1995)

David I. Kertzer, *The Popes against the Jews* (New York:
Vintage, 2001)

Hans Küng, *Infallible? An Inquiry* (Garden City:
Doubleday, 1971)

Hans Küng, *The Church* (New York: Sheed and Ward,
1968)

Richard McBrien, ed., *HarperCollins Encyclopedia of
Catholicism* (New York: HarperCollins, 1995)

Thomas P. Rausch, ed. *Catholics and Evangelicals*
(Downers Grove: InterVarsity, 2000)

Garry Wills, *Papal Sin* (New York: Doubleday, 2000)

▸ Sai Baba

Sai Baba is probably the most influential and controversial Hindu guru in the world today. According to most accounts, he was born on November 23, 1926, in Puttaparthi, southeastern India, and named Sathyanarayana Raju. His followers believe that his birth was marked by supernatural signs and that he miraculously survived a scorpion bite in 1940, the year when he proclaimed his divine essence. His first world conference was held in 1968 in Bombay.

Since the 1950s, Sai Baba has devoted funds to the building of hospitals and educational institutions in India. He has also been involved in the creation of a major waterworks project that brings clean water to hundreds of villages near his main residence. Its third phase was inaugurated in 1995 by the president of India. In 2001 Sai Baba opened a major specialty hospital in Bangalore. The guru visited eastern Africa in 1968, his only travel outside India.

Miracle stories circulate widely about him, but they are viewed as trickery and sleight-of-hand by prominent ex-members and investigators. The "anti-guru" B. Premanand has written critiques of Sai Baba's miracles in *The Indian Skeptic*. He has also accused Indian police and government officials of sloppy investigation into murders at Sai Baba's residence in 1993. Further, ex-members have charged Sai Baba with the sexual abuse of young men in his group. One of the earliest to raise this issue was Tal Brooke, one of the leaders in the Spiritual Counterfeits Project. Brooke wrote about his sojourn with Sai Baba in *Avatar of the Night*, published in 1976.

In 1999 former followers David and Faye Bailey issued *The Findings*, a report on their own disillusionment with Sai Baba, based on extensive interviews with boys and young men who had been abused by the guru. BBC2 raised the sexual abuse question in a 2004 documentary "Secret Swami." Followers usually respond by questioning the integrity of the accusers or by claiming that Sai Baba sometimes touches his devotees in order to raise their *kundalini*, or spiritual energy.

Many members, due to their complete trust in their guru, simply ignore the accusations. Indulal Shah, the top international leader in the movement, advised devotees, "We know how Bhagavan does not spare Himself in the service to Humanity. We all know that Bhagavan's Life is His Message. We also know that when we have our own experience to rely upon, we have no time or space to pay any heed to the malicious allegations that are innately false and devious."

Sai Baba claims that he lives above both criticism and adulation. He once wrote to his brother, "Have you not heard of dogs that howl at the stars? How long can they go on? Authenticity will soon win. I will not give up My Mission, or My determination. I know I will carry them out; I treat the honor and dishonor, the fame and blame that may be the consequence, with equal equanimity. Internally, I am unconcerned. I act but in the outer world; I talk and move about for the sake of the outer world and for announcing My coming to the people; else, I have no concern even with these."

There are more than twelve hundred Sai Baba centers worldwide. The American branch of the Sai Baba movement is led by Michael Goldstein.

Sai Baba

TYPOLOGY	Hindu
HOME PAGES	www.sathyasai.org
	www.srisathyasai.org.in
CRITIC SITES	www.indian-skeptic.org
	www.saiguru.net
	www.exbaba.com
	http://home.no.net/anir/Sai/
	http://bdsteel.tripod.com

▸ Satanism

The term *Satanism* can be used in at least five different ways.

First, Satanism can be a reference to those who actually worship Satan but who do not engage in any criminal behavior or ritual abuse.

Second, Satanism can refer to those who worship Satan and engage in criminal acts related to ritual worship of Lucifer. Western society allows people to worship Satan but prosecutes those who engage in satanic ritual abuse (SRA) or criminal behavior tied in with their alleged worship.

Third, Satanism refers to those who use the language of worshiping Satan but only as an expression of hedonism and an anti-Christian lifestyle and philosophy. This is the ideological position of Anton LaVey, founder of the Church of Satan and author of *The Satanic Bible*. LaVey claimed that he was both a witch and a Satanist, but he also said that he did not believe in a literal devil. The same position is adopted by Karla LaVey's First Satanic Church and John Allee's First Church of Satan. Michael Aquino's Temple of Set claims literal belief in Satan but identifies Satan with the Egyptian god Set.

Fourth, Satanism is used in popular rhetoric as equivalent to any type of witchcraft. This position is often advanced by conservative Christians, allowing for no distinction among various types of witchcraft and Satanism. On this model, it is usually argued that satanic ritual abuse is pervasive. Last, Satanism can be used to describe the practices of teenagers who dabble in the occult and use satanic imagery as a form of rebellion against social norms.

In the last three decades, a debate has taken place about the nature and extent of Satanism in contemporary society. Arguments about SRA also involve opposing views about trauma memory, multiple personality disorder (now known as dissociative identity disorder), and the extent of child sexual abuse. Several evangelical Christian writers have popularized the view that Satanism is widespread as a criminal reality. This position has also been adopted by some psychiatrists, judges, and police officers, though it has been strongly resisted by others in mental health fields and law enforcement. The controversy over Satanism has led to criminal charges involving pastors and day care workers and many legal battles over child custody. Families have been bitterly divided over claims of ritual abuse by fathers and mothers.

In reacting to the debates about modern Satanism, Christians bring two important truths to the topic. First, and most important, the Christian worldview asserts the sovereignty of God over Satan and evil. This fundamental doctrine provides a rationale for not giving undue attention to Satan or overstating the powers of the demonic. As boundless as evil seems, its scope is not infinite. Emphasis upon the omnipotence of God serves as a necessary corrective to overemphasis upon Satan.

Second, Christian recognition of the reality of evil provides the intellectual framework for taking claims about Satanism seriously. Accounts of both natural and supernatural evil can be assessed as possible, given the biblical recognition of the extent of spiritual and moral darkness in the human race and in the demonic realm. Ironically, Christian recognition of evil also presents the proper ideological ground for realizing that false claims about evil and Satanism are possible as another example of intellectual and moral depravity.

Evangelicals have often been gullible about claims of Satanism. For example, Mike Warnke, author of *The Satan Seller* (published in 1972), claimed that in 1965 and 1966 he had been the head of a satanic coven in California with fifteen hundred members. For two decades Warnke's testimony was unquestioned. Then, in 1992, *Cornerstone* magazine published "Selling Satan: The Tragic History of Mike Warnke." Authored by Mike Hertenstein and Jon Trott, this twenty-four-thousand-word exposé showed beyond reasonable doubt that Warnke had fabricated reports of his satanic activity. The article also documented his failed marriages and lavish lifestyle. The article was later expanded into a book under the title *Selling Satan* (Cornerstone Press).

Rebecca Brown, author of *He Came to Set the Captives Free*, claims that she was used by God to perform exorcisms on hundreds of demon-possessed patients while she was a doctor in Indiana. Her most significant case involved a woman named Elaine, who was allegedly the bride of Satan, having married him in a secret ceremony in a Presbyterian church. Brown also maintains that Elaine flew with Satan on his private jet to the Vatican, where she took part in planning meetings with the pope and other conspirators, including famous rock stars.

Rebecca Brown was originally known as Ruth Irene Bailey, having legally changed her name in 1986. Bailey was born on May 21, 1948, in Shelbyville, Indiana. After working as a nurse, she earned her M.D. in 1979 and performed her residency at Ball Memorial Hospital in Muncie, Indiana. The Indiana Medical Licensing Board revoked Bailey's right to practice medicine in September 1984. Bailey was charged with misdiagnosis of patients and misuse of prescriptions. One of her patients was Elaine, the woman who became the central figure in *He Came to Set the Captives Free*.

While Satanism of every type is anti-Christian, there is a radical difference between Satanists who worship themselves and do not break the law and Satanists who engage in murder. While there are Satanists who kill in the name of Satan, there is no evidence that SRA exists as an epidemic. Contrary to popular evangelical views, there are not fifty thousand ritual murders committed every year in North America. This figure has been discredited through the work of Ken Lanning, who spent many years as the lead FBI agent investigating claims of ritual abuse. He found no evidence of a massive network of criminal Satanists.

This is not to say that claims about satanic ritual abuse are impossible to believe. What Lanning's investigation demands is that every alleged instance of ritual abuse be treated on a case-by-case basis so that real instances of crime are distinguished from false allegations. Since false allegations of Satanism can ruin those accused, the testimony of alleged victims needs to be weighed seriously. Ironically, false testimony about SRA involving children has damaged the prosecution of authentic cases of child abuse because of an increased climate of distrust about the testimony of children.

Satanism

HOME PAGES	Church of Satan (Anton LaVey)
	www.churchofsatan.com
	First Satanic Church (Karla LaVey)
	www.satanicchurch.com
	First Church of Satan (John D. Allee, aka Lord Egan)
	www.fcos.us
	Temple of Set (Michael Aquino)
	www.xeper.org
ACADEMIC SITES	David Baldwin's Trauma site
	www.trauma-pages.com
	False Memory Syndrome Foundation
	www.fmsfonline.org
	False Memory Syndrome Facts
	www.fmsf.com
	Jennifer Freyd (psychologist, University of Oregon)
	http://dynamic.uoregon.edu/~jjf
	International Society for the Study of Disassociation
	www.issd.org
	Elizabeth Loftus (psychologist on memory issues)
	www.seweb.uci.edu/faculty/loftus
	PARC-VRAMC (Kathleen and Bill Sullivan)
	www.parc-vramc.tierranet.com
	Ken Pope (psychologist on memory issues)
	www.kspope.com
	Recovered Memories of Sexual Abuse
	www.jimhopper.com
	Recovered Memory Project (Ross Cheit)
	www.recoveredmemory.org
	Anna Salter (psychologist on sexual abuse)
	www.annasalter.com
RITUAL ABUSE	North American Freedom Foundation
	http://naffoundation.org
	SMART (Stop Mind Control and Ritual Abuse Today)
	http://members.aol.com/smartnews/index2.html
	Celebrations of Hope
	www.mikewarnke.org
	Rebecca Brown/Daniel Yoder
	www.harvestwarriors.com
MINISTRY TO	Refuge Ministries (Jeff Harshbarger, ex-Satanist)
SATANISTS	www.refugeministries.cc
OTHER SITES	www.cornerstonemag.com
	Personal Freedom Outreach
	www.pfo.org

READING   Daniel Brown, Alan W. Scheflin, and D. Corydon
               Hammond, *Memory, Trauma Treatment, and the
               Law* (New York: Norton, 2003)
               Paul and Shirley Eberle, *The Abuse of Innocence*
               (Buffalo: Prometheus, 1993)
               Jennifer Freyd, *Betrayal Trauma* (Cambridge: Harvard
               University Press, 1996)
               Robert Hare, *Without Conscience* (New York: Guilford
               Press, 1999)
               Kenneth V. Lanning, *Investigator's Guide to Allegations
               of Ritual Child Abuse* (Quantico, VA: FBI Academy,
               1992)
               Elizabeth Loftus and Katherine Ketcham, *The Myth of
               Repressed Memory* (New York: St. Martin's, 1994)
               Richard McNally, *Remembering Trauma* (Cambridge:
               Harvard University Press, 2003)
               Gareth Medway, *Lure of the Sinister* (New York: New
               York University Press, 2001)
               Debbie Nathan and Michael Snedeker, *Satan's Silence*
               (New York: Basic, 1995)
               Mark Pendergrast, *Victims of Memory* (Hinesburg, VT:
               Upper Access, 1995)
               Richard Ofshe and Ethan Watters, *Making Monsters*
               (New York: Scribner's, 1994)
               James T. Richardson, Joel Best, and David G. Bromley,
               eds., *The Satanism Scare* (New York: De Gruyter, 1991)
               Martha Rogers, guest editor, "Special Issue: Satanic
               Ritual Abuse," *Journal of Psychology and Theology* 20,
               no. 3 (fall 1992)
               David K. Sakheim and Susie E. Devine, *Out of Darkness*
               (New York: Lexington, 1992)
               Lenore Terr, *Unchained Memories* (New York: Basic, 1994).
               Jon Trott and Mike Hertenstein, *Selling Satan: The
               Tragic History of Mike Warnke* (Chicago:
               Cornerstone, 1993)
               Reinder Van Til, *Lost Daughters* (Grand Rapids, MI:
               Eerdmans, 1997)
               Lawrence Wright, *Remembering Satan* (New York:
               Random House, 1994)

▶ Scientology

The Church of Scientology is one of the most controversial new religious movements. The church has been involved in many major legal cases involving its tax-exempt status, its claim to be a religion, and its perceived threats to traditional medicine. The claims of Scientologists and the counterclaims of critics are so diametrically opposed to one another that it is difficult to sort through the competing views and get beyond extreme rhetoric about the church.

L. Ron Hubbard, a well-known writer, started the church in 1954. Born in 1911 in Tilden, Nebraska, he traveled widely in his youth and during his two years as a student at Georgetown University. He saw distinguished Navy service in World War II. After the war, he had contact with Jack Parsons, a disciple of Aleister Crowley, the famous occult leader. Hubbard developed an interest in the human unconscious and explored this topic in his most famous work, *Dianetics,* which was published in 1950.

During Hubbard's tenure as leader, the church was attacked by government agencies in the United States, England, and Australia. Hubbard founded the Guardian's Office (GO) in 1966 to protect the church. However, the GO engaged in illegal activities in the 1970s that resulted in a massive raid on the church by the FBI on July 7, 1977. Several top Scientologists went to jail, including Hubbard's wife, Mary Sue. Following the trial, the church went through a major reorganization in order to prevent similar illegal activity. Hubbard died in 1986.

Under its current leader, David Miscavige, the Church of Scientology has experienced major gains and significant setbacks. Scientology was featured in a major exposé by *Time* magazine in 1991 but won tax exemption from the IRS in 1993. Two years later Lisa McPherson, a church member, died at the Scientology headquarters in Clearwater, Florida, and her death created significant controversy for the church. Hollywood stars have brought prestige to Scientology, though Tom Cruise created negative publicity in the summer of 2005 because of his attack on psychiatry.

Scientology claims that humans are essentially spiritual beings. This is expressed in the belief that we are more than mind and body. Scientology teaches that human beings are really *thetans*, a term that expresses belief that humans are immortal. Our knowledge of our true identity as thetans has been blocked by a complex set of causes. Scientology calls the process of freeing the spirit/thetan of its encumbrances and reaching its true potential the "the bridge to freedom."

One of the goals along the bridge is to become "clear." This state is reached through a dual process of taking Scientology classes and engaging in a process of counseling called "auditing." In these auditing sessions Scientologists use a device known as an *e-meter*, which they believe keeps track of the workings of the inner spirit (or thetan). After a person has reached clear, instruction and counseling continue to assist the individual to attain the ultimate goal—to become an *operating thetan*, or OT. Currently, Scientology offers eight levels of OT. Amid the large body of instructional materials for the OT levels, one set of documents is viewed as confidential and sacred by Scientologists. The church has sought to keep this material off the Internet.

Scientology is a modern form of Gnosticism. Though Scientologists claim no incompatibility with Christian faith, this new religion essentially offers an alternate understanding of reality. For example, the Scientology story about Xenu (the head of a galactic federation of planets) causing thetans to be implanted in humans about 95 million years ago is distinct from the Christian narrative of creation and the Fall. Most important, the lack of focus in Scientology on Jesus Christ is proof that Scientology views and practices offer a different frame of reference than does Christian faith.

The battle over Scientology is so nasty that careful analysis is necessary to sort through false claims, wild rhetoric, and biased views. However, despite the controversy, three things are clear in terms of overall reaction to Scientology. First, in spite of what some critics argue it is obvious that Scientology is a religion. This understanding provides the best explanation for the zeal and commitment of its members and leaders. Second, the sacred texts of the Church of Scientology should be granted standard copyright protection. Finally, Scientologists deserve to be granted the same freedom to exercise their religion as members of other faiths.

Time Line of Scientology

1911	LRH is born on March 13 in Tilden, Nebraska
1924	Lives in state of Washington
1927	Visits China—1927 & 1928 (father in Guam)
1929	Studies at Swavely Prep School in Virginia
1930	Attends Woodward School for Boys
	Joins Marine Reserve in May (discharged Oct. 22, 1931)
	Studies at George Washington University
1933	Marries Margaret Louise Grubb on April 13
1934	Birth of LRH Jr. in May
1941	War duty through April 1945
1945	Meets Jack Parsons in California
1946	Marries Sara Northrup on August 10
1950	Birth of Alexis Valerie Hubbard on March 8; *Dianetics* published
1951	Divorce from Sara
1952	Marries Mary Sue Whipp
1954	Church of Scientology founded on February 18
1959	LRH Jr. leaves Scientology
1962	LRH writes JFK
1963	FDA raids Washington Church on January 4
1966	British Inquiry; John McMaster becomes first Clear; Guardian's Office founded
1968	Release of OT IV-VII
1971	Death of Susan Meister
	John Foster report
	Paulette Cooper, *The Scandal of Scientology*
1973	Rehabilitation Project Force
1975	Move to Clearwater
1976	Suicide of Quentin Hubbard
1977	FBI raid on Scientology offices on July 7
1978	Resort built at Gilman Hot Springs
1982	Religious Technology Center incorporated; *Battlefield Earth* released
1983	Raid on Toronto church in March
1984	IRS rules against Church on tax exemption

1986	LRH dies at 8 p.m. Friday January 24; Wollersheim wins court case
1988	OT VIII released
1990	*Los Angeles Times* does six part series Narconon New Life Center opens in Chilocco, Oklahoma
1991	Time cover story on Scientology (May 6) David Miscavige meets with IRS Commissioner
1992	Ted Koppel interviews Miscavige on *Nightline* Celebrity Center opened in Hollywood
1993	IRS grants tax exempt status
1994	Vicki Aznaran settles lawsuit with Church
1995	Death of Lisa McPherson
1996	Karin Spaink wins Internet case
1997	*Wall St. Journal* reports on IRS tax settlement
1999	British government denies charity status to Scientology
2000	Keith Henson charged with bomb threa; Lisa McPherson's death ruled accidental
2004	McPherson civil case settled
2005	Media storm over Tom Cruise's attack on psychiatry

Church of Scientology

TYPOLOGY	Western esoteric
HOME PAGES	Scientology
	www.scientology.org
	Religious Technology Center
	www.rtc.org
	L. Ron Hubbard
	www.lronhubbard.org
	Dianetics
	www.dianetics.org
	Narconon
	www.narconon.org
	Freedom Magazine
	www.freedommag.org
CRITIC SITES	*Special note:* I have listed below the most famous sites that are critical of Scientology. While I share many of the concerns mentioned on these sites, I urge readers to be cautious in accepting the claims of critics and the counterclaims of Scientology without further study.
	Operation Clambake (Andreas Heldal-Lund)
	www.xenu.net

Secrets of Scientology (Dave Touretzky)
www-2.cs.cmu.edu/~dst/Secrets/

Arnie Lerma
www.lermanet.com

Tilman Hausherr
http://home.snafu.de/tilman/

Scientology Watch
http://scientologywatch.org

Stop Narconon
http://stop-narconon.org/

About Lisa McPherson
www.lisamcpherson.com/

Gerry Armstrong
www.gerryarmstrong.org

Fact Net
www.factnet.org

Steve Fishman
www.xs4all.nl/~fishman

Xenu TV (Mark Bunker)
http://xenutv.bogie.nl

Narconon Exposed (Chris Owen)
www-2.cs.cmu.edu/~dst/Narconon

A.R.S Webpage Summary
www.altreligionscientology.org

READING

From Scientology
The Scientology Handbook (Los Angeles: Bridge, 1994)
What Is Scientology? (Los Angeles: Bridge, 1998)

Other reading
Jon Atack, *A Piece of Blue Sky* (New York: Lyle Stuart, 1990).
Stewart Lamont, *Religions Inc.* (London: Harrap, 1986)
J. Gordon Melton, *The Church of Scientology* (Salt Lake City: Signature, 2000)
Russell Miller, *Bare-faced Messiah* (New York: Henry Holt, 1987)

▶ Seventh-day Adventism

Seventh-day Adventist identity lies in three key notions: (a) the Bible predicts 1844 as the time when Jesus would begin an investigative judgment in the heavenly realm, (b) Christians should worship on the Sabbath, and (c) Ellen G. White is a prophet for the end-time church. Adventists are also known for their emphasis on vegetarianism and obedience to relevant Old Testament laws.

Historically, there has been considerable tension between Seventh-day Adventism and the evangelical Christian community. Relations between evangelicals and Seventh-day Adventists improved considerably through the dialogue that took place between Adventists and Donald Barnhouse and Walter Martin in the 1950s. In the last twenty-five years there has been an increase of suspicion about Seventh-day Adventism by evangelicals. This has come in part because of the handling of research from Desmond Ford and Walter Rea, two prominent scholars within the Adventist tradition.

Given the clear commitment to essential Christian doctrines, as expressed in their Fundamental Beliefs, Seventh-day Adventists should be regarded as a community of faith in essential agreement with evangelical Christianity. Adventists should be admired for their emphasis on healthy living and obedience to the ethical principles of the Old Testament. Additionally, the writings of Mrs. White deserve praise for their biblical flavor and commitment to Christ as Savior and Lord.

Evangelical Christians should also note the following concerns about key issues in Adventist doctrine and ethos:

1. The continued emphasis on 1844 as a significant date in biblical prophecy marks the weakest component in Adventist doctrine. William Miller predicted the end of the world in 1844 and was wise enough to admit his error. Unfortunately, Seventh-day Adventists

tried to rescue the prophecy by saying that it was really about the beginning of an investigative judgment in heaven by Jesus.

2. The Adventist emphasis on Ellen G. White as a prophet is not warranted, given her false teaching on certain medical issues and her mistaken prophecies. Further, it is obvious that she plagiarized from other Christians. She even claimed divine inspiration for sections of her books that were copied without credit. This has been documented beyond doubt by Walter Rea in his work *The White Lie*.

3. Adventist focus on the Law often leads to works righteousness in the movement, a fact readily evident in the testimonies of ex-members. Obedience to the commands of God is a necessary part of Christian life, but the Adventist emphasis on Sabbath keeping, Old Testament food laws, and so on can easily overshadow the doctrine of salvation by grace alone.

4. The Seventh-day Adventist love for the Second Coming of Jesus is to be admired. However, this great reality is marred by an unhealthy focus on eschatology, particularly given the ways in which Adventists write themselves into the center of God's end-time work.

5. The leadership of the Seventh-day Adventist Church has failed to address core weaknesses in their ideology. They have defended Ellen G. White at all costs. Adventist scholars who dare to question key items of Adventist doctrine are dismissed, ignored, or sidelined. This was particularly true with Desmond Ford and his case against the theory of investigative judgment. Some Adventist scholars have argued that Church leaders broke their promises about granting Ford a safe and fair hearing in 1980 when they processed his research.

Seventh-day Adventism

TYPOLOGY	Christian Protestant
KEY LEADER	Ellen G. White
HOME PAGES	www.adventist.org
	www.whiteestate.org
CRITIC SITES	The Ellen White Research Project (Dirk Anderson)
	www.ellenwhite.org
	Gary Gent site
	www.ex-sda.com

Seventh-day Adventist Outreach (Mark Martin)
www.sdaoutreach.org

Truth or Fables (Robert Sanders)
www.truthorfables.com

John Cusaac site
www.xsda.net

READING

Questions on Doctrine, annotated ed. (1957; Berrien
    Springs: Andrews University Press, 2003)
Desmond Ford, *Daniel 8:14, The Day of Atonement and
    the Investigative Judgment* (Casselberry, FL:
    Euangelion, 1980)
Gary Land, ed., *Adventism in America* (Grand Rapids,
    MI: Eerdmans, 1986)
Ronald Numbers, *Prophetess of Health* (Knoxville:
    University of Tennessee Press, 1992)
Ronald Numbers and Jonathan Butler, eds., *The
    Disappointed* (Knoxville: University of Tennessee
    Press, 1993)
Geoffrey Paxton, *The Shaking of Adventism* (Grand
    Rapids, MI: Baker, 1977)
Walter Rea, *The White Lie* (Turlock, CA: M & R, 1982)

▸ Shambhala

Shambhala is the Buddhist tradition connected with Chögyam Trungpa Rinpoche (1939–87), one of the most important Tibetan Buddhist masters of modern times. He was considered a *tulku*—a reincarnation of a bodhisattva / deity figure—of the Kagyu lineage, one of the major schools in Tibetan religion. Trungpa was also trained in the Nyingma tradition. He fled Tibet in 1959 and taught for four years in Dalhousie, India. He studied at Oxford University from 1963 through 1966. The next year he founded a Tibetan center in Scotland. In 1969, having abandoned his monastic vows, he married Diana Pybus and immigrated to America.

He founded the Tail of the Tiger (now known as Karme-Choling) meditation center in Vermont. During the 1970s, Trungpa traveled widely and began his unique program of Shambhala training. He also started Naropa University and founded the Gampo Buddhist monastery in Cape Breton, Nova Scotia, Canada. He died in April 1987. Sakyong Mipham Rinpoche (b. 1962), Trungpa's eldest son, now leads Shambhala. He was born Ösel Rangdröl Mukpo but was later viewed as Sakyong (earth protector and dharma-king) and as the reincarnation of Mipham the Great (1846–1912), a revered Tibetan lama.

The Shambhala movement has faced serious criticism about the immoral behavior of Rinpoche and also Osel Tendzin. Tendzin (Thomas F. Rich) was appointed as Trungpa's Vajra Regent, or Dharma heir, in 1976. He created an enormous scandal in 1988 when it was revealed that he had contracted AIDS in 1985 and did not inform his sexual partners about it. John Dart reported on the crisis created by Tendzin in the *Los Angeles Times* on March 3, 1989. Tendzin remained in leadership in the movement until his death in 1990.

Rinpoche was known for his wild excesses involving liquor and sex. Pema Chodron (born Diedre Blomfield-Brown), one of his disciples, admitted in an interview with *Tricycle* magazine that Rinpoche "did not keep ethical norms," and yet she said that her "devotion to him is unshakable." Chodron, who heads the Gampo Abbey, responded about his sexual indiscretions in this way: "I don't know what he was doing. I know he changed my life. I know I love him. But I don't know who he was. And maybe he wasn't doing things to help everyone, but he sure helped me. I learned something from him. But who was that masked man?" She also stated: "I can actually hold my devotion purely and fully in my heart and still say, maybe he was a madman."[17]

Sakyong Mipham Rinpoche became engaged to Semo Tseyang Palmo, the daughter of a famous Tibetan teacher, in May 2005. The Shambhala leader also took part in the Boston marathon the previous month. He is author of *Turning the Mind into an Ally*, which was released in 2004. Like his father, the Sakyong places emphasis on the Buddhist teaching of no-self. "To know the truth is to see the transitory nature of who we are—the selflessness of ourselves and others. It's to see the suffering that comes from imagining we are solid and permanent entities."

Shambhala

TYPOLOGY	Buddhist Tibetan
FOUNDER	Chögyam Trungpa Rinpoche (1939–87)
LEADER	Sakyong Mipham Rinpoche (1962–)
HOME PAGES	www.shambhala.org
	www.mipham.com

▸ Share International

Share International is one of many esoteric groups that became popular during the rise of the New Age movement in the 1970s and 1980s. This group became especially noteworthy because of the strident claims made by founder Benjamin Creme about the emergence of the Christ figure known as Maitreya.

Creme is one of the most important and fascinating figures in New Age circles. He was born in Scotland in 1922 and developed an interest in occult and esoteric writings after World War II. He was particularly shaped by the ideas of one-time Theosophist Alice Bailey, founder of the Lucis Trust and the Arcane School. Creme also had contact with the Aetherius Society, a UFO group.

Creme has concentrated on the appearance of Maitreya, a term borrowed from Buddhism and used of a Christ figure expected by many New Agers. Crème's followers formed the Tara Center and Share International to focus on the message of Maitreya's appearance. In 1974 Creme claimed that Maitreya was providing messages through him about his emergence on the planet. Creme often gave public lectures about "The Reappearance of the Christ."

On April 25, 1982, Creme even placed full-page ads in seventeen newspapers to announce, "The Christ is Now Here." Later, on May 14, he told reporters in London that it was their duty to look for Maitreya, who had taken the form of a Pakistani and was in the Brick Lane area of London. When Maitreya did not appear, Creme cast the blame on the media's apathy. As of 2005, Share International and its leader continue to focus on the soon return of Maitreya.

The movement has this to say about Maitreya: "He has been expected for generations by all of the major religions. Christians know Him as the Christ, and expect His imminent return. Jews await Him as the Messiah; Hindus look for the coming of Krishna; Buddhists expect Him as Maitreya Buddha; and Muslims anticipate the

Imam Mahdi or Messiah. The names may be different, but many believe they all refer to the same individual: the World Teacher, whose name is Maitreya." As is common in the esoteric tradition, Share International makes a distinction between Jesus and the Christ, but uniquely teaches that Jesus, who has lived in Rome since 1984, is a disciple of the Christ force.

Creme teaches that Maitreya is responsible for the fall of Communism, the end of apartheid, the emergence of environmental consciousness, and so forth. Share International expects that Maitreya will be revealed to the whole world in a Day of Declaration. Maitreya will appear on worldwide television, and all humans will be able to hear him telepathically in their own language. This apocalyptic event will include a worldwide experience of miraculous healings.

The Maitreya announcements caused much concern among evangelicals and became a central item in their critique of the New Age during the 1980s. Constance Cumbey's *Hidden Dangers of the Rainbow* (1983) gave particular attention to Creme's pronouncements. It was even popular to suggest that Maitreya fit the description of what the Antichrist would be like. Focus on the New Age as a central element in evangelical eschatology has waned since the resurgence of militant Islam.

Share International

TYPOLOGY	Western esoteric
HOME PAGE	www.shareintl.org

▸ Sidda Yoga

Sidda Yoga is the creation of Swami Muktananda, one of the most famous Hindu gurus of the twentieth century. The movement is maintained now by the Sidda Yoga Dham of America (SYDA). Muktananda, born in 1908, was a disciple of Bhagawan Nityananda (d. 1961). Muktananda brought his teaching to the West in 1970 and started more than six hundred meditation centers in North America and around the world. SYDA is based in South Fallsburg in upper New York State.

Before his death in 1982, Muktananda appointed Malti Shetty (Swami Chidvilasananda) and her brother Subhash (Swami Nityananda) as his successors. In October 1985 Nityananda (b. 1962) was removed as guru after a confrontation with his sister at the group's headquarters in India. This disruption was chronicled in an investigative report by Lis Harris in *The New Yorker* (November 14, 1994). Chidvilasananda (b. 1954) is known affectionately by her followers as Gurumayi. Nityananda now leads his own group (based in Walden, New York), but he and his sister have never reconciled.

Near the end of his life, Muktananda was accused by prominent ex-members of sexual abuse of several female devotees. These criticisms were reported by Harris and by William Rodarmor in "The Secret Life of Swami Muktananda" (*Co-Evolution Quarterly,* winter 1983).

Former member Stan Trout (now Swami Abhayananda) wrote an open letter to Muktananda in 1981 about emotional and sexual abuse. Trout stated to fellow devotees: "I sincerely regret that I must be the bearer of this news, and wish like you that it could all be proven false. I have learned, and I think you will too, that although they are hard, these sad tidings are the key to a future of freedom. And though it's a frightening and lonely vista at first, the initial anger at having been deceived for so long will subside."

Muktananda responded to Trout's accusations by arguing: "Still, this is nothing new. It is a part of the lineage that I belong to. Mansur Mastana was hanged, Jesus was crucified, and all of Tukaram's books were thrown into the river. You should be happy that I am still alive and healthy and that they haven't tried to hang me."

Critics of SYDA continue to focus on sexual abuse by Muktananda. On the other hand, Sarah Caldwell, a Hindu scholar, has sought to defend the sexual practices of the guru through his professed adoption of Tantric sexual rites, an esoteric tradition in both Hinduism and Buddhism. Caldwell was once a disciple of Muktananda. She provides evidence of Muktananda's interest in Tantric teachers and practices and conducted interviews with devotees who had sexual interaction with the famous guru.

Sidda Yoga follows the typical themes of the advaitist, or impersonalist, tradition in Hinduism. The essence of liberation involves realization that the self is divine. This is ultimately experienced through relationship with a guru who can channel divine energy to the devotee. Sidda Yoga refers to spiritual awakening as *shaktipat*, which is achieved by connection with the guru. William Mahoney, a professor of religion and a follower of Gurumayi, states, "The living master, the outer Guru, is a human being who has become totally at one with the Guru tattva, the Guru principle. Totally at one with that power of divine grace, she is identical with divine grace itself. There is no difference between the two. She is the Guru."

Sidda Yoga (Muktananda)

TYPOLOGY	Hindu
CURRENT LEADER	Swami Chidvilasananda (Gurumayi)
HOME PAGE	www.siddhayoga.org
OTHER SITES	www.leavingsiddhayoga.net
	Swami Nityananda site (Gurumayi's estranged brother)
	www.shantimandir.com

▶ Sikhism

Sikhs in North America have faced some bad press in recent years, particularly over events related to the Canadian Sikh community. There have been court battles over whether Sikh police officers can wear their turbans to work and whether Sikh children should be allowed to wear their ceremonial daggers (*kirpan*) to school. A vicious debate in British Columbia over whether chairs and tables should be used in the Sikh temple created an international storm of controversy. Most important, the crash of an Air India flight on June 22, 1985, raised questions about the militancy of the international Sikh community.[18]

Some tensions related to Sikh identity get worked out readily. The Canadian police suffered no great loss when Sikhs officers were granted the right to wear the turban. The debate over using tables was settled when Giani Rattan Singh of Surrey, British Columbia, repented of this radical departure from the traditional Sikh custom of everyone sitting on the floor of the temple.

The question of violence and Sikhism is more complicated, and we need to consider a couple of points in connection with it.

First, the Air India crash was just one part of a broader conflict between militant Sikhs and Hindus that took place two and three decades ago. The Indian government ordered a raid on the Sikh Golden Temple on June 5, 1984, a military action that left many dead. That led to the assassination of Prime Minister Indira Gandhi by two of her Sikh bodyguards. This in turn led to widespread attacks on Sikhs all across India.

Second, violence in the Sikh world has to be seen in the larger context of the religion's founding and history. The Sikh faith is rooted in the work of Guru Nanak, an Indian spiritual reformer. Nanak's religious claims put him at odds with both Hindus and Muslims. These religious differences led to both political hostility and

military campaigns against Sikhs over three centuries. This trail of
oppression and bloodshed led Sikhs to adopt a militant stance against
enemies.

Of course, Sikhs believe that the violence in their tradition does
not represent the essence of Sikhism. Rather, most important is the
belief by Sikhs that Nanak and his nine successors have been given
the ultimate revelation of truth by God. This truth is embodied in
the 1,430-page-long Sikh Bible, known as the *Adi Granth*. The *Adi
Granth* is venerated by all faithful Sikhs and is viewed as the ultimate
Guru.

Sikhs hold that there is one Creator God, who is not to be represented in images or idols. The highest spiritual duty is to praise God,
particularly in song and recitation of scripture, and to obey his commands. The faithful Sikh will follow what are known as the five k's:
(1) *kes*, uncut hair; (2) *kirpan*, wearing of dagger; (3) *kara*, wearing of
steel bracelet; (4) *kangha*, wearing of comb; and (5) *kachh*, wearing of
holy garments.

Orthodox Sikhs will not depart from the teachings of the ten
gurus. They place great emphasis upon the miracle stories connected
with Nanak and several of the other gurus. Scholars who question
the historicity of these miracles are viewed as destroyers of the faith.
Likewise, scholars such as W. H. McLeod who are skeptical about the
alleged inerrancy of the *Adi Granth* are dismissed with derision by
most Sikhs. According to orthodox Sikhs, questions should not even
be raised about the original text of the Sikh Bible.

Guru Nanak opposed the Hindu caste system and Muslim
emphasis upon pilgrimage to Mecca. He did retain the Hindu doctrine of karma and reincarnation. Sikhs believe that this life represents an opportunity to escape the cycle of death and rebirth.
Though Sikhism attributes great weight to the work of the ten gurus,
the religion generally has no clergy class. A body known as the Shri-
mani Gurudwara Prabandhah Committee, based in Amritsar, settles
issues in belief and practice.

In the last century Sikhs have maintained significant unity. However, this has come as a result of the suppression of Sikh traditions

and groups opposed to the powerful Tat Khalsa movement that came to dominate Sikh life in the last quarter of the nineteenth century. The Tat Khalsa leaders won control of the Golden Temple and the other major centers of Sikh life in India. Other Sikh traditions continued in spite of Tat Khalsa power, and the twentieth century witnessed the emergence of a few new Sikh groups. The most notable is the 3HO (the Healthy, Happy, Holy Organization), founded by the controversial guru Yogi Bhajan, who died in October 2004.

Sikh life centers in the gurdwaras, which are open to anyone as long as simple rules are obeyed. Shoes are to be removed and feet are to be washed before entering the gurdwara. On a personal note, I visited the Golden Temple, one evening and also the next afternoon in the summer of 2000. It is an amazing religious site. I witnessed firsthand the provision of free food for all visitors and witnessed the elaborate procession of the Sikh Bible being stored away for the night.

The Ten Sikh Gurus

1. Guru Nanak (1469–1539)
2. Guru Angad (1504–52)
3. Guru Amar Das (1479–1574)
4. Guru Ram Das (1534–81)
5. Guru Arjan (1563–1606)
6. Guru Hargobind (1595–1644)
7. Guru Hari Rai (1630–61)
8. Guru Hari Krishan (1656–64)
9. Guru Tegh Bahadur (1621–75)
10. Guru Gobind Singh (1666–1708)

Sikhism

FOUNDER	Guru Nanak (1469–1539)
HOME PAGES	www.sikhs.org
	http://thesikhencyclopedia.com
	http://allaboutsikhs.com
	www.sikhnet.com
READING	Hew McLeod, *Sikhism* (London: Penguin, 1997)
	Pashaura Singh and N. Gerald Barrier, eds., *Sikhism and History* (New Delhi: Oxford University Press, 2004)

▶ Solar Temple

The Order of the Solar Temple represents the darker side of new religious movements. This esoteric movement was started by Joseph Di Mambro (1924–94), a French citizen who had a background in the Rosicrucian Order AMORC (Ancient and Mystical Order Rosae Crucis) from 1956 through the late 1960s. Di Mambro started several esoteric groups in the 1970s and moved to Geneva with his followers in 1978. The Solar Temple group started in 1984. It was rooted, ideologically, in modern-day revivals of the medieval Knights Templar under Jacques Breyer and Raymond Bernard.

Di Mambro taught that his daughter Emmanuelle would become the chief spiritual guide for humanity. He also deceived followers by using hidden technology in rituals to convince them that they alone could see the masters who guided Di Mambro. The "masters" were actually holographic images.

In October 1994 fifty-three members perished in Switzerland and the Canadian province of Quebec—fifteen committed suicide and thirty-eight were murdered. The murder victims included a young Canadian couple, Tony and Nicki Dutoit, and their three-month-old baby. Tony was the chief technologist of the group and had started speaking about the use of holographs to deceive members. The couple disobeyed Di Mambro's command that they not have a child and even named him Christopher Emmanuel—a not-so-subtle reference to the founder's daughter. Di Mambro referred to the child as the Antichrist and ordered his execution, along with his parents.

Sixteen more followers died in France in December 1995, and five more perished in Quebec in March 1997. The three separate tragedies have led to much speculation about the group, including the claim that Princess Grace of Monaco was connected with the movement.[19]

Writings from Di Mambro and Jouret that survived show two leaders consumed with their self-importance and their belief that the death of the group would awaken the world to the group's sacrificial mission. "We are the Star Seeds that guarantee the perennial existence of the universe, we are the hand of God that shapes creation. We are the Torch that Christ must bring to the Father to feed the Primordial Fire and to reanimate the forces of Life, which, without our contribution, would slowly but surely go out. We hold the key to the universe and must secure its Eternity."

The apocalyptic ending of the Solar Temple leaders was impacted by ongoing financial difficulties, defections of key members, police investigations, and internal dissent over the nature and direction of the group. In the end, however, Solar Temple members lived out, through death, their group's philosophy. An internal document gave this as a hope: "Like the Phoenix We might be reborn from our ashes. Through the Sword of Light . . . Raised toward the Levels Above, what is refined should depart from the world of density . . . And ascend toward its Point of Origin."

In June 2001 Michel Tabachnik, a music conductor, was acquitted of murder charges related to the sixteen deaths of Solar Temple members that took place in the Vecors region of France in December 1995. Tabachnik claimed that he had left the Solar Temple in 1992, two years before the first suicides in Switzerland in October 1994.

Solar Temple	
TYPOLOGY	Western esoteric
FOUNDER	Joseph Di Mambro
READING	James R. Lewis, "The Solar Temple Transits," in James R. Lewis and Jesper Aagaard Petersen, eds., *Controversial New Religions* (New York: Oxford University Press, 2005)
	Jean-François Mayer, "Our Terrestrial Journey Is Coming to an End," *Nova Religio* (April 1999)
	Catherine Wessinger, *How the Millennium Comes Violently* (New York: Seven Bridges, 2000)

▶ Spiritualism

Spiritualism is traced to the alleged psychic powers of the Fox sisters (Margaret, Kate, and Leah) of Hydesville, New York, thirty-five miles east of Rochester. In 1848, Margaret, then fourteen, and her younger sister, Kate (age twelve), claimed that disturbing noises in their house were made by a spirit who would answer questions from the girls by tapping on the walls. The Fox family claimed that the spirit was that of Charles B. Rosna, a peddler who had been murdered in the house five years earlier. Margaret and Kate became national celebrities and were joined by their older sister, Leah.

Both Margaret and Kate struggled with alcoholism in later years. Leah died in 1890, Kate in 1892, and Margaret a year later. The Fox home is now owned by the National Spiritualist Association of Churches (NSAC). The NSAC is the oldest Spiritualist organization, founded in 1893 in Chicago. In 1899 the organization adopted a Declaration of Principles. The fifth principle states, "We affirm that communication with the so-called dead is a fact, scientifically proven by the phenomena of Spiritualism."

Since 1848 Spiritualism has mainly been identified by its individual practitioners. The most famous is Edgar Cayce. Born in Kentucky in 1877, Cayce gave his first "reading," or medium session, in 1901 after recovery from laryngitis. He worked as a photographer until his popularity as a medium demanded all his time and energy. Cayce gave more than fourteen thousand "readings" during his lifetime. He started the Association for Research and Enlightenment in Virginia Beach, Virginia, in 1931.

Cayce would normally do a reading while lying on a couch with his hands folded across his stomach. He would enter a self-induced sleep state and then respond to questions. Cayce believed that this psychic activity and belief in reincarnation were compatible with his Christian faith. He died in 1945.

One of the most famous modern psychics is James Van Praagh. He claims that he is able to "bridge the gap between two planes of existence, that of the living and that of the dead, by providing evidential proof of life after death via detailed messages." He calls himself a "telephone to the spirit world." After its publication in 2001, his book *Talking to Heaven* topped the best-seller list of the *New York Times*, boosted by the author's repeated appearances on major television talk shows.

A native of Queens, New York, Van Praagh was raised in a staunch Roman Catholic home but by his teen years had dismissed Catholicism as an "archaic belief system." He moved to Los Angeles after high school and worked on the fringes of show business, all the while developing the psychic abilities he says every human possesses. Van Praagh claims that his paranormal gifts were evident from his earliest years. For instance, he says that he told his first-grade teacher about injuries her son had sustained in a car crash moments before she received first news of the accident.

Van Praagh promotes Hindu teaching on karma and reincarnation. Believing each human is "perfect if we would only seek our divinity," he invites his admirers to explore the spirit world through attending séances and use of the Ouija board. He also promotes a range of practices, such as having one's aura read and developing one's *chakras* (alleged spiritual power points within the body). In *Reaching to Heaven* Van Praagh adopts the New Age message of the power of the mind. He illustrates this by writing, "If our thoughts dwell on poverty and illness, we will draw these conditions to us. If we elevate our thoughts to a higher frequency level, we will reap harmony and abundance. This is a fixed universal law that cannot be changed."

Spiritualism

TYPOLOGY	Western esoteric
HOME PAGES	National Spiritualist Association of Churches
	www.nsac.org
	Spiritualist National Union (UK)
	www.snu.org.uk

Association for Research and Enlightenment
www.edgarcayce.org

James Van Praagh
www.vanpraagh.com

CRITICAL SITES   CSICOP
www.csicop.org

Society for Psychical Research
www.spr.ac.uk

American Society of Psychical Research
www.aspr.com

READING   Ruth Brandon, *The Spiritualists* (New York: Knopf, 1983)

Martin Gardner, *Science: Good, Bad, and Bogus* (New
York: Avon, 1981)

James Randi, *Flim Flam* (Buffalo: Prometheus, 1982)

▶ Swedenborgianism

Swedenborgians trace their faith to scientist and religious leader Emanuel Swedenborg, who was born in Stockholm in 1688 and died in London in 1772. Swedenborg had a reputation as a man of letters and was involved in the political life of his country. His early work for Sweden earned him a pension from the king when he made the transition to the study of spiritual issues.

His life was changed in 1743 and 1744 when he is said to have received contact from the spiritual realm. Within two years he claimed regular communication with angelic beings. Out of this alleged divine revelation Swedenborg wrote prolifically. By 1756 he finished the twelve volumes of *Arcana Coelestia* (Heavenly Secret), which provided an esoteric commentary on Genesis and Exodus. He also wrote *Heaven and Hell* (1758), *Treatise on the Four Doctrines* (1760–61), *Conjugal Love* (1768), and many other books. The American edition of his works runs to thirty volumes.

Swedenborg remained discreet about his spiritual writings for many years. He wrote his books in Latin. It was only after he became known as a clairvoyant that attention was drawn to him as an author. His followers claim that, through psychic powers, he saw a fire that destroyed parts of Stockholm in 1759. Swedenborg did not start a church in his own country and tried to protect those who were charged with heresy for adopting his views. Though Swedenborgians often claim complete originality for him, there is evidence that he was influenced by Kabbalism, the esoteric Jewish tradition.

Swedenborg's influence went far beyond the boundaries of the several churches devoted to his teaching. His emphasis on esoteric interpretation of Christianity, use of inner revelation, and appeal to the angelic realm attracted considerable interest across Europe and particularly in London. His belief that esoteric religion can be rational was a comfort to many religious leaders in a time when

Enlightenment rationalism was undermining faith. He had an influence on Johann Wolfgang von Goethe, Immanuel Kant, William Blake, and Ralph Waldo Emerson.

Swedenborg's views also impacted early leaders in American Spiritualism, and he played a part in the development of New Thought and the broader esoteric traditions of the late nineteenth century. Zen teacher D. T. Suzuki referred to Swedenborg as "the Buddha of the north." The most famous Swedenborgians are Helen Keller and John Chapman. Chapman (1774–1845) spread Swedenborg's teaching as he planted apple trees in the Midwest. We know him as "Johnny Appleseed."

Swedenborg's theology contrasts with Christian orthodoxy at several crucial points. His understanding of the Trinity denies the affirmations of the Nicene Creed. He also taught that the Last Judgment took place in 1757 and that a New Church began in 1770, representing the Second Coming of Christ. He adopted an allegorical interpretation of the Bible, avoiding the literal or plain sense of the text. Further, his understanding of Christian faith was based on private revelation—a fact that makes Christian truth hinge on the subjective experiences of one person. This is a dangerous method for Christian theology and philosophy.

Swedenborgianism

TYPOLOGY	Western esoteric
HOME PAGES	The Swedenborg Foundation
	www.swedenborg.com Swedenborg Online
	www.heavenlydoctrines.org Swedenborgian Church of North America (Newtonville, Mass.)
	www.swedenborg.org New Church/General Church of the New Jerusalem (Bryn Athyn, Pa.)
	www.newchurch.org The Lord's New Church Which Is Nova Hierosolyma
READING	http://novahierosolyma.org Ernst Benz, *Emanuel Swedenborg,* trans. Nicholas Goodrick-Clarke (West Chester, PA: Swedenborg Foundation, 2002)

▶ Taoism

Taoism (also spelled Daoism) is one of the most complex of the world religions because of controversial issues related to its history and nature.

Taoism is traced to Laozi (Lao-tzu in the older Wade-Giles spelling), said to have lived in the sixth century before Christ. Scholars of Taoism either doubt his existence or believe that the popular legends about him have little historical value. There is even debate about whether Laozi is a person's name, since it can be translated "Old Master." Tradition states, however, that Laozi is the author of the *Tao-te Ching* (or *Daodejing*), one of the most widely translated texts in history. Again according to Taoist tradition, Laozi was a court archivist who lived at the same time as Confucius. In the more religious strand of Taoism, Laozi is viewed as a deity.

The second-best-known Taoist text is the *Zhuangzi*, which is also the name of the alleged author. Zhuangzi is said to have lived about 300 BC The current text associated with him dates from the fourth century AD, and so it is impossible to know for sure what can be traced to Zhuangzi. Most scholars view the *Zhuangzi* as a composite text. One scholar, W. C. Graham, believes that five separate voices frame the work as we know it today.

Taoism first appeared as an overt religious movement with the emergence of the Way of the Celestial Master in the second century AD From then until the rise of Communism, Taoism retained an ideological hold in Chinese life and culture and was often the preferred religion of Chinese rulers. During the Cultural Revolution, many Taoist temples were destroyed.

In both the *Tao-te Ching* and *Zhuangzi* there is frequent discussion of the Way. Tao or Dao is usually translated as "Way." The famous opening line of the *Tao-te-Ching* (which means "Classic of the Way") reads, "The Way that can be spoken of is not the constant Way."

There is no unanimity on the meaning of the "Way" in either Taoist tradition or among scholars of the religion. Is Taoism essentially religious, philosophical, ethical, or political? Alan Chan argues in his entry on Laozi in *The Stanford Encyclopedia of Philosophy* that "such categories form a unified whole in Daoist thinking and are deemed separate and distinct only in Western thought."

It is usually argued that "the Way" ultimately refers both to a path of ethics and to the ultimate source of reality. Chinese tradition often refers to the Dao as the source for *qi*, or energy, and for the cosmic forces of *yin* and *yang*. Dao is more concretely understood as a moral path for humanity, and this emphasis is dominant in Confucian usage of the term. If Dao is understood as something akin to a Creator, this is not to be understood in the sense of a personal God but rather as a supernatural force. The transcendence of the Dao is best captured by the fact that the term *Dao* is often associated with the classical Chinese notion of *Wu*, or nothingness.

Taoism

WEB SITES
Daoist Studies (James Miller), www.daoiststudies.org
Fabrizio Pregadio, http://venus.unive.it/pregadio
Russell Kirkland
www.arches.uga.edu/~kirkland
Taoism Information Page (Gene Thursby)
www.clas.ufl.edu/users/gthursby/taoism
Chad Hensen Chinese Philosophy Page
http://www.hku.hk/philodep/ch

READING
Livia Kohn, ed., *Daoist Handbook* (Leiden: Brill, 2000)
Livia Kohn, *Daoism and Chinese Culture* (Cambridge, MA: Three Pines, 2001)
Stephen Little, ed., *Taoism and the Arts of China* (Chicago: Art Institute of Chicago, 2000).
James Miller, *Daoism: A Short Introduction* (Oxford: Oneworld, 2003).
Fabrizio Pregadio, ed., *The Encyclopedia of Taoism* (London: Curzon, forthcoming)
Isabelle Robinet, *Taoism: Growth of a Religion* (Stanford, CA: Stanford University Press, 1997)
Liu Xiaogan, "Taoism," in Arvind Sharma, ed., *Our Religions* (San Francisco: HarperCollins, 1993)

▸ Thelema (Aleister Crowley)

Thelema, a Greek word that means "will" or "volition," is the term given to the religious philosophy of Aleister Crowley and the movements connected to him. Crowley had only a small following during his lifetime, but his occult views are now espoused by many groups, and he had a significant impact on Gerald Gardner, the founder of modern witchcraft.

Aleister Crowley was born on October 12, 1875, in England. He came from a wealthy and religious home. His parents were members of the Plymouth Brethren, one of the most conservative Christian groups. Crowley attended Cambridge but did not graduate. In 1898 he joined the Hermetic Order of the Golden Dawn, an occult group, but was forced out two years later by W. B. Yeats. In 1903 Crowley married Rose Kelly. The next year he traveled to Egypt with his wife.

Crowley and his disciples believe that he received supernatural dictation over a three-day period beginning on April 8, 1904. The material received became known as the *Liber Al vel Legis*, or Book of the Law. This work contains Crowley's most famous phrase: "Do what thou wilt shalt be the whole of the law." Crowley believed that the revelation in Egypt marked a new age for humanity, with Crowley as its chief prophet. He viewed his Thelemic philosophy as Magick (spelled with a *k* to differentiate it from mundane stage magic).

In 1910 Crowley developed connections to the Ordo Templi Orientis (OTO), an occult group founded in 1902 by Carl Kellner and Theodor Reuss, and eventually became its OHO (Outer Head of the Order). His first marriage ended in 1909. After his divorce he continued to travel widely, including in the United States. He settled in Sicily for several years. While there he wrote *Diary of a Drug Fiend*, one of his most controversial works. Mussolini kicked him out of Italy in 1923 after the death of Raoul Loveday, one of his students. He remarried in 1929, but his remaining years were fraught with poor health and financial woes. He died in England on December 1, 1947.

Crowley deliberately challenged the traditional mores of his time. He wrote pornography, referred to himself as a Satanist, engaged in multiple affairs with both sexes, and stated that he was the Great Beast 666. He composed the Gnostic Mass as an alternative to the Catholic Mass. Crowley taught that the greatest spiritual transformation occurs through Sex Magick and radicalized the sex rites found in the Ordo Templi Orientis. Three of the OTO degrees created by Crowley celebrate auto-eroticism, vaginal sex, and anal sex. Crowley even seemed to believe that his Sex Magick could create a divine child.

Since Crowley's death, there have been extended ideological and legal battles over which group is the proper heir to the OTO name. This story is convoluted because of ambiguity in Crowley's directives to his leading disciples and the complexities of intellectual debate about the major claimants to Crowley's throne. The top claimants are usually said to be Gerald McMurtry (1918–85), Kenneth Grant (1924–), and Marcelo Ramos Motta (1931–87).

Several U.S. court decisions have recognized McMurtry as the legal heir to Crowley's OTO, and this branch is certainly the largest. McMurtry was succeeded at his death by Frater Hymenaeus Beta, now considered head of the OTO. The U.S. branch of the OTO is led by Sabazius X. The OTO carries on its public worship through the Ecclesia Gnostica Catholica, which is the liturgical branch of Crowley's movement.

Thelema (Aleister Crowley)

FOUNDER	Aleister Crowley (1875–1947)
HOME PAGE	U.S.A. Grand Lodge (OTO) http://oto-usa.org
RESOURCE SITES	www.thelemapedia.org http://user.cyberlink.ch/~koenig www.93current.de www.redflame93.com
READING	Richard Kaczynski, *Perdurabo: The Life of Aleister Crowley* (Tempe, AZ: New Falcon, 2002) Lawrence Sutin, *Do What Thou Wilt* (New York: St. Martin's, 2002)

▸ Theosophy

Theosophy is one of the most significant religious movements of the nineteenth century. It is always associated with Helena Petrova Blavatsky. She has had a singular impact on the ideology behind New Age spirituality, even though she died almost a century before New Age became a recognized term.

HPB (as she is often known) was born in 1831 in the Ukraine and was raised in an upper-class family in Russia. Her mother died when Helena was entering her teen years, and she married a General Blavatsky when she was sixteen. After three months, she left him and then traveled the world for two decades.

She had early interests in the occult and was associated in 1858 with Daniel D. Home, a prominent medium in France. She dabbled in other forms of Spiritualism for more than a decade. After moving to New York in 1873, she had some contact with William and Horatio Eddy, two of America's leading Spiritualists. The impact of Spiritualism on Blavatsky was considerable. She would spend the rest of her life telling her own version of contact with the spiritual realm.

Madame Blavatsky claimed to transmit messages from the Great White Brotherhood, the ascended masters who guide humanity. Blavatsky taught that her messages usually came from two beings: Master El Morya and Master Koot Hoomi. Theosophists do not view the masters as angelic beings but rather as individuals who have completed the cycles of reincarnation. Also, there is nothing racist implied in the use of the word "White" in reference to the brotherhood.

Blavatsky claimed that she learned about the ascended masters through her travels in Egypt and Tibet. Her theories show knowledge of Buddhist thought and Egyptian mythology, though critics have doubted her credibility both on whether she actually traveled in Tibet and on her ideology as a whole. Her thought gives place to both Buddha and Jesus, though not in typical Buddhist or Christian fashion. The historical Jesus is identified with the eternal spirit Bodhisattva Maitreya, who is head of the love/wisdom department of the brotherhood.

Blavatsky founded the Theosophical Society in 1875 in cooperation with Henry Steel Olcott and William Q. Judge. Blavatsky's *Isis Unveiled* was released in 1877. The next year she and Olcott moved to India and settled in Adyar, near Madras, in 1882. They had a working relationship with a Hindu group until Blavatsky was suspected of trickery.

In 1884 Emma Cutting Coulomb, a longtime confidante, charged Blavatsky with making fraudulent claims about having psychic power. Richard Hodgson investigated Coulomb's charges on behalf of the Society for Psychical Research. In December 1885 Hodgson wrote a damning report against Blavatsky that plagued her for the rest of her life and continues to affect the image of the Theosophical Society to the present.[20]

In 1887 Blavatsky settled in London and worked on her book *The Secret Doctrine*, which was published two years later. She died on May 8, 1891. Theosophy underwent schism after Blavatsky's death. One group, following Olcott, has its headquarters in India, while the other, following Judge, established headquarters in Pasadena, California. Theosophy has formed the ideological basis for many esoteric movements not formally connected with the two major Theosophical groups.

Theosophy

TYPOLOGY	Western esoteric
MAJOR FIGURE	Helena Petrova Blavatsky (1831–91)
HOME PAGES	http://ts-adyar.org (India-based group)
	www.theosociety.org (Pasadena-based group)
OTHER SITES	www.blavatskyarchives.com
	www.blavatsky.net
	www.theohistory.org (James A. Santucci)
READING	Peter Washington, *Madame Blavatsky's Baboon* (New York: Schocken, 1995)
	K. Paul Johnson, *The Masters Revealed* (Albany: State University of New York Press, 1994)

▶ Toronto Blessing

The term *Toronto Blessing* refers to the charismatic renewal that started at the former Toronto Airport Vineyard Church on January 20, 1994. In late 1995 and early 1996 the church left the Association of Vineyard Churches and became known as the Toronto Airport Christian Fellowship (TACF). Pastors John and Carol Arnott, a husband-wife team, lead the congregation.

The blessing renewal began under the ministry of Randy Clark, a Vineyard pastor from St. Louis, who was holding a revival campaign in early 1994. Clark outlined his own experience of spiritual awakening through the work of Rodney Howard-Browne, a Pentecostal evangelist from South Africa, who now heads Revival Ministries International in Tampa, Florida. Howard-Browne gained renown through the "holy laughter" that characterized his revival meetings.

The initial campaign in Toronto continued after Clark returned to St. Louis. The blessing gained international attention as news spread throughout the charismatic Christian world about a supernatural revival in Toronto. By the summer and fall of 1994, thousands were flocking to Toronto for the meetings held six nights every week. *Toronto Life* magazine billed the blessing as the top tourist attraction of 1994. Visitors continued to come to Toronto by the thousands from every part of the globe throughout 1995 and early 1996. Since then, TACF has focused more on special conferences and on travel to various countries to export the renewal.

From the outset of the renewal, critics such as Hank Hanegraaff, author of *Counterfeit Revival*, accused TACF leaders of using hypnotism and psychological control to manipulate the crowds into bouts of laughing, shaking, rolling on the floor, moaning, groaning, crying, and falling down (known as being "slain in the Spirit"). What drew particular concern from Vineyard leader John Wimber were episodes of people acting or sounding like animals during the worship services.

In early 1996 TACF formed Partners in Harvest, a nondenominational organization that seeks to unite charismatic ministries and churches. There are now about one hundred participating member organizations from the United States, Canada, Europe, the United Kingdom, Africa, and South America.

TACF became the target of fresh criticism in 1999 following reports from the church leaders that God was filling people's cavities with real gold. TACF released a video about the alleged miracles called *Go for the Gold*, and their Web site featured pictures from people who claimed that God had performed dental work on them. Attendance increased as reports circulated about the supernatural claims. As further research on the claims undermined their veracity, the focus on dental miracles subsided.

TACF has an enormous worldwide outreach through its weekly television program, renewal magazine, and school of ministry. In addition, the church has been visited by several million people since 1994 and maintains links with prominent leaders in the charismatic and Pentecostal worlds, including Benny Hinn.

Toronto Blessing leaders are sincere Christians who do not deserve the wild polemics against their character and motives. The Blessing has led to many conversions to Christ and to authentic spiritual renewal. These gains cannot be denied. However, the movement has also hurt charismatic Christian life through its wild excesses and through overemphasis on being slain in the Spirit.[21]

Toronto Blessing

TYPOLOGY	Christian Protestant charismatic
HOME PAGE	Toronto Airport Christian Fellowship www.tacf.org
READING	John Arnott, *The Father's Blessing* (Lake Mary, FL: Creation House, 1995)
	James A. Beverley, *Holy Laughter and the Toronto Blessing* (Grand Rapids, MI: Zondervan, 1995)
	Guy Chevreau, *Catch the Fire* (London: Marshall Pickering, 1994)
	Margaret Poloma, *Main Street Mystics* (Lanham, MD: AltaMira Press, 2003).

▸ Transcendental Meditation

TM is one of the most recognized modern movements in the study of religion. The meditative program, made famous by guru Maharishi Mahesh Yogi, has been the subject of endless controversy about its purported status as a science. Followers claim that it combines the best of Western science with Vedic science (or SCI: science of creative intelligence) and should not be dismissed as a religion. Critics argue that the techniques of TM involve explicit religious practices, including the recitation of Hindu mantras. They also point to a groundbreaking court case in 1978 in New Jersey when TM was banned from public schools because of its religious nature.

Maharishi learned the methods of TM from Guru Dev and then went public in the late 1950s. TM grew dramatically in the late 1960s and through the 1970s and was viewed by many participants as a helpful, nonreligious meditation exercise. Maharishi has aimed for every person on earth to engage in TM. A World Plan Executive Council is in charge of implementing the wide-ranging vision.

The claims made by TM are astounding. It is argued that if 1 percent of the world population would meditate via TM, it would bring wars to an end. Any city that has 1 percent of its population meditating would experience a drop in crime. The movement claims that more than five hundred scientific studies have proved that TM works. There is, of course, evidence that meditataton in itself is beneficial for the individual in reducing stress. This would apply to the techniques in TM but to other forms of meditation as well.

Maharishi's vision is expressed through his Open University, the Natural Law Party (led by John Hagelin), and his Corporate Program. He offers products from Vedic medicine and even offers advanced courses in yogic flying. Ex-members have said that the "flying" amounts to learning to bounce from a sitting position on a mattress to one or two feet in the air with a forward motion of three or four feet.

Early advertisements about TM promised levitation, invisibility, and supernormal hearing and sight.

The claim that TM is not religious is difficult to sustain in the face of Maharishi's Hindu roots, the explicit use of Hindu mantras, his overall ideology, and his own clear statements made in private publications and conversations over the years. Two court cases that affirmed the religious element in TM are *Malnak v. Yogi, Appeal from the United States District Court for the District of New Jersey (D.C. Civil Action No. 76-0341)* and *Malnak v. Yogi, Nos. 78-1568, 78-1882, United States Court of Appeals, Third Circuit, 592 F.2d 197*, December 11, 1978, argued February 2, 1979.

Transcendental Meditation	
TYPOLOGY	Hinduism
FOUNDER	Maharishi Mahesh Yogi
HOME PAGES	www.tm.org
	www.alltm.org
	www.natural-law.org
CRITIC SITES	TranceNet
	www.trancenet.org
	Falling Down the TM Rabbit Hole (Joe Kellett)
	www.suggestibility.org
	Meditation Information Network (Mike Doughney)
	http://minet.org
	Behind the TM Façade
	http://unstress4less.org

Twelve Tribes is the latest designation for a Christian commune led by Elbert Eugene ("Bert") Spriggs. The group was known for years as the Northeast Kingdom Community Church, based in Island Pond, Vermont. Spriggs and his followers moved to Vermont in 1978, after six years of ministry based in Chattanooga, Tennessee. Spriggs is known as Yoneq in the group.

In the 1980s the group experienced intense scrutiny from cult-watching groups and from Vermont law enforcement. There were concerns about child abuse involving excessive discipline of children. Ex-members also accused the leadership of authoritarianism, hypocrisy, and illegal activities (involving failure to comply with birth registries and burial permits). Tensions heightened in 1983 over claims that a young girl named Lydia Mattatall was taken away by Spriggs and his wife, Marsha, without the consent of her father, Juan (who had legal custody of Lydia). Furthermore, Eddie Wiseman, the number-two leader in the group, was blamed for beating a young girl named Darlynn Church in May 1983. (The criminal case against him was eventually dropped.)

These issues and others led Vermont state officials to authorize a police raid on the homes of church members. The raid took place in the predawn hours of June 22, 1984, and involved ninety Vermont police officers. A total of 112 children were taken from their homes in order to be examined by social workers. However, the legality of the raid was questioned immediately and the children were allowed to return home. A Vermont judge ruled that the raid was unconstitutional. In the last two decades the communal group has continued to face child custody issues, though not in the fashion of the 1984 raid.

On a personal note, I was involved in public debates about this group in the 1980s. After careful investigation, I concluded that the Mattatall case should be viewed in favor of the Twelve Tribes. Lydia's

father, Juan, was a pedophile and the group was right in their arguments in court that the mother should have had retained custody of
Lydia and the other children. Juan lied to me and others about himself and the group. Juan was murdered by his own mother in 1990
just before she committed suicide.

The Twelve Tribes have homes in the USA, Canada, the United
Kingdom, Australia, Argentina, Brazil, France, Germany, and Spain.
Group members view themselves as the body of Christ, dismissing
both the Catholic and the Protestant traditions. The Twelve Tribes
refer to Jesus as Yahshua and believe that communal living is necessary for salvation. They do not send their children to public schools,
colleges, or universities. They do not allow the use of television but
maintain an attractive Web site.

Evangelical Christian scholars argue that the Twelve Tribes is sectarian in its ideology. The movement is prone to legalism and works
righteousness. Leaders put too much emphasis on issues such as
dress codes and hairstyles. Twelve Tribes leaders would do well to
foster more independence among members and abandon their simplistic dualism that creates unnecessary conflicts with ex-members,
courts, and the world outside their group. Yoneq fosters dependence
upon his rule through false comparisons with New Testament apostles, developing an antirational mindset in the group, and equating
his word with the direction of the Lord. His teachings are rarely self-
critical, and he is obsessed with the Twelve Tribes as the only work of
God on the earth.

Twelve Tribes

TYPOLOGY	Christian Protestant sectarian
HOME PAGE	www.twelvetribes.com
CRITICAL SITES	NEIRR research (Bob Pardon)
	http://neirr.org/mcconclu.html
	Twelve Tribes-Ex
	www.twelvetribes-ex.org
	Jacob Eberhardt site
	www.twelvetribesteachings.info

▶ UFO Cults

"UFO cults" is the term for small, diverse, and independent groups who believe that alien beings are "out there" and that their existence is of vital importance to human life on earth. Speculation about life beyond earth's boundaries has existed for centuries, but contemporary interest dates to June 24, 1947, when Kenneth Arnold, a pilot, claimed to see nine unidentified flying objects, or UFOs, near Mount Rainier, Washington.

The major UFO-style New Age groups are the Aetherius Society, the Unarius Academy of Science, and the Raelian movement. The suicide debacle of the Heaven's Gate group in 1997 cast a gloom over New Age UFO groups, and over UFO interests in general, but the passing of time has dulled the impact of Heaven's Gate on believers in the New Age UFO groups. The religious-based UFO groups have a dogmatic commitment to the claims of their leaders and the alleged spiritual revelations from aliens.

Of course, even secular-minded UFO advocates believe passionately in the truth of their claims about extraterrestrial life and in the widespread belief that the United States government is engaged in a cover-up about spaceships. In addition to the Kenneth Arnold case, there is agreement among advocates that a spaceship crashed in Roswell, New Mexico, in the first week of July 1947. This is known as the Roswell incident. The U.S. military claims the incident was simply a case of a crashed weather balloon. There is a UFO Museum and Research Center in Roswell.

Another significant case involves the allegation that the U.S. government operates Area 51, a military compound ninety miles north of Las Vegas, as a site where alien craft can be examined. Bob Lazar, a leading UFO advocate, made this notion famous with his assertion in 1989 on the Art Bell *Coast to Coast* radio program that he had worked with alien spacecrafts in the area. Area 51 is a military site used by the

Air Force to test new fighter planes, but the Air Force denies Lazar's claims.

J. Allen Hynek, who died in 1986, was one of the world's leading UFO advocates. He was a professor of astronomy and a consultant to the U.S. Air Force's Project Blue Book, which investigated UFO claims until the project was shut down in 1969. In 1973 Hynek published the classic work *The UFO Experience: A Scientific Study*. Also, along with Philip Imbrogno and Bob Pratt, he coauthored *Night Siege*, a book on the Westchester County "Boomerang" sightings, involving hundreds of reports in the 1980s about a V-shaped craft hovering both north of New York, in the Hudson River Valley, and over Connecticut.

Critics of UFO sightings and UFO religions reject claims that there is proof of alien visits to planet earth. The skeptics do not argue that every claim can be disproved or that the believers are all liars. Their approach is to argue that most of the cases can be explained better by alternative explanations. One of the major groups attacking the credibility of UFO reports is the Committee for the Scientific Investigation of the Claims of the Paranormal, popularly known as CSICOP. Their UFO specialist is Philip J. Klass, author of *UFOs: The Public Deceived*, a number of other books, and "The Klass Files."

UFO Cults

TYPOLOGY	Western esoteric
GENERAL SITES	Mirrored site with focus on Area 51
	www.ufomind.com
	The International UFO Museum and Research Center
	www.iufomrc.org
	The National UFO Reporting Center
	www.nuforc.org
	Art Bell
	www.artbell.com
	Center for UFO Studies (J. Allen Hynek)
	www.cufos.org
	Committee for the Scientific Investigation of Claims of the Paranormal
	www.csicop.org
	Center for the Study of Extraterrestrial Intelligence
	www.cseti.com

▸ Unarius

Unarius is a UFO-oriented movement founded in Los Angeles in 1954 by Ernest L. Norman (1904–71), aka Archangel, and his wife, Ruth E. Norman (1900–93), aka Archangel Uriel. Unarius is an acronym for Universal Articulate Interdimensional Understanding of Science. Unarius teaches that a "Pleiadean star ship" will bring missionary-like "Space Brothers" to the earth and we will become "the final world to join an alignment of 33 planets forming an interplanetary confederation for the spiritual renaissance of humankind on Earth."

The Unarian Science of Life curriculum is based on mastering the "mind-body system." To progress spiritually, followers undergo "past life therapy" for unresolved problems from previous lives. Ruth Norman claimed fifty-five past lives, including that of Mary Magdalene. Mrs. Norman announced that, as Mary Magdalene, she had been engaged to Jesus of Nazareth, who was a previous incarnation of Ernest L. Norman. She claims that in her current incarnation she was once again "by the side of the man who had taught from the hillsides of Galilee, before the plots against him resulted in his crucifixion and the subsequent distortion of his true teachings by his disciples, under the negative leadership of the one who changed his name from Saul of Tarsus to Paul."

After Ruth died in 1993, the leadership of the movement passed to Charles Spiegel, who used the spiritual name of Antares. Spiegel joined the movement in 1960 and wrote many volumes about Unarius themes. Spiegel believed that he had previously lived as Napoleon Bonaparte and wrote an autobiography about this past life called *The Confessions of I, Bonaparte.* He also claimed to have channeled messages from Ruth Norman after her departure. Spiegel died on December 22, 1999.

On October 12, 1984, Ruth Norman said that she had received contact from a being named Alta, from the planet Vixall, who told her that a spacecraft from Myton would land in the Bermuda Triangle in the year 2001. By 2010, thirty-one other spaceships will have arrived, each holding a thousand "Space Brothers" who will work out of the seventy-three-acre plot reserved for them near El Cajon, California. When the 2001 prediction failed, members were told that earth's leaders were not mentally receptive to the Space Brothers' visit.

In the mid-1970s an earlier failed prophecy was explained on similar lines. When the Space Brothers were about to come to earth, Ruth Norman and other Unarians were recalling their past lives in Egypt. It was revealed that some Unarian students had killed the great masters Isis and Osiris just as their Space Brothers were about to take them back to their planet. Ruth taught that she was the incarnation of Isis and her husband, Ernest, had been Osiris in a previous life. In the words of the Unarius Web site: "These two beings had returned to the earth plane, overshadowed by the Archangels Raphiel and Uriel, to help the very same souls who had murdered them in the past!"

Unarius	
TYPOLOGY	Western esoteric and UFO oriented
FOUNDERS	Ernest L. Norman (1904–71) and Ruth E. Norman (1900–93)
HOME PAGE	www.unarius.org

▶ Unification Church

The Unification Church is one of the best-known and most controversial new religious movements. It is led by Sun Myung Moon, a native of Korea. Moon was born on January 6, 1920. Unificationists believe that Jesus appeared to Moon on April 17, 1935, and that Moon was asked to fulfill the mission of Jesus. Moon has been married twice. His first marriage lasted ten years (1943–53), and he married Hak Ja Han, his current wife, in 1960.

Moon officially launched the Holy Spirit Association for the Unification of World Christianity in 1954. In 1959 Young Oon Kim, one of the most important Unification theologians, was sent to the United States of America. The church received scrutiny for its giant rallies at Madison Square Garden (September 18, 1974), Yankee Stadium (June 1, 1976), and the Washington Monument (September 18, 1976). By this time, Moon was probably the most visible target of the anticult movement.

The United States government charged Moon with income tax evasion on October 15, 1981. Though powerful religious groups protested Moon's indictment, the Korean leader was found guilty and sentenced to eighteen months in prison. He began his term in a prison in Danbury, Connecticut, in the summer of 1984 and was released from a Brooklyn halfway house on August 20, 1985.

Moon's followers were elated with Moon's meetings with Mikhail Gorbachev on April 11, 1990, and with North Korean leader Kim Il Sung in November 1991. These strategic meetings were viewed as evidence of Moon's supremacy over Communism. Moon took credit both for the fall of the Berlin Wall in 1989 and for the victory of the Allied forces in the Persian Gulf War in 1991.

In 1998 Nansook Hong, Moon's former daughter-in-law, published a devastating memoir about life inside the church. Titled *In the Shadow of the Moons*, Hong accused her ex-husband, Hyo Jin Moon, of adultery, drug addiction, and physical and emotional abuse. Further, she claimed that Sun Myung Moon had an illegitimate child who was raised by another Unification family.

The Unification Church utilizes Christian themes in its thought, but draws equally from the beliefs and practices of Korean folk religion. The church is committed to monotheism but does not adopt a trinitarian understanding of God. Moon teaches that Satan seduced Eve sexually and then she engaged in sex with Adam before the time allowed by God. Moon's private teachings about Jesus build upon explicit views given in *Divine Principle* (the Unification Bible) that Jesus was not sent to die on the cross and that the ideal plan for Jesus was to have found a true Eve to restore humanity.

Moon contends that Jesus is the product of a sexual relationship between Mary and Zechariah, the father of John the Baptist. According to Moon, Mary never told Joseph who was the real father of Jesus. Moon states that Mary and Joseph purposely left Jesus behind in Jerusalem when he was visiting at Passover at age twelve.

Moon teaches that Jesus failed in several crucial ways. Unificationists believe that God has had to look to Sun Myung Moon as the new Adam, as Messiah, as Lord of the Second Advent.

Moon has placed great emphasis on direct revelation from the spirit world. This has included claims of supernatural messages from Moon's deceased son, Heung Jin Nim, from Moon's mother-in-law, from a deceased Unification scholar, and even from various religious and political leaders who have died. This list includes Buddha, Marx, Hitler, and dead U.S. presidents. These messages have been channeled mainly through two women in the Unification Church.

Unification Church

TYPOLOGY	Christian sectarian
FOUNDER	Sun Myung Moon (1920–)
HOME PAGE	Family Federation for World Peace and Unification www.ffwpui.org

True Parents Organization
www.tparents.org
Unification Home Page (Damian Anderson)
www.unification.net

CRITIC SITES
Craig Maxim
www.geocities.com/craigmaxim
Allen Tate Wood
www.allentwood.com

READING
Eileen Barker, *The Making of a Moonie* (Oxford: Basil
Blackwell, 1984)
James A. Beverley, "Spirit Revelation and the
Unification Church," in James R. Lewis and Jesper
Aagaard Petersen, eds., *Controversial New Religions*
(New York: Oxford University Press, 2005)
George Chryssides, *The Advent of Sun Myung Moon*
(New York: St. Martin's, 1991)
Michael Inglis, ed., *40 Years in America* (New York: HSA,
2000)
Massimo Introvigne, *The Unification Church* (Salt Lake
City: Signature, 2000)
Nansook Hong, *In the Shadow of the Moons* (Boston:
Beacon, 1998)

▶ Urantia

Urantia is a modern esoteric movement connected to followers of *The Urantia Book*, a work of 2,097 pages said to be a revelation from celestial beings for Urantia (planet earth). The book was first published in 1955 and is promoted by the Urantia Foundation. Its earthly story owes most to two people: psychiatrist William S. Sadler (1875–1969) and one of his patients, who claimed to receive the divine revelations that became *The Urantia Book*.

In 1923 Sadler, who had a Seventh-day Adventist background, organized a forum to discuss material from the patient. They met at 533 Diversey Parkway in Chicago. *The Urantia Book* presents a complex cosmology, with hundreds of constellations, each with hundreds of inhabited worlds. Urantia describes five "epochal" events in the history of humankind, the fourth being the life of Christ and the fifth being the writing of *The Urantia Book* itself.

The Urantia Book teaches that God used beings called "Creator Sons" to create various universes in time and space. Earth's Creator Son is Michael, who created Nebadon, our local universe. Michael incarnated on earth as Jesus of Nazareth. *The Urantia Book* claims to provide a huge amount of new information about the life of Jesus, in addition to offering radical interpretations of classical Christian teaching about Jesus.

The legal case has centered on a dispute with the Michael Foundation and Harry McMullan III. The Urantia Foundation was upset with the Michael Foundation and McMullan for publication of *Jesus: A New Revelation*. This volume contains material from section 4 of *The Urantia Book*. In March 2003 a U.S. appeals court ruled that the Urantia Foundation could not renew its copyright on *The Urantia Book*. In October of the same year the U.S. Supreme Court refused to review the decision.

As the case suggests, there has been considerable controversy over the nature of *The Urantia Book* and the manner of revelation with Sadler's patient. Martin Gardner, a writer on fringe science, suggests in his work *Urantia: The Great Cult Mystery* that the individual in question was Wilfred Custer Kellogg, Sadler's brother-in-law. Gardner also argues that *The Urantia Book* makes major errors on scientific issues and that it plagiarizes from other sources.

The plagiarism charge relates to the exhaustive research done by Matthew Block. Block was a believer in Urantia and viewed the connections between the sacred text and human sources as a signal of the brilliant creativity of the revelators who spoke to and through Sadler's patient. However, recently Block has become more skeptical and has expressed greater appreciation for the work of Gardner.

The divide between Urantia and classical Christian faith is fundamentally about whether one accepts *The Urantia Book* as divine revelation and as an accurate commentary on God and Christ and cosmology. Urantia apologists repeatedly rest their case on the trust that Dr. Sadler and his patient were recipients of modern revelation. Given the human sources at work in *The Urantia Book*, its key errors on testable items about the universe, and its denial of major biblical teaching, Christians should resist claims that it is new revelation from God.

Urantia

TYPOLOGY	Western esoteric
FOUNDER	William S. Sadler (1875–1969)
HOME PAGES	The Urantia Foundation
	www.urantia.org
	The Official Urantia Foundation Truth Page
	www.freeurantia.org
	The Urantia Book Fellowship
	www.urantiabook.org
	Square Circles Publishing
	www.squarecircles.com
	A New Picture of Jesus
	www.truthbook.com
READING	Martin Gardner, *Urantia: The Great Cult Mystery*
	(Buffalo: Prometheus, 1996)

▶ Vampire Religion

Since the release of Bram Stoker's *Dracula* in 1897 and its movie version in 1930, vampires have increasingly captured the human imagination. This has been illustrated in the last several decades by the success of various novels (Anne Rice's *Interview with a Vampire*), television shows (*Buffy the Vampire Slayer*), comic books (*Vampirella*), and even scholarly studies (J. Gordon Melton's *The Vampire Book*).

While the great majority of people who identify with vampires are simply fans of vampire fiction and movies, what makes the vampire theme most significant is that a small but growing number of humans claim to be vampires. Further, vampire life and ideology is being considered as a religious path. Internet sites provide details on how to get blood from donors, where to get the best fangs, and what are the best ways to handle "the Beast" (the inner urge to drink blood). While some "vampires" are actually into drinking blood, the majority stress the psychic-vamp path, that is, the alternative lifestyle of avoiding blood sports and simply feeding off human energy.

Self-professed vampires usually describe themselves as light-sensitive, prone to nocturnal living, susceptible to migraines, and capable of sensing the presence of other vampires. They also claim above average strength and intelligence. A few vampires say the essence of being a vampire is the need for blood. "We require blood to survive. Why this is I do not know, but it does not change the fact it is necessary. To feed charges a vampire—renews them, strengthens them, simply invigorates them and sets every nerve on fire." Blood is usually obtained through a donor and seldom involves biting on the neck.

Most vampires recognize they have an image problem. Michelle Belanger and Father Sebastian, two famous leaders, coauthored a thirteen-point code of ethics known as *The Black Veil*. It was even mentioned in an episode of *CSI: Vegas* that dealt with vampires. One of the codes reads: "Do not allow your darkness to consume you.

You are more than just your hunger, and you can exercise conscious control. Do not be reckless. Always act with a mind toward safety."

Vampire elders warn that the vampiric life is difficult. One vampire states: "There are far more depressed (and manic-depressive) vampires out there than healthy, happy ones. We're a horribly unstable lot prone to deep and even suicidal bleakness and tend to mostly suffer through various bi-polar-esque see-saws of stability. It's not easy fighting a primal, horridly powerful need to feed your Hunger." Night Angel, another vampire, writes: "This isn't something I want nor would I want it if I did not have it already."

Though some vampires claim to be Christians, the ethos of the vampire culture is antagonistic to the gospel. Generally, vampires who are spiritually inclined are more attuned to witchcraft and the New Age than to any form of Christian faith. Some vampires are openly hostile about Jesus. Many show a distinct preference for sadomasochism and the bondage scene. Often the blood rituals in vampire life take place as part of sexual encounters. The Temple of the Vampire is one of the better-known groups for vampires inclined to religion.

Vampire Religion	
TYPOLOGY	Western esoteric
WEB SITES	www.sanguinarius.org
	www.drinkdeeplyanddream.com
	http://sphynxcatvp.nocturna.org
	www.vampiretemple.com
	www.lionsgrove.com
READING	J. Gordon Melton, *The Vampire Book* (New York: Visible Ink, 1998).

The Association of Vineyard Churches is most commonly associated with John Wimber, one of the leading charismatic Christians of the twentieth century. Wimber was born in 1934 in the American Midwest. His alcoholic father left the family when John, an only child, was young. He had no introduction to Christian faith in his youth. In 1955 he married Carol, a nominal Roman Catholic. Gifted in music, he began his career as a writer for the rock group the Righteous Brothers. John and Carol separated in 1962, but their marriage was saved when John turned to God for help.

In the early 1970s Wimber served as copastor of an evangelical Quaker church in Southern California. From 1974 to 1978, he worked with the Fuller Institute of Evangelism and Church Growth. In 1977 Wimber became identified with Chuck Smith and the Calvary Chapel movement. On Mother's Day in 1980, Wimber's Calvary church in Yorba Linda experienced a major revival, one that included radical charismatic behavior. In 1982 Wimber left Calvary Chapel and became leader of a small group of churches known as the Vineyard, founded in 1974 by Kenn Gulliksen.

Wimber started teaching course MC 510 on "Signs and Wonders and Church Growth" at Fuller Seminary, Pasadena, in 1982. This class, cotaught with Peter Wagner, acquired worldwide attention after *Christian Life* published a special report on the course. In 1985 Fuller Seminary put Wimber's popular and controversial course on hold. It was later brought back into the curriculum, and Wimber remained an adjunct faculty member until 1992.

The Vineyard movement went through internal reorientation in 1988 when Wimber embraced the prophetic movement connected with Mike Bickle's Kansas City Fellowship (KCF). In the next three years Wimber traveled internationally with Bickle and with Paul Cain, Bob Jones, and John Paul Jackson, the three leading prophets connected with the Kansas City movement. Wimber distanced himself from the prophetic focus in 1991.

In 1994 and 1995 Wimber and other Vineyard leaders were drawn into the controversy surrounding the Toronto Blessing, the renewal movement that originated at the Toronto Airport Vineyard. Wimber had grown increasingly concerned about some of the religious ecstasy involved, particularly duplication of animal behavior. In December 1995 Wimber pressured the Toronto congregation, led by John Arnott, to leave the Association of Vineyard Churches.

The Vineyard has often been targeted as heretical and occultic by right-wing Christians. These charges are far too extreme. Vineyard leaders follow standard evangelical doctrine and have no interest in the darker side of religion. The Vineyard movement has, however, been prone to subjectivity and too much focus on sensationalistic elements in charismatic Christian life. These weaknesses were corrected by Wimber in his reaction to the Kansas City Prophets and the Toronto Blessing.

Wimber died in 1997. The Vineyard, currently led by Bert Waggoner, has about six hundred churches in the United States.

The Vineyard

TYPOLOGY	Christian Protestant
HOME PAGES	Association of Vineyard Churches, USA
	www.vineyardusa.org
	Vineyard International Consortium
	www.vineyard.org
READING	James Beverley, *Holy Laughter and the Toronto Blessing* (Grand Rapids, MI: Zondervan, 1995)
	Carol Wimber, *John Wimber: The Way It Was* (London: Hodder & Stoughton, 1999)

▶ The Way International

Victor Paul Wierwille is the founder of The Way International (TWI), based in New Knoxville, Ohio. Born on December 31, 1916, Wierwille was ordained in 1941 in the Evangelical and Reformed Church and started a radio ministry known as Vesper Chimes in 1942. He pastored St. Peter's Church (Van Wert, Ohio) until 1957. He claims that he received the baptism of the Holy Spirit through speaking in tongues in 1951. Two years later he produced the first version of his Power for Abundant Living course. He resigned from his denomination in 1958.

TWI became the target of the countercult movement in the 1970s. The most notorious charge had to do with allegations of weapons training for TWI membership. The Way leadership said that these charges were a result of misunderstanding the Way's participation in a state program on hunting safety. TWI also underwent an internal crisis in 1986 and 1987 over evidence of sexual libertarian practices by Wierwille and other Way leaders.[22] John Juedes has provided extensive evidence that Wierwille plagiarized from various sources and that he was careless about major claims in his spiritual journey.

Religious positions of the TWI founder raise concerns. Wierwille believed that the Bible was originally written in Aramaic (it was actually mostly written in Hebrew and Greek). Wierwille taught that Christians are not subject to the Gospels and the Book of Acts; he placed emphasis instead on Paul's later epistles. The Way leader also denied the Trinity in his work *Jesus Christ Is Not God*.

Similar problematic positions occur in TWI's theology. The group rejects water baptism and Communion. Members believe that it is necessary to speak in tongues to be a Christian. And while they affirm the atonement of Jesus and his resurrection from the dead, they believe that Jesus died on a Wednesday and rose on Saturday.

Craig Martindale became the second president of The Way International in 1982, three years before the death of the founder in 1985. Martindale and his wife, Donna, adopted an aggressive policy against members who were not totally devoted to Way leadership. Donna stated that a female follower died in a plane crash because the girl's father was not obedient to the group's leadership. The Way had its most serious internal crisis in 1987 when ex-members provided evidence of sexual indiscretions by Wierwille, Craig Martindale, and other top leaders.

In early 2000 Paul and Frances Allen sued for fraud, sexual assault, and breach of contract against TWI. Frances claimed in the suit that she was coerced into sex with Craig Martindale. Martindale resigned as president shortly after the Allen suit was launched. He denied the assault charge but admitted to having an affair. The Allen couple accepted a settlement from the group in late 2000. Their case created a crisis on the movement. After Martindale's multiple sexual affairs were made known to the Way's board, it moved to suspend him from office, investigate the charges, and eventually removed him from any leadership role in the organization.

The TWI home page makes no mention of Wierwille or Martindale. Rosalie F. Rivenbark is the current president.

Several splinter groups formed because of objections to either Weirwille or Martindale. The largest group is Christian Educational Services, based in Indianapolis and led by John Schoenheit, John Lynn, and Mark Graeser. A lot of members left the Way after reading Chris Geer's account of Wierwille's last days in "The Passing of a Patriarch." Christian Family Fellowship formed in 1996 and is based in Tipp City, Ohio.

The Way International

TYPOLOGY	Christian Protestant sectarian
FOUNDER	Victor Paul Wierwille (1916–86)
HOME PAGE	www.theway.com
SPLINTER GROUPS	Christian Family Fellowship, www.cffm.org
	Christian Educational Services (CES)
	www.christianeducational.org
CRITIC SITES	No Way Out, www.trancenet.org/noway
	www.ex-wayworld.com
	The Path of Christ Ministry (Patrick Roberge)
	www.waychrist.com
	The Cult That Snapped (Karl Kahler site)
	www.ex-way.com

▶ Witchcraft

There may be nothing more important in the correct interpretation of witchcraft than making careful distinctions among its types. Since the Middle Ages, it has been commonplace to believe that all witches are worshippers of Satan who engage in ritual killing, sexual orgies, and various diabolical acts. This image of the witch continues today, both in secular and in religious circles. Many evangelical Christians have spread this stereotype. For the sake of accuracy, witchcraft should be understood in four different ways in relation to actual beliefs and practices.

First, the term *witchcraft* can refer to the practice of sorcery done by witch doctors in pre-industrial, nontechnological societies. This involves tribes in Africa and South America and applies to practitioners of voodoo in Haiti and other countries. This type of witchcraft can involve actions ranging from the effective use of potions as medicine to gruesome rites such as grave robbing and the ritual killing of babies.

Second, *witchcraft* is a term given to those who follow the pagan path idolized in *The Da Vinci Code*. Such witches worship gods and goddesses, honor Mother Earth, participate in covens, celebrate sexuality in their rituals, and follow the cycles of nature for their holy days. Such practitioners are often known to outsiders as "white witches" because they do not believe in Satan and explicitly deny intent to harm anyone. These witches follow various traditions, both ancient and recent.

Third, there are witches in the industrialized world who call themselves Satanists. They follow "the dark side" and believe that true living involves being self-centered and engaging in all the lusts of the flesh. This type of witchcraft is exemplified by Anton LaVey, founder of the Church of Satan and author of *The Satanic Bible*. LaVey (1930–97) and his followers deny that they believe in Satan as traditionally understood. Rather, LaVey invokes Satan as a metaphor for a life lived in direct opposition to Christian principles of peace, gentleness, and love. Further, the Church of Satan denies involvement in satanic ritual abuse or any other criminal acts.

Finally, there are witches who follow Satan, call themselves Satanists, and engage in satanic ritual abuse. They form a criminal element in a number of countries of the world. Usually such Satanists operate as loners or in concert with a handful of others. Some serial killers represent themselves as Satanists. In the 1980s it was popular to believe that Satanists killed fifty thousand people every year in the United States. This satanic panic died down as law enforcement, including the FBI, and court officials were unable to find evidence to back up such an astounding claim.

Contemporary understanding of witchcraft has been shaped by the frenzy about witches that dominated Western society from the fifteenth through the eighteenth century. Catholic, Protestant, and secular leaders engaged in an inquisition against alleged witches. This campaign of fear was fueled by superstitious theories about sorcery, zealous prosecutors who used torture to force confessions, and a readiness to condemn anyone who stood for even minimal justice for accused witches. More women were targeted than men. The Salem witch craze took place in 1692.

Modern Neo-Pagan witchcraft, or Wicca, can be traced to the work of Gerald Gardner, a British civil servant, who brought Wicca into public light in 1954 with his book *Witchcraft Today*. Gardner (1884–1964) claims that he was introduced to a coven in 1939, and he became one of its leaders. Though Gardner claimed that the group's rituals go back through the centuries, modern research, especially that of Aidan Kelly, has shown that Gardner composed most of the rituals himself. He also borrowed from a wide variety of modern literary and occult sources, not the least being Aleister Crowley (1875–1947).

Most informed Wiccans now acknowledge that there is little proof that modern pagan rituals have a long historical pedigree. While Kelly's research was initially greeted with hostility, it is now commonplace for witches to argue that pagan ideology does not depend on any chain of transmission from one generation to the next. Kelly used theories learned from textual criticism of the Bible and applied them to source analysis of *The Book of Shadows*, the main ritual book used by Gardner in witchcraft ceremonies.

Christian testimony to Western-style witches is often ruined by the false claim that all witches are Satanists. We need to imagine what it is like for peaceful, loving witches to be accused of worshipping Lucifer and engaging in ritual murder. It would be difficult for them to be open to the gospel from Christians who confuse them with Satanists of any variety.

Witchcraft ultimately fails in the mythic and legendary nature of its gods and goddesses. The Roman, Celtic, Nordic, and Greek deities dwell only in the imagination of the followers. The lack of historical trustworthiness concerning Artemis or Zeus or Diana or Isis is in direct contrast to the historical nature of the Gospel accounts of Jesus Christ. Here Christians can remember the point that C. S. Lewis often made about the myths and legends from other times: while they are not historically true, they can prepare individuals with a sense of anticipation and longing for God's real intervention in history. One can also remember Paul's reference to the faint realities of Greek religion (Acts 17) as a pointer to the story of Jesus that "was not done in a corner" (Acts 26:26).

Christian leaders should process accusations of satanic ritual abuse against specific witches (or others) with extreme caution. This is necessary for two reasons. First, if the charges are true, this involves the most serious crimes, and anyone dealing with the criminals involved is in serious danger. Second, if the claims are not true, the accused can face ruin through gossip and rumor.

Time Line of Modern Witchcraft

1884	Gerald Brosseau Gardner born in England (June 13)
1889	*The Key of Solomon the King* published
1899	Charles Leland publishes "Aradia: Gospel of the Witches"

1890	Sir James Frazier publishes *The Golden Bough*
1908	Gardner moves to Borneo
1909	Aleister Crowley publishes *The Equinox*
1921	Margaret Murray publishes *The Witch Cult in Western Europe*
1929	Birth of Alexander Sanders
1929	Aleister Crowley publishes *Magick in Theory and Practice*
1936	Gardner settles in England
1939	Gardner allegedly initiated into a witch coven
1947	Gardner meets Aleister Crowley on May 1
1947	Death of Aleister Crowley (December 1)
1948	Robert Graves publishes *The White Goddess*
1949	Gardner publishes "High Magic's Aid" under pseudonym of Scire
1951	Death of Dorothy Clutterbuck (January 12)
1951	Britain repeals witchcraft laws (June)
1953	Doreen Valiente joins Gardner's group and becomes High Priestess
1954	Gardner publishes *Witchcraft Today*
1955	The *Sunday Pictorial* equates witchcraft and Satanism
1956	Violet Firth (aka Dion Fortune) publishes *Moon Magic*
1957	Fred Lamond joins Gardner's coven
1957	Valiente and Ned Grove leave Gardner's coven in summer
1962	Tim Zell and Robert Christie found The Church of All Worlds
1963	Raymond Buckland starts Gardnerian coven in USA
1964	Gardner dies
1964	Doreen Valiente initiated by Robert Cochrane into new coven
1968	Zell begins publication of *The Green Egg*
1969	*King of the Witches* published about Sanders
1971	Stewart Farrar is initiated into Alexandrian coven
1972	Susan B. Anthony Coven formed By Z. Budapest
1973	Tim Zell marries Morning Glory
1973	Raymond Buckland leaves Gardnerian movement
1974	Selena Fox forms Circle Sanctuary
1975	Covenant of the Goddess formed
1979	Margot Adler publishes *Drawing Down the Moon*
1979	Starhawk publishes *The Spiral Dance*
1983	Isaac Bonewits starts Druid group *Ár nDraíocht Féin* (ADF)
1984	*The Witches' Bible* published

1986	Five members protest ADF policies at Pagan Spirit Gathering
1988	Alexander Sanders dies
1991	Publication of Aidan Kelly, *Crafting the Art of Magic*
1997	*The Witches' Voice* Internet site started
1999	Death of Doreen Valiente
2000	Death of Stewart Farrar

Witchcraft

TYPOLOGY	Western esoteric
WITCHCRAFT SITES	*Ár nDraíocht Féin* (ADF)
	www.adf.org
	Isaac Bonewits
	www.neopagan.net
	Raymond Buckland
	http://geocities.com/SoHo/Workshop/6650/
	Circle Sanctuary
	www.circlesanctuary.org
	Church of All Worlds
	www.caw.org
	Covenant of the Goddess
	www.cog.org
	Stewart and Janet Farrar (and Gavin Bone)
	www.wicca.utvinternet.com/
	Selena Fox
	www.mhtc.net/~selena/
	Gerald Gardner
	www.geraldgardner.com
	Henge of Keltria (Druid)
	www.keltria.org
	Order of Bards, Oviates, and Druids (OBOD)
	http://druidry.org
	Reformed Druids of North America
	www.geocities.com/mikerdna
	Doreen Valiente
	www.doreenvaliente.com
	The Wiccan-Pagan Times
	www.twpt.com
	The Witches' Voice
	www.witchvox.com
	Z. Budapest
	www.zbudapest.com
	Oberon Zell-Ravenheart

www.caw.org/clergy/oberon
Academic sites about the witchcraft inquisition
Gender Studies and witchcraft
www.gendercide.org
Brian Pavlac
www.kings.edu/womens_history/witch
Shantell Powell
www.shanmonster.com/witch
Doug Linder on the Salem trials
www.law.umkc.edu/faculty/projects/ftrials/salem/sal
em.htm
Salem Witch Trials Project
http://jefferson.village.virginia.edu/salem/home.html
Seventeenth-Century New England
www.17thc.us/index.php?id=12

MINISTRY Ex-witch Ministries
www.exwitch.org

SCHOLARLY WORKS Graham Harvey, *Contemporary Paganism* (New York: New York University Press, 1997)

Ronald Hutton, *The Triumph of the Moon* (London: Oxford University Press, 1999)

Aidan A. Kelly, *Crafting the Art of Magic* (St. Paul: Llewellyn, 1991)

T. M. Luhrmann, *Persuasions of the Witch's Craft* (Cambridge: Harvard University Press, 1989)

Sarah Pike, *Earthly Bodies, Magical Selves* (Berkeley: University of California, 2001)

Charles Clifton, ed. *The Pomegranate: The International Journal of Pagan Studies.*

Shelley Rabinovitch and James Lewis, eds., *The Encyclopedia of Modern Witchcraft and Neo-Paganism* (New York: Citadel, 2002)

READING Bengt Ankarloo and Stuart Clark, eds., *The Athlone History of Witchcraft and Magic in Europe* (London: Athlone, 1999), 5 vols.

Robin Briggs, *Witches and Neighbors: The Social and Cultural Context of European Witchcraft* (New York: Penguin, 1998)

Carlo Ginzburg, *Ecstasies: Deciphering the Witches' Sabbath* (Chicago: University of Chicago Press, 2004)

Brian P. Levack, *The Witch-Hunt in Early Modern Europe* (New York: Addison-Wesley, 1995)

Darren Oldridge, *The Witchcraft Reader* (London: Routledge, 2002)

Jeffrey B. Russell, *A History of Witchcraft* (New York:
  Thames & Hudson, 1980)
Geoffrey Scarre and John Callow, *Witchcraft and
  Magic in Sixteenth and Seventeenth-Century
  Europe* (London: Palgrave, 2001)

BY MODERN WITCHES   Margot Adler, *Drawing Down the Moon,* 2nd ed.
  (Boston: Beacon, 1986)
Stewart Farrar, *The Witches' Way* (London: Robert Hale,
  1985)
Gerald B. Gardner, *Witchcraft Today* (Rider, 1954)
Ellen Hopman and Lawrence Bond, *Being a Pagan*
  (Rochester, Vermont: Destiny, 2001)
Starhawk, *The Spiral Dance* (New York: Harper & Row,
  1979)
Doreen Valiente, *The Rebirth of Witchcraft* (London:
  Robert Hale, 1989)

CHRISTIAN RESPONSE   Brooks Alexander, *Witchcraft Goes Mainstream*
  (Eugene: Harvest House, 2004)
David Burnett, *Dawning of the Pagan Moon*
  (Nashville: Thomas Nelson, 1991)
Craig Hawkins, *Goddess Worship, Witchcraft, and Neo-
  Paganism* (Grand Rapids: Zondervan, 1998)

▶ Worldwide Church of God

The Worldwide Church of God was started as the Radio Church of God in 1933 by Herbert W. Armstrong. Armstrong was born in 1892 and joined the General Conference of the Church of God, part of the Adventist tradition, in 1927 and was ordained in 1931. In 1933 Armstrong linked with the newly formed Church of God, 7th Day, led by Andrew N. Dugger. Armstrong lost his credentials with that group in 1937 but continued an independent ministry. He moved his base of operations to Pasadena in 1947. He ordained his son Garner Ted (1930–2003) in 1955. The Radio Church of God was renamed the Worldwide Church of God (WCG) in 1968.

The WCG became well-known in the late 1960s and early 1970s through its television program, *The World Tomorrow*, and its free magazine, *The Plain Truth*. In his teaching Herbert W. Armstrong focused on some themes common to Adventists: eschatology, Old Testament law, and the Sabbath. However, he also taught that the WCG was "the" Church of Christ and that he was the only apostle of God's end-time work. Armstrong and his son also advocated a form of British-Israelism, arguing that the Jews of the Old Testament became the people of the British Empire and the United States.

Prior to his death in 1986, the Worldwide Church of God became embroiled in controversy. Several ex-members wrote critically about Armstrong's wealth and dictatorial style. The most prominent critic was John Trechak, who began publishing *The Ambassador Report* in 1976. In 1978 Herbert excommunicated Garner Ted, who then started the Church of God, International, based in Tyler, Texas. In 1979 the State of California initiated legal action against the Worldwide Church of God in relation to alleged financial improprieties, but the suit was quickly dropped.

After Herbert's death, the WCG went through major doctrinal changes under Joseph Tkach Sr., its new pastor general. In his boldest move, Tkach preached a sermon on Christmas Eve in 1994 that clearly spelled out that church members were not obligated to obey Old Testament law related to diet and Sabbath. Tkach was succeeded in 1995 by his son Joseph Tkach Jr. The WCG continued to become more evangelical in its ideology, adopting a trinitarian understanding of God and a grace-based understanding of salvation. The church became part of the National Association of Evangelicals in 1997.

The departure of the WCG from many of Armstrong's views created a crisis among its membership. Many WCG pastors broke away and started their own groups. The best-known new groups that follow traditional Armstrongism are the Philadelphia Church of God, the United Church of God, Church of God—An International Community, and the Living Church of God. After six years of litigation, the Philadelphia Church of God, founded by Gerald Flurry, reached an agreement with the WCG to hold copyright on the writings of Herbert W. Armstrong.

In 1998 Garner Ted was ousted from the Church of God, International, and formed the Intercontinental Church of God. He died in 2003 and leadership passed to his son Mark. Joseph Tkach Jr. believes that he and his father helped move the WCG toward biblical orthodoxy. He wrote about this in his 1997 work *Transformed by Truth*. "We searched the Scriptures diligently to discover the right twist to this doctrine or the correct slant to that one. We got lost in minutiae and largely missed the real treasure, Jesus Christ Himself."

Worldwide Church of God

TYPOLOGY	Christian Protestant Adventist
FOUNDER	Herbert W. Armstrong (1892–1986)
CURRENT LEADER	Joseph Tkach Jr.
HOME PAGE	www.wcg.org
MAJOR WCG SPLITS	Church of God, International (1978–) Founder: Garner Ted Armstrong www.cgi.org Philadelphia Church of God (1989–) Founder: Gerald Flurry www.pcog.org

Global Church of God (1992–99)
Founder: Roderick Meredith
Christian Educational Ministries (1995-)
Founder: Ron Dart
www.cemnetwork.com
United Church of God (1995–)
Founder: David Hulme
www.ucg.org
Church of God—An International Community (1998–)
Founder: David Hulme
www.church-of-god.org
Intercontinental Church of God (1998–)
Founder: Garner Ted Armstrong
www.intercontinentalcog.org
Living Church of God (1998–)
Founder: Roderick Meredith
www.livingcog.org
Sites about the WCG and other Church of God groups
Servants' News
www.servantsnews.com
Exit and Support Network
http://home.datawest.net/esn-recovery
The Journal: News of the Churches of God
www.thejournal.org
The Painful Truth
www.herbertwarmstrong.com

READING   Joseph Tkach Jr., *Transformed by Truth* (Sisters, Oregon: Multnomah, 1997)
J. Michael Feazell, *The Liberation of the Worldwide Church of God* (Grand Rapids: Zondervan, 2001)

▸ Zen

Zen is one of the better-known, though most difficult, forms of Buddhism. While Zen is normally associated with Japan, it actually emerged in China as part of the larger Mahayana tradition. In China this form of Buddhism is known as Ch'an (Zen is the Japanese rendition of Ch'an). The Chinese origin of Ch'an is usually linked to the famous Mahayana teacher Bodhidharma. The classical period in Ch'an Buddhism began with Hui-neng (638–713), a leader in the dominant southern school. Two forms of southern Ch'an, Rinzai and Soto, spread to Japan in the twelfth and thirteenth centuries, respectively.

Zen Buddhism places emphasis on trying to achieve sudden enlightenment. This is attempted through sitting meditation and concentration, particularly on *koans*—paradoxical teachings or stories used to help students reach a new level of comprehension. More than five hundred koans are popular in Zen, particularly in the Rinzai school. The most famous koan is "What is the sound of one hand clapping?" The purpose of the koan is not to inspire confidence in rationality, as if a riddle was being solved, but to reach insight that is beyond reason.

The story of Zen in America is mainly connected to two individuals: Daisetz Teitaro Suzuki and Philip Kapleau.

Suzuki is one of the most famous Buddhist scholars of the last two centuries. He was born in Japan in 1870 and studied Zen at Tokyo University. He moved to America in 1897 and worked with Paul Carus at Open Court Publishing. In 1909 he moved back to Japan, teaching in his native land over the next four decades. He started the Eastern Buddhist Society in 1921 and became a professor at Otani University in Kyoto. He wrote extensively on Zen and Japanese religion. He was also a frequent visiting professor at Columbia University. He died in 1966.

Philip Kapleau is the author of *The Three Pillars of Zen*, one of the most influential guides to Zen Buddhism. He was raised in New

Haven, Connecticut, and became a court reporter, eventually chosen to work at the Nuremberg trials and the war crimes rrials in Tokyo. In Japan he met D. T. Suzuki. He returned to the United States in 1950 and studied with Suzuki at Columbia University. In 1953 he moved to Japan and spent thirteen years in Zen training. He was ordained by Hakuun Yasutani-roshi in 1965, the same year his popular book was published and also the year he founded the Rochester Zen Center. Kapleau died in May 2004.

Zen must be distinguished from the teachings of Frederick P. Lenz III, one of the more controversial gurus of the twentieth century. He was known as Zen Master Rama and was author of the best sellers *Surfing the Himalayas* and *Snowboarding to Nirvana*. He died in April 1998 at his Long Island mansion. He was born in San Diego in 1950 and grew up in Connecticut. Lenz had a PhD in English literature from Stony Brook.

He was once a follower of Sri Chimnoy, the Hindu guru based in Queens. After 1981 he started his own group in California, and used the Zen vocabulary to create his own version of enlightenment. He demanded both intense emotional and financial commitment from his followers, and he was accused of sexual abuse by former members of his group.[23]

Zen	
TYPOLOGY	Buddhist Mahayana
HOME PAGES	Rochester Zen Center (Philip Kapleau, d. 2004)
	www.rzc.org
	DharmaNet on Zen teachers
	www.dharmanet.org/infowebz.html
	Frederick P. Lenz III (Zen Master Rama)
PRO-LENZ SITES	www.himalaya.com
	www.fredericklenz.com
	www.ramalila.com
CRITIC SITES	www.ex-cult.org
	www.trancenet.org
READING	Philip Kapleau, *The Three Pillars of Zen* (New York: Anchor, 1989)

Notes

1. Details about alleged sexual abuse by Adi Da can be found at many posts in the Daism forum: http://lightmind.com/daism/daism.mv.

2. For details see http://www.perefound.org/xcsob_90.html.

3. See Julius Rubin, "Contested Narratives," Benjamin Zablocki and Thomas Robbins, eds., *Misunderstanding Cults* (Toronto: University of Toronto Press 2001), 452–477.

4. See Simma Holt, *Terror in the Name of God* (Toronto: McClelland and Stewart, 1964).

5. See David Lane, *The Making of a Spiritual Movement* (Del Mar, CA: Del Mar Press, 1983).

6. For a prophetic warning about evangelicalism by an insider, see Mark Noll, *The Scandal of the Evangelical Mind* (Grand Rapids: Eerdmans, 1994).

7. For a sober assessment of the Family's sexual practices, see J. Gordon Melton, *The Children of God* (Salt Lake City: Signature, 2004).

8. See William Bowen's personal story at www.silentlambs.org. The Web site contains his letter of resignation in protest of Watch Tower policies on reporting pedophiles.

9. See the chapter on the Kansas City Prophets in James A. Beverley, *Holy Laughter & The Toronto Blessing* (Grand Rapids: Zondervan, 1995).

10. Witness Lee was deeply influenced by a Plymouth Brethren view of ecclesiology. This will be explored in a forthcoming book by Mark Steinacher, church historian at Tyndale Seminary in Toronto.

11. The news archive of the United Methodist Church at www.umc.org provides comprehensive coverage of both the Dammann and Stroud cases.

12. See the discussion in Mattias Gardell, *In the Name of Elijah Muhammad* (Durham, NC: Duke University Press, 1996).

13. For very critical interpretation of the New Apostolic Reformation, see www.cephasministry.com.

14. See various news reports about the group at www.rickross.com.

15. See the discussion at http://www.sannyasnews.com.

16. For ex-member testimony and report on the Aberdeen incident see www.peebs.net.

17. The Pema Chodron interview about Rinpoche is from *Tricycle*, Issue 9 (Fall 1993).

18. For news reports about the Air India crash, see www.cbc.ca.

19. The ideological framework of the Solar Temple is explored in George Chryssides, "Sources of Doctrine in the Solar Temple," at www.cesnur.org.

20. For an essay by Richard Hodgson on the Coulomb issue, see www.blavatskyarchives.com. This site also provides replies to Hodgson.

21. On a personal note, I have seen Toronto Blessing participants "shoot" the Holy Spirit at one another and attempt to throw the Spirit across the room. I have also witnessed a man acting like a cow, allegedly from the Holy Spirit.

22. For discussion of sexual issues in the Weirwille years, see Karl Kahler's www.ex-way.com.

23. See the reports on Lenz at www.ex-cult.org.

General Internet Resources on World and New Religions

Academic and General Sites

Adherents.com
www.adherents.com
American Religion Data Archive
www.thearda.com
Beliefnet
www.beliefnet.org
Center for Millennial Studies
www.mille.org
Center for the Study of Global Christianity
www.globalchristianity.org (Todd Johnson and David Barrett)
CESNUR (Massimo Introvigne)
www.cesnur.org
Hartford Institute for Religion Research
http://hirr.hartsem.edu
INFORM (Eileen Barker)
www.inform.ac
NCC Denominations List
www.electronicchurch.org
NRM Article Archive
www.skepsis.nl/nrm.html
Nurelweb (Irving Hexham)
www.acs.ucalgary.ca/~nurelweb
Ontario Consultants for Religious Tolerance
www.religioustolerance.com
Pluralism Project at Harvard (Diana Eck)
www.pluralism.org
Religion, Religions, Religious Studies (Gene Thursby)
www.clas.ufl.edu/users/gthursby/rel
Religious Movements Home Page (Jeffrey Hadden/Douglas Cowan)
http://religiousmovements.lib.virginia.edu
ReligioScope (Jean-Francois Mayer)
www.religioscope.com

Religious Studies Resources on the Net (John L. Gresham)
http://sim74.kenrickparish.com
Virtual Religion Index (Rutgers University)
http://religion.rutgers.edu/vri/

Evangelical Sites
Alpha & Omega Ministries (James White)
www.aomin.org
Ankerberg Theological Research Institute
www.ankerberg.com
Answers in Action (Bob and Gretchen Passantino)
http://answers.org
Apologetics Index (Anton Hein)
www.apologeticsindex.org
Apologetics Information Ministry (Craig Hawkins)
www.apologeticsinfo.org
Apologetics Resource Center (Craig Branch)
www.apologeticsresctr.org
Apologetics.com (Robert Bowman)
www.apologetics.com
Apologia Report (Rich Poll)
www.gospelcom.net/apologia
Christian Apologetics and Research Ministries (Matthew Slick)
www.carm.org
Christian Research Institute
www.equip.org
Christianity Today
www.christianitytoday.com
Dialog Center International
http://www.dci.dk/index.html
Evangelical Ministries to New Religions
www.emnr.org
Institute for Religious Research
www.irr.org
New England Institute of Religious Research (Bob Pardon)
http://neirr.org
Personal Freedom Outreach
www.pfo.org
Probe Ministries
www.probe.org

Reasoning from the Scriptures
http://home.earthlink.net/~ronrhodes
Sacred Tribes
www.sacredtribes.com
Spiritual Counterfeits Project
www.scp-inc.org
Stand to Reason
www.str.org
Walter Martin's Religious Info
www.waltermartin.org
Watchman Fellowship
www.watchman.org

Secular Cult Awareness Sites

Cult Information Centre (UK)
http://www.cultinformation.org.uk
Ex-cult Resource Center
http://ex-cult.org/
Freedom of Mind Center (Steven Hassan)
www.freedomofmind.com
Info-cult
www.infocult.org
International Cultic Studies Association
www.csj.org
Refocus
www.refocus.org
TranceNet
www.trancenet.org
Wellspring Retreat & Resource Center
http://wellspringretreat.org

Religious Liberty Sites

Christian Solidarity International
www.csi-int.org/
Freedom House
www.freedomhouse.org
Human Rights Watch
www.hrw.org
Human Rights Without Frontiers
www.hrwf.net

International Association for Religious Freedom
www.iarf.net
International Coalition for Religious Freedom
www.religiousfreedom.com
International Religious Freedom (U.S. State Department)
www.state.gov/g/drl/irf/
International Religious Liberty Association
www.irla.org
J. M. Dawson Institute of Church-State Studies
www.baylor.edu/Church_State/
Liberty Magazine
www.libertymagazine.org/
United States Commission on International Religious Freedom
www.uscirf.gov
Voice of the Martyrs
www.persecution.com
WEF Religious Liberty Commission
www.worldevangelical.org/rlc.html

Resources on World and New Religions

General Scholarly Resources

Anderson, Allan H. *African Reformation*. Trenton, NJ: African World Press, 2001.

Barrett, David, George Kurian, and Todd Johnson. *World Christian Encyclopedia*. Oxford: Oxford University Press, 2002.

Burgess, Stanley M., ed. *The New International Dictionary of Pentecostal and Charismatic Movements*. Grand Rapids, MI: Zondervan, 2002.

Lewis, James R. and Jesper Aagaard Petersen, eds., *Controversial New Religions*. New York: Oxford University Press, 2005.

Marshall, Paul, ed. *Religious Freedom in the World*. Nashville: Broadman & Holman, 2000.

McBrien, Richard P., ed. *The HarperCollins Encyclopedia of Catholicism*. New York: HarperCollins, 1995.

Melton, J. Gordon. *Encyclopedia of American Religions*. Detroit: Gale, 2003.

Melton, J. Gordon, and Martin Baumann, eds. *Religions of the World*. Santa Barbara ABC-CLIO, 2002.

Miller, Timothy, ed. *America's Alternative Religions*. Albany: State University of New York Press, 1995.

Partridge, Christopher, ed. *New Religions: A Guide*. New York: Oxford University Press, 2004.

Richardson, James T. *Regulating Religion*. New York: Kluwer, 2004.

Sunquist, Scott W., ed. *A Dictionary of Asian Christianity*. Grand Rapids, MI: Eerdmans, 2001.

Evangelical Scholarship

Corduan, Winfried. *Neighboring Faiths*. Downers Grove, IL: InterVarsity, 1998.

D'Costa, Gavin, ed. *Christian Uniqueness Reconsidered*. Maryknoll, NY: Orbis, 1990.

Enroth, Ronald, ed. *A Guide to New Religions* Downers Grove: InterVarsity, 2005.

Hexham, Irving, Stephen Rost and John W. Morehead, eds. *Encountering New Religious Movements: A Holistic Evangelical Approach*. Grand Rapids: Kregel, 2004.

Kraemer, Hendrik. *The Christian Message in a Non-Christian World*. London: International Missionary Council, 1938.

Kyle, Richard. *The Religious Fringe*. Downers Grove, IL: InterVarsity, 1993.

Martin, Walter. *The Kingdom of the Cults*. Minneapolis: Bethany House, 2003.

Neill, Stephen. *Christian Faith and Other Faiths*. Downers Grove, IL: InterVarsity, 1984.

Netland, Harold A. *Dissonant Voices*. Grand Rapids, MI: Eerdmans, 1991.

Pinnock, Clark. *A Wideness in God's Mercy*. Grand Rapids, MI: Zondervan, 1992.

Tiessen, Terrance L. *Who Can Be Saved?* Downers Grove, IL: InterVarsity, 2004.

Tucker, Ruth. *Another Gospel*. Grand Rapids, MI: Zondervan, 1989.

Zacharias, Ravi. *Jesus Among Other Gods*. Nashville: W Books, 2002.